Talk To Me

Communication moves to get along with anyone

Dr. Dennis O'Grady

PUBLISHER'S NOTE

New Insights Communication
7501 Paragon Rd., Suite 200
Dayton, OH 45459
Phone: 937-428-0724
Fax: 937-428-0824

Contact information for Dr. Dennis O'Grady at *www.drogrady.com*

Edited by Sue MacDonald *www.surgerysucks.com* or *www.rossiter.com*
Designed by The Next Wave *www.thenextwave.biz*
Cover design by David Esrati *esrati@thenextwave.biz*
Text design by Linda Malie
Diagrams by Carl DeCaire

Printed in the United States of America

Library of Congress Cataloging-in-Publication Data

O'Grady, Dennis Evan

Talk To Me/Dennis O'Grady

1. Interpersonal Communication. 3. Married people—Psychology.
3. Personal Growth—Change. 4. Entrepreneurial Leadership.

ISBN 0-9628476-2-3
ISBN 978-0-9628476-2-2

New Insights Communication Web site address: *www.drogrady.com*

New Insights Communication

I dedicate this book to my beloved mother, Elizabeth Merrill O'Grady

And to the spirit-filled women in my life: Kerry Lee O'Grady, Erin Ashley O'Grady, Riley Anne O'Grady, Kasey Lee O'Grady, and Sierra O'Grady.

To all of you: The power of your love re-makes me.

And oh, hasn't it been a barrel of fun to truly know who are the Empathizers and Instigators among us?

DEO
Dayton, Ohio, 2005

TABLE OF CONTENTS

INTRODUCTION GETTING ALONG WITH ANYONE

TALK TO Me teaches you about two different styles of communicators—Empathizers and Instigators.

INTRODUCING YOUR LEADER IN COMMUNICATIONS

One of my goals as a psychologist is to help people succeed in the world around them. I help them confront challenges with optimism. I help them cope with change. I teach them about feelings. And in this new book, I offer a powerful new communication program called *Talk to Me.* I firmly believe that communications problems are at the heart of many difficult challenges in life, and that's why I've put 30 years of professional experience as a family psychologist into action in *Talk to Me*.

Talk to Me teaches you about two different styles of communicators—Empathizers and Instigators. Empathizers and Instigators believe, think and speak differently about communication problems. They don't know those differences, of course, and problems arise because Empathizers and Instigators alike assume that everyone else believes, thinks and communicates just like they do. Until they understand themselves, their communication styles and each other's communication styles, Empathizers and Instigators will continue to struggle with the basic act of communication. *Talk to Me* provides the understanding and insights needed to move beyond assumptions. Think of me as your communications coach, the instructor who will tell you how to read the unique maps of the two communication styles in order to make communication easier and more fun on the highway of life.

Think of me as your communications coach, the instructor who will tell you how to read the unique maps of the two communication styles in order to make communication easier and more fun on the highway of life.

In fact, think about this learning experience in the same way that you think about how you learned to drive a car. Becoming a capable driver required a lot of preparation, didn't it? You had to take a driver's ed class, study the laws and rules that govern driving, read road signs, get some practice in a real live automobile and learn about the driving behaviors of other people on the road so that you could avoid running into them. You emerged from all that training with one style of driving and also became aware that other people on the road drive entirely differently from you. Eventually, you learned how to handle them too. That's what *Talk to Me* does for the act of communication. It gives you the background, the knowledge and the experience to be a better communicator—and to understand others' styles in the same way that experience and knowledge behind the wheel make you a better driver.

Instead of getting stuck in communication traffic or constantly running into others, you are going to *learn,* with my help, how to make your point of view heard without making an enemy. Think of me as your driving coach, the guy who explains the rules of the road, provides encouragement from the passenger's seat, offers new strategies and communications tips, and helps you understand why everyone else on the communications highway is reacting, driving and maneuvering in ways that are different from your style. Call me "Coach Dennis," the guy who will make you practice (and practice and practice some more) until you become an excellent communicator.

Does *Talk to Me* work? My communication trainees and seminar members alike are grateful for this approach. Says one: "I learned what I already knew at some level inside, but I didn't have the words to describe it. Now I can make these communication concepts a part of my awareness and routine as I go through my day. The light has been turned on in the shadows, and now I can see what I'm doing instead of banging into everything."

"The light has been turned on in the shadows, and now I can see what I'm doing instead of banging into everything."

Why is communication so important? Make no mistake about it: The success or failure of your personal and work relationships depends upon your ability to shed negative feelings and to develop effective relationships and positive communication skills.

In fact, I feel a personal responsibility to teach peak communication skills in people's private lives and in the public arena. *Talk to Me* will help you understand the two basic styles of communication and the four modes of talking that each style uses. Once you understand those basic concepts, you can be successful in any situation, from dealing with your top customer at work to strengthening your marriage at home. Company profits can take

Talk to Me will help you understand the two basic styles of communication and the four modes of talking that each style uses.

flight on the wings of positive communication, and raising healthy kids depends on it, too.

I developed the powerful *Talk to Me* communication system to help people just like you learn how to communicate better by understanding two very distinct communication styles. *Talk to Me* includes training seminars and car study programs, and it stems from my expertise in the field of communications at New Insights Communication, the practice I founded 30 years ago in Dayton, Ohio. I'm also a Clinical Professor at the Wright State University School of Professional Psychology, have been practicing positive psychology in academic and community settings since 1975, and have written two other books, *Taking the Fear Out Of Changing* and *No Hard Feelings.*

Allow me now to teach you how to move out of communication ruts. Learn what exactly makes the difference between an effective and an ineffective communicator. By the end of this training, you will stop feeling frustrated by talks that go nowhere.

By the end of this training, you will stop feeling frustrated by talks that go nowhere.

I consider myself a lucky family man, and I get plenty of time to practice what I preach. My roots are rich, and anchored in the love I feel for my wife and three daughters. As the sole guy in the O'Grady household, believe me: communicating is a daily workout and a constant opportunity for real growth.

Please share my knowledge and experience as you learn to develop better communication skills, patterns and behaviors in your own life.

TALK TODAY

The buck stops here...but it's not my fault.

YOU DON'T UNDERSTAND ME

TRAINING GOAL

To determine your communicator type and your co-communicator's type: Empathizers (E-types) and the Instigators (I-types)

"You don't understand me" is a guilt trip that drains the energy battery of any positive talking communication system.

As a family psychologist, I'd be wealthy if I earned a dollar for every time I heard the words: "You just don't understand me." Those five simple words form a wedge that splits people apart. Those five succinct words divide relationships, as if each partner is on opposite sides of a canyon, yelling across a bridgeless, deep divide.

Clients who come to my firm, New Insights Communication, frequently joke with me that my office is their mental gym, and I am their very own personal psychological trainer. I like the metaphor.

I like it because my customers get a real mental workout, and a good laugh, about once a week. A regular mental and emotional workout improves not only emotional stamina but mental balance as well. It builds a bridge across the rising river of emotional exhaustion caused by negative communication.

Talk to Me is a communications workout. My goal as a trainer is to get you back in great communications shape. I want to make sure you don't slack off your goals, don't turn weak and flabby and that you understand the principles behind good communications training so that you begin to see results from your new thought patterns and tactics.

Similarly, *Talk to Me* will help you learn the principles and skills that turn you into communications bodybuilders—knowledgeable about what communication is, and trained in the exercises, mindsets and activities that get them there. Are you ready? Let's find out quickly if this new communication training program is worth your time, attention and investment.

THE NEW INSIGHTS COMMUNICATION INVENTORY (NICI)

Positive communication doesn't just happen. Good talks take work, smarts and guts.

When your most important personal relationships are working right, they're plenty of fun. But when a communication mix-up occurs or when communication wires get crossed, strong words can hurt a relationship.

Let's start by finding out what type of communicator you are: Empathizer or Instigator.

The following 12 items in Chart 1.1 on the New Insights Communication Inventory, or NICI, have been carefully selected to help you determine your communicator type. The NICI takes the pulse of your communication preferences and beliefs.

As you read each "yes" or "no" question, please pick the first answer that comes charging into your mind. An equal tally of "yes" and "no" answers isn't necessary. If you feel mixed or on the fence about some answers, think about your daily life and then try to pick the best answer—the one that is mostly true or mostly false for you.

1.1	New Insights Communication Inventory (NICI)	Yes	No
1	Do you try hard not to hurt anyone's feelings?		
2	Are your feelings easily hurt?		
3	Do you think of yourself as being too sensitive?		
4	Do you believe talking about feelings makes things better?		
5	Are you surprised when your strong words or actions make someone else feel bad?		
6	Do you believe you have the power to get out of a relationship rut?		
7	Do you believe that communication gaps are correctable?		
8	Do you believe the adage that women are more moody than men?		

		Yes	No
9	Do you think you are 50% responsible for any communication breakdown?		
10	Do you "give in" to avoid conflict?		
11	Do you tend to blame other people or situations for your feelings or actions?		
12	Do you find yourself helping other people to the exclusion of yourself?		
	Total		

QUICK-SCORING YOUR NICI

It's plenty easy to find out if you are an Empathizer, or E-type communicator or whether you are an Instigator, or I-type communicator.

All you have to do is add up the total number of your "yes" and "no" answers out of the 12 questions that you answered honestly.

Now, tally up how many "yes" and "no" answers you gave.

COPING WITH YOUR INTERPERSONAL RELATIONSHIPS

Since I want to be extra careful in correctly verifying your score, I want to ask you a couple of additional questions, found in Chart 1.2. These questions help in case your score doesn't lean strongly one way or the other. These extra questions help most if your yes/no tallies fall into an either/or middle ground on the NICI.

1.2 Life-Coping Questions

		E/S	L/R
A	Overall, do you cope with life stress by using <u>emotions and sensitivity</u>, or by using <u>logic and reasoning</u>?		

1.2 Relationships

B Overall, does your relationship partner cope with life stress by using emotions and sensitivity, or by using logic and reasoning? E/S L/R

C Overall, did your mother (or mothering figure) cope with life stress by using emotions and sensitivity, or by using logic and reasoning? E/S L/R

D Overall, did your father (or fathering figure) cope with life stress by using emotions and sensitivity, or by using logic and reasoning? E/S L/R

E Emotionally, do you have a more difficult time coping with sadness, or do you have a more difficult time coping with anger? Sad Mad

F On a 1–10 scale—with 1 indicating "not at all stressed" and 10 indicating "maximum stress"—how distressed would you say your romantic relationship is at this time?

THE SCORING KEY FOR THE NICI

Let's make communication simple for a change!

Tally your NICI scores again by entering your total number of "yes" and "no" answers below. Then read through the scoring key, and use the tips to determine your type.

Which communicator category does your score place you in? Do you agree or do you disagree, why or why not?

EMPATHIZER OR E-TYPE COMMUNICATORS

If you answered eight (8) or more of the 12 survey questions "yes," then chances are that you are an *Empathizer communicator.*

INSTIGATOR OR I-TYPE COMMUNICATORS

If you answered six (6) or fewer of the 12 survey questions "yes," then chances are that you are an *Instigator communicator.*

EITHER EMPATHIZER (E-TYPE) OR INSTIGATOR (I-TYPE)

If you answered, seven (7) of the 12 survey questions "yes," then you could be either an *Empathizer or Instigator communicator.* You'll be able to tell for sure which type you are by reviewing the emotional vs. logical side of your answers or by reviewing again the additional relationship clarifying questions.

Other type tip-offs: Tally your answers to the first three questions. If you answered two out of three of the first three questions "yes," then chances are you are an E-type. Conversely, if you answered two out of three of the first three questions "no," then chances are that you are an I-type.

Remember, the reasons you gave for your answers will determine your communicator style.

MIXED EMPATHIZER/INSTIGATOR COMMUNICATOR (E/I TYPE):

I do not believe there is a mixed *Empathizer/Instigator communicator type,* or E/I or I/E type, at least not until after you work extensively with this material or have had many years of intensive psychotherapy.

Therefore, for accuracy and triple-checking purposes, I offer this additional perspective. If you feel your NICI score is in the middle of the E/I type somewhere and you're wondering which way to turn, try this:

ARE YOU MORE SENSITIVE OR INSENSITIVE? YES, I TEND TO BE...

If you answered, "Yes, I tend to be a *sensitive* communicator" to the question above, then chances are you are an Empathizer (E-type) communicator.

If you answered, "Yes, I tend to be more *insensitive* when it comes to communication," then chances are you are an Instigator (I-type) communicator.

It matters not if you are a boy or a girl, rich or poor, young or elder. You will avoid many feuds and disputes when you use this easy-to-learn new theory.

EMPATHIZER Communicator Style

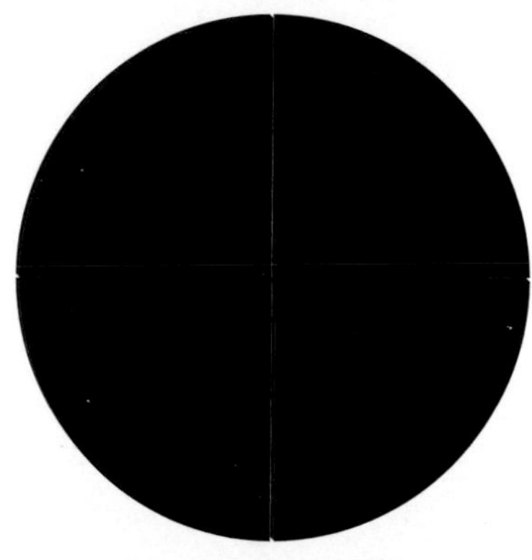

figure **#1**

If you like to think of yourself as a logical person but really believe your emotions run your life more than you would like them to—you probably are an Empathizer.

Empathizer

If you like to think of yourself as a logical person but really believe your emotions run your life more than you would like them to—you probably are an Empathizer. Also, if you struggle with the emotion of sadness, then you are probably an E-type. Likewise, if you value talking to others about situations that make you feel anxious, then you are probably an E-type.

E-type communicators are:

- Sensitive
- Empathetic
- Feel deeply
- Relationship experts

I-type communicators are:

- Insensitive
- Genuine
- Think deeply
- Problem-solving experts

Statistically, 40% of all people are Empathizer communicators (E-types) while 60% of all people are Instigator communicators (I-types).

INSTIGATOR Communicator Style

figure **#2**

Instigator

If you qualified many of your answers, then chances are you are an Instigator-type. Also, if the emotion you struggle with is anger, then you probably are an I-type. If you value making strategic action plans to reduce your anxiety, then chances are you are an I-type. Lastly, if think you are a combination E/I type anyway, chances are that you are an Instigator communicator because you qualify your world rather than globalize it.

If you qualified many of your answers, then chances are you are an Instigator-type.

STILL ON THE FENCE AS TO WHETHER YOU ARE AN E-TYPE OR AN I-TYPE COMMUNICATOR?

Did the previous exercise and the additional questions help you better determine your type? If you are still on the fence, and a few of you might be, no sweat. The next best way to determine your type is to review the Life-Coping question "A" on Page 7.

Namely, if you primarily cope with life stress by using emotions and sensitivity, then you are an Empathizer communicator.

If you primarily cope with life stress by using logic and reasoning, then you are an Instigator communicator.

Now let's get down to it, my dear E-types and I-types!

Communicator Style

My communicator style according to the NICI:	E I
My relationship partner's communicator style is (either an E-type or an I-type):	E I
Our co-communicator match-up:	E-E E-I I-I

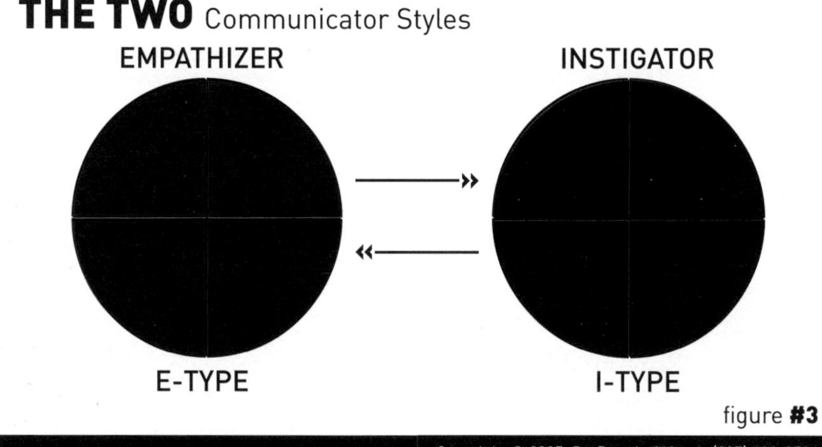

figure **#3**

COUPLED CO-COMMUNICATORS

Soon you will be able to easily and accurately identify what communicator type your co-communicator is and work within that frame of reference to achieve far superior results. In some couples, for instance, both people are E-types or I-types, while in other couples, one is an E- and the other is an I-type.

Work with the notion that coupled co-communicators fall into thirds according to their type.

Work with the notion that coupled co-communicators fall into thirds according to their type. Thus, one third of coupled co-communicators are E-E types, one third of coupled co-communicators are E-I types, and one third of coupled co-communicators are I-I types. I have purposely used "coupled" out of respect for the rich variety of relationships that exist in our world. Nonetheless, "coupled" also in my mind means two people

"Coupled" also in my mind means two people who are committed to really trying to get along well and communicate accurately.

who are committed to really trying to get along well and communicate accurately.

In Question B, I asked you to determine if your relationship partner (if you have one) copes with life stress by using emotions or logic. In my experience, you will be very accurate in quickly determining the communicator type of your partner.

Emotional honesty is just one example of an E-type Empathizer strength, while Intellectual honesty is just one example of an I-type Instigator strength.

Emotional honesty is just one example of an E-type Empathizer strength, while Intellectual honesty is just one example of an I-type Instigator strength.

We're going to use both of these strengths to get you where you need and want to go.

IF YOU'RE SINGLE, DIVORCED, WIDOWED, FACING DIVORCE

I want to give a very warm welcome to all of you who are single, divorcing or divorced, or widowed. Howdy!

Part of my special outreach mission for the past 20 years has been to work with single, divorced and widowed people in churches and organizations in my community. I am familiar with your struggles to get beyond the hurt, anger, pain and guilt of breakups or losses.

Part of my special outreach mission for the past 20 years has been to work with single, divorced and widowed people in churches and organizations in my community.

First, I encourage you to accept a couple of important facts. In my experience, most divorces or breakups occur because of *mismatching.* Enough already of the guilt albatross strung around your neck! When I use the word "mismatch," I'm not talking about co-communicator mismatching, since any match-up can work out just fine with these new talk tools. My definition of "mismatching" means that at some point, you elected subconsciously not to place yourself in a loving relationship. Instead, you chose some other type of relationship.

If you are widowed, you can love again or you can love for the first time. "Love" is a very misused word, and it's no wonder so many people become confused by love. Romance and monetary security are not the same as love, and people often mistake advantages or security for love. "Everyone else is partnering up" is not love. "I lust after him/her" is not love. It's even possible to love someone who isn't good for you and with whom you shouldn't create a partnership.

"Love" is a very misused word, and it's no wonder so many people become confused by love.
If you're divorcing or divorced, it is entirely possible that you are lugging around a big gunnysack stuffed with guilt.

If you're divorcing or divorced, it is entirely possible that you are lugging around a big gunnysack stuffed with guilt. "I am a failure" …"I failed to see the light"…"I feel ashamed of myself"…"I'll look like a failure to all my family and friends" are common negative beliefs about divorce. But I would suggest you think differently about the change you're going through, such as: "The relationship was a mismatch!"…"The deck was stacked against us from the beginning!"…"Maintaining a long-term but unsatisfying relationship isn't my notion of success!"

If you are divorced, chances are (in my opinion) that you felt or thought you were in a loving relationship, when in actuality you were in a controlling relationship or friendship relationship.

LOVE REQUIRES MATURITY

Half of all men and half of all women, at some point in life, have been immature.

Immaturity means you aren't able to love, or that you are able to love only in small ways.

Immaturity means you aren't able to love, or that you are able to love only in small ways. Maturity is required to be able to love unconditionally and to keep plowing forward when you both feel real stuck. For now, accept that half of men and half of women are immature and unable to love. What does that mean?

You can't make someone love you, and you shouldn't allow it even if you could.

If you are divorced, it means that you might not have enjoyed co-equal love in your relationship. By coequal, I mean love that exists when one partner loves the other partner about equally. You can't make someone love you, and you shouldn't allow it even if you could.

If you are divorced, quit blaming yourself. It's entirely possible that you and your ex-partner were not both in love in equal amounts at the same time.

My conclusion: If you are divorced, quit blaming yourself. It's entirely possible that you and your ex-partner were not both in love in equal amounts at the same time. If you can't accept this new insight yet, at least be open to the possibility. Imagine how you would feel about your life and your future if you thought what I said was true? I bet you would go into entirely new, more exciting and positive directions to change your life if you could be free of that guilt.

After all, love is a force—love is the only thing that lasts. That's something I've come to realize from personal and extensive professional experience in all three types of relationship combinations—loving, controlling and friendship (see more in Chapter 3).

LOVING YOURSELF IS REQUIRED BEFORE YOU ENTER INTO A LOVING RELATIONSHIP

Don't expect to be in a loving relationship if you hate yourself. It's just not possible.

The partner you choose will be based on your attained level of self-esteem or self-love. You can't move "up," you can't move "down" in this regard. You will match with a partner based on how confident you are in loving yourself.

I've come to believe that a loving relationship requires personal maturity. You must love yourself before you can expect someone else to love you! If you can't love yourself, why should anyone else want to? How can you feel secure if you don't love yourself through thick and thin, and in spite of all the negativity and rejections? You are complete and good enough no matter the negative words you hear, but if you don't believe that about yourself, why would others?

How can you feel secure if you don't love yourself through thick and thin, and in spite of all the negativity and rejections?

Through my life and work experience, it's been apparent that each of the three relationship categories is quite separate and distinct. Therefore, you can't step up from a controlling relationship to a friendship relationship to a loving relationship with the same person. It's just not possible. Changing partners is required. You might not like to hear such talk, but it is the truth.

You can't step up from a controlling relationship to a friendship relationship to a loving relationship with the same person. It's just not possible.

Furthermore, I believe the only relationship that has any lucky or serious chance of going the distance is the loving relationship. Why? There are several reasons.

Controlling relationships are filled to the gills with angry power plays and negativity. Likewise, a friendship relationship is like having a roommate, teammate or best friend. Once the relationship's "mission" has been accomplished—such as raising kids, or getting one partner through college or medical school—then the purpose for the union has been completed and there's nothing left to fill in or take its place.

No one's perfect, of course. I'm the first to admit that I'm far from perfect or ideal in any way. But so long as I love myself and my partner chooses to love me, everything will be okay. A loving relationship allows both co-communicators to make thousands of unintended communication mistakes (which admittedly I do!), mistakes that need to be forgiven freely as we go about changing, growing and moving on together.

If you're single or "partner-free," your double talk partner is yourself. The person with whom you carry on communication is that other self inside your head, and whatever communicator type you are, double it! Are you an E-E type (E-E inner-personal) or are you an I-I type (I-I inner-personal)? What a blast! I want you to build a very loving relationship with yourself—whatever type you are! And get ready: By using these principles, you may discover that finding the person of your dreams becomes a reality instead of a pep talk.

COMMUNICATOR TYPE OF YOUR PARENTS

The NICI relationship questions C and D on Page 8 try to determine the communicator types of your mother and father.

If your mother (or the mother figure in your childhood) coped with life's challenges by using emotions, then she is an E-type, and if mom used logic and reasons more, then she was an I-type. Similarly, if your father (or the father figure in your childhood) coped by using emotions and sensitivity, then he was an E-type, but if dad used logic and reasons, then it's more likely that he was an I-type.

Were you the same or a different type from mom and dad?

So what types of co-communicators were mom and dad? Did your mom and dad match as the same type (E-E or I-I)? Or did they have differing types? (E-I or I-E)? Were you the same or a different type from mom and dad? (If you're not sure, it's okay to take a wild guess). Or use the chart below to help.

Parental Communicator Style

My mother figure was either an E-type or an I-type:	E	I
My father figure was either an E-type or an I-type:	E	I
My mother-father figures were this combination of either E-E types, E-I types, or I-I types:	E-E	E-I I-I

As I bet you've guessed by now, your communicator type was molded and shaped as you were growing up by your parents and in your sibling/family environment. Even today, it's possible your talk style is still influenced through signs of parental or sibling approval or disapproval. Usually, your type was either encouraged, or discouraged, in the family atmosphere—or a little of both.

After all, even as adults, we're still family members and co-communicators, and sometimes we still exist in a desert-like, emotionally illiterate world of interpersonal relationships. But now we have the experience and maturity to understand the dynamics.

THE 50% CO-RESPONSIBILITY RULE

I've learned a lot of things in my clinical practice over the past 30 years, and I'd like you to accept a few "facts" as I've experienced them.

First, to avoid codependency in your relationships, I suggest you adopt the *50% co-responsibility rule.* What does that mean? It means that no matter how frustrated you feel with your co-communicator (and this can include you speaking to your inner self), stop the anger/blame game dead in its tracks. Here's how: Firmly remind yourself that you are half of every problem and half of every solution. You have control only over your half—but that's a considerable positive chunk of responsibility that requires positive change.

Firmly remind yourself that you are half of every problem and half of every solution.

In a relationship, the 50% co-responsibility rule also means that co-communicators are each 50% responsible for the mood and communication results of the relationship, whether the relationship is fine or failing. If you believe you aren't to blame—or if you believe you are at total fault for the communication impasse—then you won't see the light of change.

If you believe you aren't to blame—or if you believe you are at total fault for the communication impasse—then you won't see the light of change.

I very much dislike the word "fault," as in, "It's all your fault." Assigning "fault" is a guilt trip meant to place blame somewhere else. Assigning "fault" stymies positive change. Everyone is vulnerable to projecting their weaknesses onto others and then blaming everyone else for what they can't accept in themselves. During power plays, blame is tossed back and forth like a live grenade. Sooner than later, someone is going to get their talk legs blown off.

Assigning "fault" stymies positive change.

During power plays, blame is tossed back and forth like a live grenade. Sooner than later, someone is going to get their talk legs blown off.

Still, if you must assign fault, you have two options. First, neither of you is at fault or secondly, both of you are equally at fault. Those two options, in my opinion, are the only choices. It matters not to me because I know you and your co-communicator are 50% co-responsible (most of the time) for what you have co-created. But if you keep playing the anger/blame game, you'll never be able to experience love.

Lastly, I would like to ask you to accept, for the time being, another notion I've developed from my clinical experience, and that is this: even though most people believe that love relationships are the ideal, two-thirds of all couples are dissatisfied, distressed, and feel hopeless and helpless as to what to do about their distress as a couple. It's also possible that two-thirds of all couples are involved in controlling or friendship relationships.

I know I am asking you to change some of your basic ideas about relationship dynamics, but I can't help it! By using these new positive ideals, you will obtain speedier results, especially if you adopt the guilt-freeing idea that you are 50% responsible for the mood of your relationship and for your own personal satisfaction and happiness.

I know I am asking you to change some of your basic ideas about relationship dynamics, but I can't help it!

If you stubbornly refuse to believe that you are 50% responsible, you are not going to go anywhere fast, and I cannot willingly permit that to happen.

SEEK TO BE CURIOUS, NON-JUDGMENTAL, OPEN-MINDED

It's also okay to be open-minded and curious about your communication type. I certainly was when I first began working with the theory.

Don't settle in too fast, or be too black-and-white about which type you are, or you might just take the zip out of the process. Argue in your mind how you might be an Empathizer—and how you might be an Instigator. Get to know the key traits of each type, then decide for yourself which communicator size fits you the best. Argue for and argue against what type you are, and what type your co-communicator happens to be.

Don't settle in too fast, or be too black-and-white about which type you are, or you might just take the zip out of the process.

Argue for and argue against what type you are, and what type your co-communicator happens to be.

By working with these concepts, you are going to find yourself blending the two types together, and it's a process that can be miraculous yet predictable. Thus, if you're an E-type, you will become an Empathizer/Instigator communicator. And if you're an I-type, you will become an Instigator/Empathizer communicator.

Although you will always prefer your original style, you're going to like the features and strengths of your opposing style. In fact, you

In fact, you will create rapid change when you take on or adopt the strengths of the opposing style—and the changes are positive ones that happen fast and that last!

will create rapid change when you take on or adopt the strengths of the opposing style—and the changes are positive ones that happen fast and that last!

SEX ROLE STEREOTYPES AND COMMUNICATOR TYPE

One of the first things trainees new to this material assume is that men and women have definite communicator types. They figure that since Empathizers are keen on empathy, while Instigators are keen on results and fixing things, more women (perhaps 70% or higher) are E-types and that an equal percentage of men are I-types.

However, I have not found this to be the case in real life. When I gave the NICI to 100 college students from different degree programs, a group evenly split between male and female, I found out that about half of all E- and I-types are men and half of all E- and I-types are women.

This finding was at first confusing but now it's amazing. Sex role stereotypes can look like one communicator type but will be in fact the other type. For instance, I know big, burly, gruff-talking mountain men guys who are diehard Empathizer communicators. And I know super-feminine, soft, easygoing, demure total-female gals who are drop-dead Instigator communicators. E-types love to love, and they create great power by intensely identifying with and loving the dimensions of their sex or gender roles. Likewise, I-types love power, and female or male beauty can be powerful!

I know big, burly, gruff-talking mountain men guys who are diehard Empathizer communicators. And I know super-feminine, soft, easy-going, demure total-female gals who are drop-dead Instigator communicators.

If you're still confused about your own type, remain calm, and don't panic. Clarity is on the way if you just stay tuned to find out which communicator type you really are! After all, you will be learning that positive communication moves aren't razzle-dazzle maneuvers. Instead, they happen reliably in a preset pattern according to the temperament (E-type or I-type) of the communicator.

Things are about to get interesting on the communication highway, so buckle up and adjust your mirrors.

EMOTIONS AND YOUR TYPE

You are now on the road to being a more flexible and accurate communicator as we begin to delve into the differences in communicator style.

Later on in this book, I will be exploring four negative emotions that have a huge impact on each and every communicational transaction you make. These four emotions are Dysphoria (or feeling blue), Anxiety (or feeling edgy and agitated), Anger (or feeling rejected and resentful) and Guilt (or feeling undeserving of joy and enjoyment). Each of these four emotions can be used in either negative or positive ways in interpersonal interactions. Also, if we had more time and space, I would have also liked to include a discussion of boredom and loneliness—two additionally and frequently misunderstood emotions.

For now, please realize that Empathizers struggle with feeling dysphoric, blue, crushed down, and hurt because they are *naturally sensitive and empathetic.* Instigators, on the other hand, often struggle with unhealthy anger, intolerance and irritation because they are *naturally insensitive and genuine.* Therefore, E-types and I-types can collide, crash and burn up if they aren't watching where they're going.

For now, please realize that Empathizers struggle with feeling dysphoric, blue, crushed down, and hurt because they are naturally sensitive and empathetic. Instigators, on the other hand, often struggle with unhealthy anger, intolerance and irritation because they are naturally insensitive and genuine.

Driving is a good example of how the Empathizer and Instigator communicator types differ. For the most part, E-types don't get all huffy because of the flaky driving behaviors of their fellow travelers on the two-way communication highway. They're pretty forgiving at heart. They'll slow down to let someone else merge, and they feel bad for the old-lady driver that other drivers are honking at because she's too slow.

By contrast, I-types struggle with impatience, irritation and even "road rage" episodes because they believe that poor driving is a hallmark of stupidity, not paying attention and impracticality by their fellow drivers. They'll honk at people to get out of their way and feel justified for doing so. I-types want to get to their destination fast, while E-types want to enjoy the trip.

(As an aside, I think "road rage" should be changed to "driver rage." "Road rage" is a misnomer, and it says something about how society is confused and cops out over healthy vs. unhealthy anger. No one's enraged by a road, which is nothing more than blacktop and the occasional pothole. Drivers become enraged at other drivers whom they justly but insensitively condemn. By the way, I can usually cure "driver rage" in just a few sessions, especially if the person wants to relax and enjoy the trip more).

Lastly, Empathizers fear the anger of Instigators, while Instigators fear the sadness and sorrow of Empathizers. It's very true that E-types need to learn how not to take things so personally, while I-types need to learn how to take things less impersonally.

Always. . .always. . .always insist in your mind and persist in your emotions that one type is not better than the other type. They are just different. And the only time one type is "up" while the other is "down" is when a controlling power play is underway.

Empathizers fear the anger of Instigators, while Instigators fear the sadness and sorrow of Empathizers.

E-types need to learn how not to take things so personally, while I-types need to learn how to take things less impersonally.

Always...always...always insist in your mind and persist in your emotions that one type is not better than the other type. They are just different.

EMOTIONAL CHALLENGES—COMMUNICATION SOLUTIONS

In my worldview and from where I stand, here are some of the real reasons you and I struggle with emotional challenges:

1. *You feel dysphoric, sad and pessimistic or you may feel anxious or mad. In essence, you feel loved less.*
2. *You feel all the negative feelings from No. 1 (and more) because your relationship(s) is in distress.*
3. *Your relationship is in distress because you and your co-communicator(s) are making mistakes by using negative communication moves.*
4. *Your overall effectiveness at work and home suffers and declines as a result of your distress. So do your health and your positive attitude.*

EMOTIONAL CHALLENGES—POSITIVE TALKING

Here's how we're going to change all that by "positive talking":

1. *You feel happy, excited about your life, in charge of your relationship mood. In essence, you feel loved more.*
2. *You feel all the positive feelings from No. 1 (and more) because your relationship(s) is deepening in the areas of emotional intimacy and personal satisfaction.*
3. *Your relationship is emotionally intimate and personally satisfying because you and your co-communicator(s) are making positive communication moves.*
4. *Your overall effectiveness at work and home improves appreciably as a result of your new communication patterns and behaviors. So do your health and your positive attitude.*

Did you follow the emotional logic above? Do you understand now why it's just not fair to judge your co-communicator as having his or her front porch light burned out?

What a difference positive communication moves will make in so many of your life areas. Just you wait and see!

KEY DIFFERENCES BETWEEN EMPATHIZER AND INSTIGATOR RESPONDERS TO THE NEW INSIGHTS COMMUNICATION INVENTORY

If you're like most respondents to the NICI, you might have had trouble answering two or more of the questions. Answers sometimes can go either way, and that is why I carefully check why you said what you did. I appreciate you getting off the fence in those cases and making a clear choice.

I created a composite portraiture or signature for the classic Empathizer and the classic Instigator communicator.

About my process in this work: First, I created a composite portraiture or signature for the classic Empathizer and the classic Instigator communicator. Then I administered the NICI communicator survey to people I knew socially and people I have respected for many years. Their real-life answers didn't exactly fit the template and I was happy about that. Their real-life answers, sometimes, surprised me. . .and that's a very good thing when the rubber of theory meets the road of real life. I hope you will be surprised and delighted, too.

I hope you'll gain a new awareness of the differences that exist in and between Empathizer and Instigator communicators.

I've included some of their responses here in Chart 1.3. By hearing the responses in their words, I hope you can begin to understand some of the uncommon differences in feeling and thinking styles that exist within the definitions of E- and I-types. I hope you'll gain a new awareness of the differences that exist in and between *Empathizer* and *Instigator* communicators:

1.3 Empathizer	Instigator
1 Do you try hard not to hurt anyone's feelings?	
Yes. I believe you should respect the feelings of others, since I don't like my own feelings being hurt.	**No.** Of course, I don't ever want to hurt anyone's feelings, but sometimes you can't help it if you tell the truth.
2 Are your feelings easily hurt?	
Yes. Sometimes my feelings are hurt easily but other times they're not.	**No.** I don't logically think it's very useful to ever take things too personal.
3 Do you think of yourself as being too sensitive?	
Yes. I've been told that I am too sensitive and too tuned in to what others are saying or doing.	**No.** I've been told most of my life that I can be too insensitive and tuned out to what others are feeling.
4 Do you believe talking about feelings makes things better?	
Yes. I believe that talking never hurts and always helps everyone to get along better.	**Yes.** But not necessarily—I've learned that some problems will go away if you don't think about them too much.
5 Are you surprised when your strong words or actions make someone else feel bad?	
No. I am usually able to anticipate when someone is going to feel bad by what I say or do.	**Yes.** Sometimes I feel disappointed and surprised when I find out someone feels bad about something small I said or did.

1.3	Empathizer	Instigator
6	Do you believe you have the power to get out of a relationship rut?	
	No. Feelings just come over me and I can't help or control how I feel, but sometimes I feel like a victim to sad feelings.	**No.** I wouldn't exactly say I choose how I feel, but sometimes I speak too bluntly and end up feeling like an out-of-control and angry prosecutor.
7	Do you believe that communication gaps are correctable?	
	Yes. That is, if your partner cooperates instead of avoiding the problem and building a wall of mistrust.	**Yes.** If your partner works with you, of course. But sometimes it's better to agree to disagree or you can make things worse.
8	Do you believe the adage that women are more moody than men?	
	No. Of course, women can be moody and men can be moody too—we just show it differently.	**Yes.** Women are more moody than men but men aren't angels, either.
9	Do you think you are 50% responsible for any communication breakdown?	
	Yes. I play a part in the problem, but don't ignore me and make me feel guilty or I'll come back at you.	**Yes.** I may play a part in the problem, but don't blame me and make me feel guilty or I'll strike back at you.
10	Do you "give in" to avoid conflict?	
	No. Although I dislike conflict intensely, I won't back down on something that feels very important to me.	**Yes.** I try to avoid conflict but I won't back down if the issue is big enough.

1.3	Empathizer	Instigator

11 Do you tend to blame other people or situations for your feelings or actions?

No. Of course I don't use power plays to get my way and cover up my mistakes because I am a loving and relationship-centered person.

Yes. I've got to be genuine and honest here. Of course, sometimes I blame or get mad at others when I'm feeling insecure.

12 Do you find yourself helping other people to the exclusion of yourself?

Yes. Sometimes, I try too hard to help others who don't want to help themselves, and I end up getting hurt or run over in the process.

No. The bottom line is that I believe I've got to help myself or I won't be much good in helping others.

SCORING THE SHORT FORM OF THE NICI

Let's score your NICI again, but this time by using only the first three questions. Please tally your "yes" and "no" answers to items #1, #2 and #3. Got it?

NICI Short Form	Yes	No
My NICI short form answer total is:		

If you answered "yes" to Nos. 1, 2 and 3, then chances are that you are an *Empathizer, or E-type, communicator.*

However, if you answered "no" to Nos. 1, 2 and 3, then chances are you are an *Instigator, or I-type, communicator.*

Many times, E-types will provide at least two "yes" answers to items #1, #2 and #3—while I-types will provide at least two "no" answers to items #1, #2 and #3. This is because the dimension of interpersonal sensitivity vs. insensitivity is predictably different between the two types. Another signpost of your communicator type is what emotions you struggle with and how you choose to cope with them.

Well, how are we doing so far? By now, hopefully, we have pieced together your communicator puzzle type for starters, at least, and maybe your co-communicator's style to boot! Now, in your opinion, which is it going to be? From your brief peek into the inner world of each communicator style, are you approaching this material as an *Empathizer communicator*—or as an *Instigator communicator?* You can go forward without knowing your type, but your progress will be much faster with your type in the center of your mind.

Now think about the talk antagonist in your life…the person with whom communication is most difficult. Which communicator type do you think your talk antagonist happens to be?

You're doing great so far, by the way. I know you are with me, and trust me—we are going to travel to some very new and exotic "talk places."

Coach O'Grady will show you how the different, or diametrically opposed, communication moves between *Empathizer communicators* and *Instigator communicators* are similar to the vast difference between night and day circadian rhythms. You are going to learn how to use powerful, new communication moves to the mutual advantage of all communicators on the planet. This is no lame joke, and I am not pulling your leg!

You are going to learn how to use powerful, new communication moves to the mutual advantage of all communicators on the planet.

Once you understand and use the new talk moves, your life will never feel the same way—nor will you ever think the same way. Plus, your talk antagonists won't bug you as much.

MEET EMPATHIZER–EMPATHIZER (E-E), EMPATHIZER–INSTIGATOR (E-I), AND INSTIGATOR–INSTIGATOR (I-I) COUPLED CO-COMMUNICATORS

Recall my saying that Empathizers and Instigators are equal in number, and equally divided between men and women? It's a mistake to assume that all men are Instigators and all women are Empathizers. Likewise, it is a mistake to assume that all coupled partnerships, whether straight, gay or lesbian, are of the same communicator type.

It's a mistake to assume that all men are Instigators and all women are Empathizers. Likewise, it is a mistake to assume that all coupled partnerships, whether straight, gay or lesbian, are of the same communicator type.

Two-thirds of couples are not in a loving relationship, in my clinical studies. I have purposely selected couples who are in loving relationships for this next section. With their permission, and my gratitude, here are their real-life answers to the NICI.

The instructions I gave to the core group of NICI takers were simple: Answer the survey separately, write a brief sentence or two giving the reason for the answer, and talk about the answers only after each partner couple had recorded his/her answer. I did not want answers to be modified or changed because of the partner's input. The answers are shown in Chart 1.4.

Chart 1.4 Pages 28–35

Here again is the communicator style score key:

If you answered, eight (8) or more of the 12 survey questions "yes," then chances are you are an *Empathizer communicator.*

If you answered seven (7) of the 12 survey questions "yes," then you could be either an *Empathizer* or *Instigator communicator.* However, by reviewing the emotional vs. logical side of your answers, or by reviewing again the additional relationship clarifying questions, you will be able to tell for sure.

If you answered, six (6) or fewer of the 12 survey questions "yes" or you gave six or more "no" answers, then chances are you are an *Instigator communicator.*

Other tip-offs to determine your type: Tally your answers to the first three questions. If you answered two or three of the first three questions "yes," then chances are you are an E-type. If you answered two or three of the first three questions "no," then chances are you are an I-type.

Remember: in a pinch, the reasons you gave for your answers will determine your communicator style.

PROTOTYPICAL EMPATHIZER AND INSTIGATOR RESPONSES TO THE NICI AND COACH O'GRADY TALK

One of my first jobs writing this book was to draw up the typical styles of the Empathizer and Instigator, based on what I gleaned from my clinical and field studies. I had to put pen where my mind and mouth are all day.

1.4 E-E Couple / E-I Couple

	SUE	RICHARD	SUZANNE
1 Do you try hard not to hurt anyone's feelings?	**Yes.** "I try as much as possible to watch how my words affect other people, and I try as much as possible to run a gut-check through my own mind sometimes about what to say before the words come out of my mouth."	**Yes.** "Sure, I try to be tactful before just blurting something out."	**Yes.** "I wouldn't exactly say I try 'hard' not to, but I try to be aware of others' feelings."
2 Are your feelings easily hurt?	**Yes.** "I try not to let it slow me down, but it's impossible not to feel that zing through your heart or gut when someone says something that hurts my feelings. It's a very physical sensation inside, like a jolt of electricity sometimes."	**Yes.** "I guess I'm self-conscious, and my feelings are part of who I am, so when someone says something hurtful, I feel it inside."	**Yes.** "Sometimes my feelings can get hurt initially, but if I have a chance to think a little I can get a better perspective. I really try not to have a "knee jerk" reaction."
3 Do you think of yourself as being too sensitive?	**No.** "I'm told just the opposite by people. People often remark at how "cool" I manage to stay, even when everyone else is on edge or being driven crazy."	**No.**	**Yes.** "If I'm being poked fun at or teased about things I do, I don't always think it's funny."

I-I Couple

JIM	SHERI	JERRY
No. "'Hard' is the operative word. I mean, I don't try to hurt feelings, but I don't try hard not to."	**Yes.** "I try to be considerate of others' feelings."	**No.** "Most of the time, I don't need to try. I don't like to hurt people's feelings. It isn't something that I try to do or that comes naturally for me. On occasion, I will unintentionally hurt someone's feelings. I would guess it's family more than anyone that takes the brunt."
No.	**No.** "Not usually."	**No.** "I don't think so. Only if I'm made to feel inadequate or if my integrity is questioned. Then I don't handle it well."
No. "I have been told that I am insensitive."	**No.**	**No.**

1.4	E-E Couple		E-I Couple
4	Do you believe talking about feelings makes things better?		
	Yes. "It drives me crazy when there's something bothering me or someone close to me, and everybody just ignores it or refuses to talk about it."	**Yes.** "Sometimes I don't want to talk about it right away. I might need to go off by myself and think about things for a while before I'm ready to talk, but I don't like things left hanging, either."	**Yes.** "But, not always."
5	Are you surprised when your strong words or actions make someone else feel bad?		
	No. "I know how I feel when someone says something that hurts, so I assume everyone else does, too."	**No.** "Sometimes you just have to blurt out the truth, no matter what. And you know what they say. . .sometimes, the truth hurts!"	**No.** "I'm surprised especially if it's someone who cares about me, because I'm sure what I say or feel matters to them."
6	Do you believe you have the power to get out of a relationship rut?		
	Yes. "I have the power, but I can't do it alone. Maybe I've read too many other books, but I prefer to think of problems as a two-way street, and I'm willing to pull my half of the load if the other person is willing, too."	**Yes.** "As long as everything's out there in the open."	**No.** "I don't choose how I feel but I choose how I react or respond to those feelings."
	SUE	**RICHARD**	**SUZANNE**

I-I Couple

JIM	SHERI	JERRY
No. "Understanding people who wish to talk about their feelings can make things better."	**Yes.** "In most situations, when things are verbalized, it's a starting point to trying to understand why you are feeling a certain way."	**Yes.** "But only if the person you're talking with is open about the feelings and willing to talk about solutions more than problems."
No. "I used to be but it has happened so often that it no longer surprises me."	**No.** "Strong words and actions usually do put people on the defense. It is not intentional to hurt someone on purpose, but in the heat of the moment, it's possible that you'll say something without thinking about what you're saying, instead of taking time to reflect on how to handle a situation."	**Yes.**
No. "Initially you cannot help how you feel, but long-term, it's a decision."	**Yes.** "When you feel stuck you are not making good choices. But you can make a choice to work it out or get out of the situation that is making you feel stuck. It is interesting how you word some of the questions."	**Yes.** "It's been so long, I don't know what that feels like [a relationship rut]."

1.4	E-E Couple		E-I Couple
7	Do you believe that communication gaps are correctable?		
	Yes. "I've also realized that some people aren't willing to try to correct gaps. They're stuck in their ways. I hope I've learned to stay flexible and willing to learn."	**Yes.** "I'm in my 50s, and I still learn new things about how to get along better and communicate with people."	**Yes.** "'Correctable' is strong, but if both parties are focused it could happen; more likely people just adapt to them."
8	Do you believe the adage that women are more moody than men?		
	No. "Having raised one of each, I know they're sometimes equally moody but often have very different ways of showing, hiding, or masking their feelings."	**Yes.** "Maybe that's because I grew up the oldest in a family with four other sisters. I was surrounded by moody girls until my two younger brothers showed up."	**Yes.** "I think I am more emotional and, therefore, subject to more emotions showing."
9	Do you think you are 50% responsible for any communication breakdown?		
	Yes. "If there's two of us in the relationship and I think there's trouble with my partner, who else could share the other half but me?"	**Yes.** "Everything's connected, and everybody's responsible for their own stuff."	**Yes.** "One of two things (or both) usually happens between two people—one person doesn't explain effectively and/or the other doesn't listen closely."
10	Do you "give in" to avoid conflict?		
	Yes. "Sometimes it's just easier to give in and move on and forget."	**Yes.** "But it doesn't mean I have to like it."	**No.** "It's not worth it in the long run."
	SUE	**RICHARD**	**SUZANNE**

I-I Couple

JIM	SHERI	JERRY
Yes.	**Yes.** "I believe this to be true in most cases."	**Yes.** "Again, only with all parties working at it."
No. "But I do believe their moodiness lasts longer."	**Yes.** "I think it's true most of the time."	**Yes.** "I believe adages and unfortunately perpetuate some of them myself."
Yes. "Not always, but probably half the time."	**Yes.**	**No.**
No. "Not usually."	**Yes.** Sometimes, not always—but I try to avoid it.	**No.** "Not normally, unless needless pain is caused by pursuing rather than giving in. Otherwise, I'll seek to find a win/win or reason to work out whatever it is."

1.4 E-E Couple E-I Couple

11 Do you tend to blame other people or situations for your feelings or actions?

No. "Why should I blame someone else for what's inside of me?"	**Yes.** "Sometimes, other people do things or say things that they know are going to hurt, and they do them anyway. That's not my fault… it's theirs."	**No.** "I feel responsible for my own feelings, words and actions."

12 Do you find yourself helping other people to the exclusion of yourself?

Yes. "I can't stand to see other people hurt or suffer sometimes."	**Yes.** "It makes me uneasy to see someone else in pain."	**No.**

	SUE		RICHARD		SUZANNE	
Total	**8**	**4**	**10**	**2**	**7**	**5**
	Yes	No	Yes	No	Yes	No

I-I Couple

JIM	SHERI	JERRY
Yes.	**No.** "It depends on the circumstance. It may be my first reaction to blame someone else because it is easier to blame others than it is to look at your responsibility in a situation."	**Yes.** "In certain situations (traffic, et cetera) that are out of my control, I do. Normally, no."
Yes. "But only because I usually don't need help."	**No.** "Maybe sometimes."	**No.** "No, although I haven't played a game of golf since 2003. I don't do choir or piano or tennis or several other things I used to do. Golf is pretty much to avoid the time away from family during what would normally be 'family' time—Saturday/Sunday, especially. Other than that, it's not that the time isn't available, because I'm spending it helping someone else."
4 Yes, 8 No	7 Yes, 5 No	6 Yes, 6 No

To get started, I thought of prototype automobiles—you know, the original mockups of cars that engineers build before they mass produce the real thing. I wondered: How on earth, could I help you, the reader, tell the two very different talk styles apart? How could I interact with you when you don't spend the whole day with me in my office? Well, this is how: I imagined the questions that you would want to ask me whenever you are in a face-off with a co-communicator who is frustrating you.

Chart 1.5 Pages 38–59

So in the spirit of good science, this is what I did. I created the 12-item NICI as the instrument to tell you and me which car is which on the communication highway—who is really driving?
I concluded there are two communicator styles that are the skeleton of the body of talk. I also decided to pretend to imagine how a composite portrait of my clients would respond to the questions. This composite portrait is referenced in Chart 1.5. Since I held the essential group communication data bank in my experience, I thought that it was only fair to speak from both Empathizer and Instigator voices. It turned out to be some hard mental stretching and flexing, but it was worth all the hard work. I hope the process will be easier for you but just as enriching.

The short story here is that an Empathizer's feelings are too easily hurt—while an Instigator's feelings are not hurt easily enough.

The short story here is that an Empathizer's feelings are too easily hurt—while an Instigator's feelings are not hurt easily enough. We all know that! Each style is simply different and simply astonishing. Empathizers and Instigators need interaction with each to fully do their thing and feel their zing! As one of my clients ripped, "I feel intensely. My partner thinks intensely. It's not fair to judge either of us as right or wrong, good or evil." My response to that: Amen.

Using this beginning prototype model or skeleton, let us begin to understand how Empathizer and Instigator communicators operate differently when driving down the two-way communication highway.

Whew! What a workout. Do you feel like you need to stop and catch your breath? You're awesome in piecing together new information into a comprehensible whole.

You probably noticed in the earlier diagrams of Empathizer and Instigator communicators that the circle has a cross in the middle dividing the circle in four equal quadrants. Figure 4 shows you *why* these four communicator modes are going to become some of your truest friends:

THE FOUR COMMUNICATOR MODES

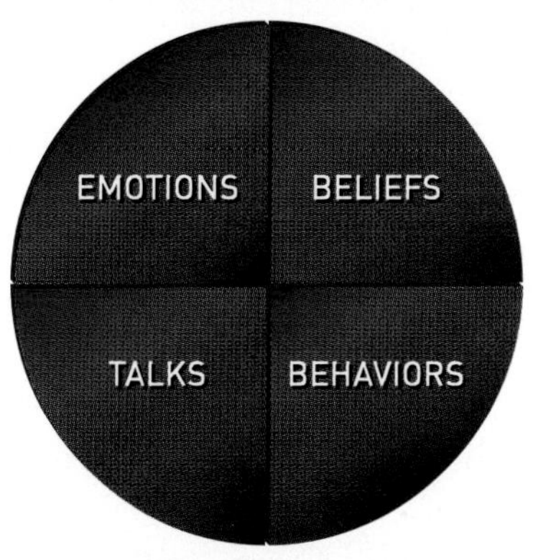

figure **#4**

Wow! You've really surpassed the goal of this chapter, which was to identity your communicator type and learn a little bit about it. And there's more to come, but it's just about time to take a break and rest.

Let's end this session on a note about strengths.

ADOPTING THE STRENGTHS OF YOUR OPPOSITE COMMUNICATOR STYLE: MEETING IN THE MIDDLE OF THESE TWO EXTREMES

Depending on whether you come from the inner world of an Empathizer (E-type) communicator or the outer world of an Instigator (I-type) communicator, your world is the only one in which you feel comfortable maneuvering. Empathizers and Instigators who meet on middle ground between these two worlds create and promote positive communication and intense emotional intimacy, the kind of intimacy from which love pours. Learning the communication world of an E-type or an I-type truly is only half of the whole story of effective communication. My goal is to encourage you to *adopt the strengths* of your opposite communicator style when it suits you to do so.

My goal is to encourage you to *adopt the strengths* of your opposite communicator style when it suits you to do so.

Since you are probably now aware of your type—and aware of your co-communicator's type—here are just a few of the different strengths that E-types and I-types apply differently in their interpersonal exchanges and decisions.

1.5 Empathizer | Instigator

1 Do you try hard not to hurt anyone's feelings?

Yes. I don't want to hurt anyone's feelings. I consider myself a sensitive and caring person. I try hard to make people feel better. Sometimes, my energy feels drained out of me.

No. I wouldn't exactly say I try hard not to hurt everyone. Now I don't want anyone to feel bad and I certainly don't want to be the cause of a problem. However, sometimes you can't help hurting others if what you have to say or your opinion is disliked or unpopular.

2 Are your feelings easily hurt?

Yes. I live in an emotional inner world where my feelings do get easily hurt. I've known that ever since I was a young child. When my feelings are hurt as an adult, my world stands still until I can get my bearings again.

I try to be honest and positive in all my relationships. I struggle with feelings of sadness, of feeling good enough, but I don't thrive on the negative. I am a big believer in emotional honesty and transparency. Honesty and trust make a positive relationship world go around.

Put-downs, even accidental slights, stick to me like a bad smell. Don't talk down to me, or I will feel intimidated and back off. My hurt feelings take a while to go away, sometimes they never do.

No. I don't wear my emotions on my sleeve because I'm a strong person.

I need the positive to plus up my life, I hate talking negative. I am a big believer in good works that last the test of time. Don't take this wrong, though. I'm a selfish person.

I admit, I do get mad, probably too often, and I wish I could control my temper better. I am definitely impatient. I can shrug off slights because I try my best not to take things too personal. I forgive and forget and move on.

Put-offs and cross-ups in communication bug me and stick into my back like a knife. Don't talk down to me or I will get angry and cross you off my list.

Empathizers strive hard to get along with others and understand how everyone feels. An Empathizer is loaded with empathy and is able to walk a mile in another person's moccasins. E-types lead from their emotions.

On the other hand, Instigators instigate change and handle interpersonal conflict more confidently. They don't beat around the bush when they talk. Instead, they get straight to the point. I-types lead from their beliefs. Instigators also often feel disappointed in the actions of Empathizers. Both communicators are responsible for the emotional welfare and happiness of one another in the relationship.

An Empathizer is loaded with empathy and is able to walk a mile in another person's moccasins.

Instigators instigate change and handle interpersonal conflict more confidently.

On the talk road, Empathizer communicators first sort through their emotions before they share or talk about the emotions with the co-communicator. Telling an E-type what to do or what action to implement when they're feeling sad is rude.

The Instigator communicator's path is to work from the facts, and clarify them logically by thinking through beliefs, and then making new plans of action. Forcing an I-type to talk when they are in the sorting process is agitating.

Conflict occurs when honest emotional disclosures get a cutting comeback line, such as "you're being too sensitive," "you're taking this way too personal," "you don't understand what I'm trying to tell you," or "tell me what you feel right now." Conflict is the result of unfair power plays that seek to win a debate or point at the expense of mutual understanding or love.

Both communicators are responsible for the emotional welfare and happiness of one another in the relationship.

Telling an E-type what to do or what action to implement when they're feeling sad is rude.

Forcing an I-type to talk when they are in the sorting process is agitating.

1.5 Empathizer Instigator

3 Do you think of yourself as being too sensitive?

Yes. Absolutely, I've been told scores of times that I'm too sensitive. I cannot argue with that indictment of me.

Whenever I hear statements like "you think too much," "you're being too sensitive," or "you're taking this way too hard," I feel scolded for feeling what I do.

No. I'm rarely told that I'm too sensitive. In fact, I am accustomed to being accused of being too insensitive—but I do really have a big heart! When I feel backed into a corner or confronted unfairly and criticized for feeling too little, I back off from the relationship. My ego stings when I feel in the wrong about anything.

There is a time to be sensitive and a time to be insensitive.

There is a time to be sensitive and a time to be insensitive.

Although empathy and sensitivity are the biggest blessings of Empathizers, both traits can result in Empathizers' relationship downfalls. Conversely, although genuineness is a priceless gift of Instigators, their insensitivity can put them into emotional bankruptcy in many relationships, both business and personal.

Each communicator type needs to adopt some of the positive attributes of the opposing style to get along better—if we all genuinely care to get along better.

Communication cross-ups are not your fault, but they are certainly your responsibility and your finest opportunity for a new positive moment to change.

Take hold of that moment.

1.5 Empathizer

Instigator

4 Do you believe talking about feelings makes things better?

Empathizer

Yes. I believe talking about feelings or disappointments keeps the relationship on track. I believe honesty, trust and coming to compromise are the glue that keeps relationships strong. However, sometimes I get anxious when I can't talk about an issue with my co-communicator. When talks break down, I feel stranded and all alone.

I try hard not to miscommunicate, but when I do, I stew and go over in my head what I could have said or done differently. I can second-guess myself and drive myself nuts sometimes. I might even feel sorry for myself and throw a pity party, but eventually I get back up and get going again. I don't feel happy, or loved, and I dry up inside when we all can't get along and connect emotionally.

Also, I like to help others as much as I can. I struggle with perfectionism because I'm an idealist who believes you can resolve any conflict with teamwork.

Overall, I'm a caring person who values relationships and plays by the rules.

Instigator

Yes. Talking about feelings can help, but only if you focus on solutions instead of griping. I believe in logical problem-solving more than I believe in analyzing emotions. I give only one ear when I have to listen to someone else's emotions.

People have to take more responsibility for their actions. When my point of view isn't heard, I can quickly become impatient and feel resentment. I don't want to get bogged down in feelings. I want to get over them and move on.

I don't miscommunicate often, because I'm pretty blunt and to the point. I'm a glass-is-half-full kind of a person and I dislike the pessimistic "poor me" crowd who can suck the energy right out of me. When I make a communication mistake, I apologize and set the record straight or make up for the wrong.

I'm accused of coming on too strong when I feel miffed or slighted. But hey, I don't practice sidewalk psychology. I don't have the time to have a long memory for small slights. I just want to get past problems and move on.

Overall, I'm a responsible person who values results that come from forming relationships.

All humans wrestle with basic individual feelings: mad, sad, scared and glad.

There are other basic interpersonal emotions that co-communicators struggle with, including dysphoria (or feeling blue), anxiety (or feeling agitated), anger (or feeling resentful), and guilt (or feeling unworthy).

Empathizers struggle with sad feelings when relationship matters aren't going well.

Empathizers struggle with sad feelings when relationship matters aren't going well.

Instigators struggle with mad feelings when relationship matters aren't going well.

Instigators struggle with mad feelings when relationship matters aren't going well.

When misunderstandings or conflicts erupt, both E-types and I-types become anxious, but they show their anxiety differently. E-types will want to talk out their anxiety, and I-types will want to act out or take action to quell their anxiety. The truly negative communicator's credo is: "If you don't talk or think about what's painful, everything will be okay."

E-types will want to talk out their anxiety, and I-types will want to act out or take action to quell their anxiety.

Overall, when anxiety runs high, you and your co-communicator make far more unintended communication mistakes. Guilt results. Guilt trips are used against you to make you feel as if you're solely at fault for the communication breakdown—which isn't true. When you pick up and lug the entire guilt load around with you, you become self-defeating and resist pursuing your positive goals.

Lastly, anxious E-types move toward the relationship in order to repair it while anxious I-types move away from the relationship to feel more secure.

Lastly, anxious E-types move toward the relationship in order to repair it while anxious I-types move away from the relationship to feel more secure.

1.5 Empathizer Instigator

5 Are you surprised when your strong words or actions make someone else feel bad?

No. I am not often surprised when something I've said or done upsets someone. Although I try hard to be nice, to tread lightly and not step on any toes—I realize it's still possible for me to upset people. I constantly scan the face of my co-communicator to be aware of how my words are coming across.

I make an extensive effort to include others' feelings and not hurt anyone, so much so that I feel like I am walking on eggshells, sometimes. I am intimidated when someone gets mad at me. I'm afraid of angry feelings and words. I back down and go into myself, and agree to do things that I really don't care to do.

I believe everyone has the power to make you feel good or bad by what they say or do.

Yes. I feel taken off guard when my words are taken wrong or come across too strong because I didn't mean anything by it. I was just being forthright, and telling it like I see it without sugar coating anything. People are too indirect and need to come to the point more often and deal with it. I don't have the patience to constantly wave a magical wand to make everyone feel all warm, and fuzzy and nice. People are responsible for their own minds and emotional states.

I constantly scan my mind and may look off into space when I'm thinking abou the next point I want to make when I open my mouth. I don't play mind games, though. I'm a strong person, and I like to exude confidence and live by a positive attitude. But I'm not a pushover, so if you come at me I will be aggressive right back. I stand my ground and don't back down if I think I'm in the right and the issue is a big one to me.

I feel everyone has the power and ultimate responsibility to make themselves feel good or bad by what they say or do.

E-types create positive new results when they discuss their beliefs—why they believe as they feel and do. I-types create positive new results when they encounter their emotions and discuss them. Positive communicators are flexible to get the job done, which requires ongoing awareness of your feelings, thoughts, deeds and words. In each communicator mode, you must feel able and free to choose the positive over the negative.

E-types create positive new results when they discuss their beliefs—why they believe as they feel and do. I-types create positive new results when they encounter their emotions and discuss them.

Negative communicators give the impression that no one, especially themselves, can make another person feel bad by what they say or do, which isn't true. "You alone are responsible for feeling bad," they'll croon to others. Instead of being 50% responsible for any communication mishap, negative talkers hold themselves harmless. Negative communicators believe that others are free to choose to feel negative, neutral or positive about an upsetting event. So, why doesn't everyone just step up and choose to be optimistic, they wonder? This lets the negative communicator off the hook for his/her negativity.

Negative communicators give the impression that no one, especially themselves, can make another person feel bad by what they say or do, which isn't true.

In truth, when relationship efforts and energy are not mutual, and when power plays or avoidance replace cooperation and satisfaction, everyone will experience an energy drain that must be plugged. And simply being optimistic may not be the cure!

Empathizers and Instigators alike share the common belief that they are either a negative or a positive communicator—inside their skulls and outside in the real world. As either an E-type or an I-type, you get to choose. You are not stuck in the negative because of past conditioning. When you put a positive Empathizer communicator together with a positive Instigator communicator—the fireworks display will be beautiful and rich.

When you put a positive Empathizer communicator together with a positive Instigator communicator—the fireworks display will be beautiful and rich.

In reverse, as you might expect, a negative Empathizer with a negative Instigator communicator causes nasty explosions that you don't want to witness.

1.5 Empathizer Instigator

6 Do you believe you have the power to get out of a relationship rut?

Yes. When I'm stuck in a relationship rut, I may not exactly choose how I feel, but I do choose what I'm going to do about it, if anything. When I feel stuck, I can feel my mood start to bring me down, but I still take ownership of my feelings. I'll ask for help when I'm stuck in order to make better choices.

I believe honesty is the best policy when things aren't going well. I don't trust anyone who says, "Wait, can I be honest for a moment here?" What are they doing the rest of the time, lying like a bad rug? Also, when a relationship crash occurs, I often think it must have been my fault. I can also feel distracted, unfocused and I can underperform at work when I feel stuck in a muddy pit of negative emotions that sap my energy. My physical health can suffer, too.

As a rule, I measure relationship success by how positive I feel and how happy we are. I believe that happiness should be the rule, not the exception, in a positive, adult-to-adult relationship.

No. I don't choose how I feel because the situation makes me feel what I do. I don't value reacting to situations. I prefer instead to think of it as being responsive to a situation. Since my problem-solving skills are so developed, I like the challenge of tackling a crisis and getting my wheels unstuck from a relationship rut.

Often I don't quite know what I feel, and I'm not sure I even care to. I really have to think about it, because feelings come in and feelings go out like the tide. My partner says you have to drag emotions out of me, which I don't think is entirely true. To be honest with you, many times I blame the other person in my mind for causing the difficulty. It's not all my own fault. I'm not trying to cause trouble here, but I have noticed that ignoring a problem sometimes makes it go away over time. Talking wears me out.

I'm at my best in the midst of a crisis. You can count on me to take the lead and put out the fire! I don't like hearing myself complain, so I don't often ask for help or hire a communications coach. When I am disappointed or angry I am worked up, and being worked up motivates me to tackle projects. I fear striking back out of anger when I don't mean to. If I stopped to think about it, I often feel alone in my primary relationships.

As a rule, I measure the success of a relationship by the goals that are accomplished. I also believe a solid positive relationship with my partner should be the norm, not the exception.

Relationship ruts make an Empathizer feel hopeless and an Instigator feel powerless. During relationship distress, both E-types and I-types are prone to behave in emotionally irresponsible and blaming ways by playing The Anger Game. This is a problem because blame is a compounding negative emotion. Blame steams ahead into self-fulfilling negative beliefs/thinking and into negative, self-defeating, behaviors/actions that escalate the problems and issues. Instead, talking honestly about emotions without blaming the co-communicator pulls couples up and out of many relationship/ communication ruts.

Empathizers hate feelings of interpersonal hopelessness, whereas Instigators hate feelings of interpersonal helplessness. The Anger Game is the second-biggest reason for relationship breakups, right behind mismatching. Distressed couples are more likely to fight in unfair ways, and the ways they fight unfairly are standard across distressed couples. An example of this is "Kitchen Sinking," where two people stand around in the kitchen and yell at each other without resolving anything, day are day after day. Empathizers like to feel connected, while Instigators like to feel in control.

Boredom and loneliness, two emotions that live in couples/families dealing with depression, must be addressed on a regular couple basis or emotional intimacy will stagnate. Fun activities, such as "date nights," and emotionally meaningful dialogue can create excitement and keep couple energy levels high. Experimenting sexually with juicy, mutually agreed upon fantasy/activities is also important to sustaining the loving couple. E-types feel most sexual when emotional bonds are the strongest, while I-types believe that a strong achievement drive creates positive emotions in couples. We all have heard from the pulpit that without a satisfied couple, family cohesion weakens, but few of us take this advice to heart.

When feelings run high, Empathizers can't hide their feelings. When feelings run high, Instigators don't want to show their feelings. Both communicators are prone to going into emotional seclusion—or coming on too strong—when negative feelings are too intense. Positive communicators try to be proactive when their dysphoric, anxious and angry feelings are running wild.

When Empathizers or Instigators feel cornered in a relationship conflict, each becomes riddled with self-doubts, such as: "I feel worthless and unloved and something must be wrong with me." When defensive, everyone forgets how lovable and important they are. Get a grip! Any way you turn it, throwing up your hands in exasperation and handing the wheel of your power over to a passenger in your life car isn't safe.

Responsive vs. Reactive Communicators are flexible, accurate, non-victim types who choose to drive in new directions instead of spinning their tires and cursing about the unfairness of it all.

Distressed couples are more likely to fight in unfair ways, and the ways they fight unfairly are standard across distressed couples.

When feelings run high, Empathizers can't hide their feelings. When feelings run high, Instigators don't want to show their feelings.

When defensive, everyone forgets how lovable and important they are.

Responsive vs. Reactive Communicators are flexible, accurate, non-victim types who choose to drive in new directions instead of spinning their tires and cursing about the unfairness of it all.

1.5 Empathizer | Instigator

7 Do you believe that communication gaps are correctable?

Yes. I believe that communication gaps are normal and can be corrected if people are willing to work on them. Partners who go in different directions for too long eventually run into a communication wall. Even when a relationship bridge blows up, I believe you can repair and rebuild it.

I am by nature a little pessimistic, I guess. Sometimes I feel like the glass is half-empty and has a hole in the bottom. In order to span a communication gap, I have to get the listener's attention and talk honestly about what I'm really thinking and feeling. Talks break down when different ideas aren't heard, and blame is tossed back and forth like a lit stick of dynamite.

Negative communicators expect me to give in to their needs. Negative communicators also expect me to give up my identity and independence. They say, "I didn't mean to blurt out something that hurt your feelings, so accept my apology and get over it." I am a big-hearted giver, and I don't keep score of good deeds done. I am usually not a big fan of change because I like stability and security, but I don't think of myself as someone who resists change, either. In fact, my co-communicator accuses me of being a wee bit phobic about change.

Whenever I feel like I am doing all of the communication work, I don't feel good about myself or the other party. I feel misunderstood, under-appreciated and quietly resentful.

Yes. I know you can close a communication gap when both parties want to. Now you can't always stay cool or talk sane during tense times—that's understandable—but that doesn't make me a goat on a rope. Words are just that—words. Why get all bent out of shape by them? Partners who use a decent map of goals and plans don't run into a communication wall or stalemate.

I am by nature an optimist, so I believe the glass is always half-full, so full it's overflowing. In order to span a communication gap, I have to release resentments, let them go and not think about them too much or they will fester and I will stop being positive. Talks break down when I can't agree to disagree.

Negative communicators expect me to be dependent and one down, or what feels like one step below everyone else. Negative communicators also expect me to give up my identity and independence. They say, "I've been giving in to your agenda and meeting your needs and I'm finally fed up with selfish old you." I am big-hearted, but I value putting my head over and above my feelings. I keep score, and I occasionally do keep track of favors done. Typically, I am a huge fan of change because I like excitement and adventure and hate to be bored. In fact, my co-communicator accuses me of being compulsive about change, never satisfied with the status quo.

Whenever I feel like I am getting all the criticisms and none of the praise, I don't feel good about myself or my co-communicator. I feel misunderstood, under-appreciated and quietly resentful.

Empathizers believe that Instigators try to talk them out of their feelings. Instigators feel that Empathizers back down too quickly and don't stand up to their logical arguments fast or strong enough. When communicating effectively, the goal isn't to score points but for co-communicators to understand, cooperate and feel heard.

E's approach change by trying to understand the problem, whereas I's approach change by trying to fix the problem. Empathizers experience Instigators as using a defense I call "head-spinning," while Instigators experience Empathizers as using a defense I call "gut-dropping." Both E- and I-types are right to believe or think that their vulnerabilities are known to their co-communicator, and that the co-communicator knows full well which buttons to press at any time to get a reaction or rise.

Empathizers experience Instigators as using a defense I call "head-spinning," while Instigators experience Empathizers as using a defense I call "gut-dropping."

What do I mean by head-spinning and gut-dropping? Head-spinning is a misguided attempt by I-types to bridge the communication gap by using negative talk to throw off the focus or turn the spotlight away from emotions.

Gut-dropping is a misguided attempt by an Empathizer to bridge the communication gap by using negative talk to throw off the focus or turn the spotlight away from beliefs or logical thinking.

Instigators can spin your ideas around until you feel like an idiot.

Instigators can spin your ideas around until you feel like an idiot.

Empathizers can rip open your heart and emotions and make you feel like a guilty fool.

Empathizers can rip open your heart and emotions and make you feel like a guilty fool.

I believe positive communicators can purposely steer the communications car back on track during difficult times. In doing so, positive communicators also invite positive change to come along for the ride.

	Empathizer	Instigator
1.5		

8 Do you believe the adage that women are more moody than men?

Yes. I think everyone has deep emotions—women as well as men do. If you are a human being and not an alien, you feel deeply, as deep as the ocean. I agree that women are moody. I disagree if you are implying men aren't just as moody or emotionally standoffish sometimes, because they are. Men and women are equal, which means women have access to deep emotions and men do, too. Love means becoming friends with all of your emotions.

Yes. We're all moody sometimes but I believe that you shouldn't get too carried away with emotions. Emotions can lead to your undoing. I come alive and work at my best during a crisis but there's a price I pay for it. A man or woman who stuffs big feelings into the back of a closet is trying to de-escalate tensions to get the job done and make things better. Sure, you can get a little jittery and crabby when you shove issues to the back of the mind. I know women who are pretty darn gruff, tough and inexpressive. I also know men who are pretty darn open, sensitive and expressive. It's all in how you look at it, because knowledge is power.

Empathizers suffer from what I call relationship attention-surplus disorder. They tune in when they ought to tune out.

Instigators suffer from relationship attention-deficit disorder—they tune out when they ought to tune in.

The point of talking positively is to meet emerging needs in diverging communicators. Both men and women are often in the mood for a good talk. The question is: do we ever allow ourselves such delicious pleasures on a regular basis?

In my observation, people in general are very moody and filled to the brim with dramatic emotions that make adults behave like children. How a man or woman chooses to behave in response to these emotional tides or energy charges is both an individual matter and a relationship matter. Too often, communicators give up or attack when they are feeling overwhelmed.

Communication isn't about gender as much as many people presume. In my opinion, your Communicator type is more important than your gender type. Men at work or at home can be grumpy, grouse about the boss, snap when an unexpected event unfolds or whine to co-workers when they're anxious or angry as much as or more than women can. Conversely, I've worked with many professional men and women who can be cool as cucumbers at work—and who may snap, gripe and snipe at home.

But both E- and I-types agree on one thing, and so do I: blaming bad/negative behaviors on bad/negative feelings, or blaming bad/negative talking on bad/negative logic, is ducking the issue of responsibility, and doing so never helps to repair the relationship bridge.

Empathizers suffer from what I call relationship attention-surplus disorder. They tune in when they ought to tune out.

Instigators suffer from relationship attention-deficit disorder—they tune out when they ought to tune in.

The point of talking positively is to meet emerging needs in diverging communicators.

Communication isn't about gender as much as many people presume.

1.5	Empathizer	Instigator

9 Do you think you are 50% responsible for any communication breakdown?

Empathizer

Yes. I believe that it takes two to tango and two to get untangled when a communication breakdown occurs. I am at least half-responsible for any communication that has gone off track. I don't cast stones of blame, even though I might feel at fault. I always give people the benefit of the doubt.

The biggest road block I face is when my co-communicator is not aware of his or her part in the problem and dodges responsibility for talking effectively about the issues. Although I have a very long fuse, I can go off when I feel burned up.

I'm accountable for my actions, although sometimes I think I overlook and put up with problems more than I care to admit.

Instigator

Yes. I am the responsible nucleus that holds everything together. Don't take this wrong, but I often don't feel at fault for the communication mix-up. I am not a control freak, but I need to have a sense of positive control, so I come up with answers and provide guidance to others. In doing so, I try to negotiate logical, fair settlements during communication standoffs or breakdowns. If I can't lead the way to a solution, then I feel like a failure. I don't like to point fingers and assign fault, but there is a right and a wrong way to go about doing things. Just to joke with you, yes, I'm not always 50% responsible, but probably I am half the time.

The biggest roadblock I face is when my co-communicator is not aware of his or her part in the problem and dodges any responsibility for talking rationally and sanely about the issues. Or my partner will become over-emotional and I dislike handling that messy stuff. Although I have a very short fuse, I can hang tough during a crisis and stand strong.

I go numb when I'm overwhelmed. I need my life areas of home and work to be upbeat. I'm like a shark. I need to continue to move forward in order to breathe and survive. I know I should put more work into my relationship, but career comes first. I can do better if given the chance. When I feel frustrated, one of my goals now is to avoid being short or saying mean words that I can't take back. I am not a shell empty of emotions.

I'm accountable for my actions, although sometimes I think I cause more of my problems than I care to admit.

The 50% communicator responsibility rule states that you are half-responsible for any relationship outcome. It is a good rule to help you keep a perspective about any mind game that you are struggling to resolve. This rule makes you take responsibility mentally for a problem that is co-invented. This rule also keeps you from being mentally lazy and lapsing into a blame game.
This rule strives to put the power back in your hands instead of the lap of your antagonist. This rule helps you escort a troublemaker to the exit of your mind to take time off from thinking about him/her. This rule keeps a negative communicator from occupying the center stage of your mind long enough to get your attention focused again on your life goals.

The 50% communicator responsibility rule states that you are half-responsible for any relationship outcome.

1.5 Empathizer | Instigator

10 Do you "give in" to avoid conflict?

Yes. I dislike conflict. And yes, I must admit that I give in sometimes to avoid making a conflict worse when I probably should stand firm or refuse to shut up. Unfortunately, I give in because I feel intimidated and that sends the wrong message to my antagonist. I need to learn how to press on and make my point heard when the co-communicator acts aggravated with me. I've noticed lately that in order to be heard, I have to really speak up and be firm and stay focused on the topic at hand.

I do best during a conflict if you listen to how I feel instead of get your next point ready to throw at me. Once my feelings are out, then I can brainstorm new options to old problems with you—but don't rush me. I believe you hear me best when I state my feelings concisely and assertively, without a hidden agenda. I believe you respect me more when I push back and don't let myself be pushed around. Because I dislike fighting, bickering and arguing, I will give up my good ideas to appease the debater—or absorb negative thinking. Some people I know love to fight rather than change ideas, but that doesn't include me.

I will stand up for my values if I'm pushed pretty hard, but I've got to convince myself it's worth it. I work hard at getting along. I think I am well liked and accepted. I feel uneasy when someone doesn't like me. Thus, a manipulative person can act mad and use threats to make me do something I don't want to.

I need to stop worrying so much about what everyone thinks about me. I feel stupid when hurtful words are hurled my way because I feel guilty—like I've brought the misunderstanding on myself.

Yes. I really try to avoid conflict but I won't giv in when I know I'm in the right. I realize I can be intolerant at times, especially when I'm sure what has to be done. People depend on me for leadershi I like taking charge and settling conflicts.

I do best when I state my beliefs assertively. Howev sometimes I'm not congruent and my actions don always match my words. I put more effort into my work life than my relationship life. I get bored eas I don't think many people tell me what they truly think of me, and that's okay by me. I tend to bark out orders like a commander when my emotions a bursting or bristling. I will stand up for my values because without them, I feel like a ship without a rudder or a car without a steering wheel. I feel gui when I hear secondhand that I have run over someone I work with or care for and have made them feel bad because I pushed and pushed until I got my way.

I need to worry more about what everyone thinks about me and what emotional impact I have on people. I have always been pretty dynamic and charismatic, so I know people accept me even wh my actions don't fulfill my word or the commitments I've made about a relationship. I feel uneasy when someone doesn't agree with me, although I say we can still stay friends. I prefer to follow through on my timetable—not yours—ar when I'm in the mood to.

I feel guilty when my words or actions cause hurt misunderstanding. When an attempt at communication goes bust, I try not to feel bad for very long and instead try to do something positive myself—or somehow make up for the aggravatio with the other person. When I've done wrong, I fe owe it to the other person to give them some type extra compensation to even the score.

Empathizer and Instigator communicators are both big believers in the philosophy that responsible and accountable individuals do not run away from problems. Instead, they agree to disagree maturely.

Nevertheless, in my clinical studies, Empathizers are voted most likely to back down during a conflict of opinion the fastest, while Instigators won't back off even when their position isn't a very effective one to stick to. Also, I-types are more opinionated while E-types are more open-minded. In general, E-types go with the flow of the relationship and accept the limits inherent in a situation while I-types need to improve a situation by going against the grain of the relationship.

Empathizers are voted most likely to back down during a conflict of opinion the fastest, while Instigators won't back off even when their position isn't a very effective one to stick to.

Empathizers can be on the shy side when it comes to focusing on one's self, seeking pleasure or basking in the spotlight. Instigators are more at ease having their needs met and dominating a situation because they enjoy being liked and being active. Instigators speak strongly and then move on, while Empathizers don't speak up enough and thus don't get ahead. When either type uses guilt trips, they set themselves up to give up who they really are in exchange for being liked.

1.5 Empathizer | Instigator

11 Do you tend to blame other people or situations for your feelings or actions?

No. I refuse to pin blame on anyone because blame games are a total waste of my time and energy. People skills, civility and self-awareness are in short enough supply nowadays.

I have mixed feelings about change. I believe motivation is a personal inner decision and not inspired by outside factors or rewards to fire me up. I am criticized often for making a mountain out of a molehill and not being able to let things go. Perhaps I care too much about what others are feeling.

I don't have the power to make someone else feel bad enough to change. I shouldn't have to beg someone else for time and attention. I dislike blame games and unhealthy anger. However, I get very angry sometimes and I feel guilty about it. When my partner makes a unilateral decision that negatively affects me, I may be quiet.

I've definitely noticed that I take communication mishaps more seriously than others do. Sometimes I can't stop ruminating about how I could've said something different, or done something different, to get my message across better.

No. I think blame games are useless. I try to engineer solutions, not cause additional problems. However, I do feel blamed a lot by other people. I also often hear a long list of excuses about why someone hasn't followed through on their agreements or responsibilities.

I love change. I motivate myself by using external reinforcements like money, cars and vacation trips. I am responsible for my own actions and reactions. You are responsible for your actions and reactions. I am competitive and I hate feeling like a loser.

When you impact me with a poor decision, don't expect me to say nothing. If you push me into a corner, I will fight back. I put up walls to protect myself when I'm treated unfairly because insensitivity is a mental pain blocker.

I'm criticized for letting things go too eas and not taking relationship issues serious enough. Perhaps I care too little about wh others are feeling.

"Don't take it so personally" is good advice for an Empathizer to use. "Do take it more personally" is good advice for an Instigator to adopt. "Go easy on yourself and your partner until you calm down!" is great advice for Empathizer and Instigator communicators who are in a power play. The solution to failures of communication is often to add empathy or an emotional gut-check to the talk process. Pinning your problems on your partner doesn't create positive communication loops where deep joy and peace are experienced. Nor should you talk to anyone as if they're beneath your dignity or easily influenced, because doing so only doubles your trouble and causes communication problems to multiply. It's important to acknowledge to yourself that a communication gap results in frustration and loss for both parties across that great emotional divide. Telling the emotional truth closes every communication gap.

"Don't take it so personally" is good advice for an Empathizer to use. "Do take it more personally" is good advice for an Instigator to adopt.

1.5 Empathizer — Instigator

12 Do you find yourself helping other people to the exclusion of yourself?

Yes. I put high value on helping others and helping them climb up the ladder of success. I am a hard worker who works now and plays later. There is always someone in crisis who needs my help and emotional support. However, a crisis or other upsetting event drains my energy and depresses my spirit.

I am a giver, not a taker. I feel sorry for people who can't express their feelings and who make bad choices. I feel responsible for making the world a better place. I believe in harmony and trying to get along. I feel tremendous sympathy for people who don't cope well with painful life happenings.

I believe that I co-create the positive or negative quality of any relationship. I may dislike what you say, but I like to know how you truly think and feel. I can get distracted with other people's problems and lose track of emotional intimacy. I can pick up the negative feelings of people I care for. I am known to be naïve and idealistic. I often put myself last on the list of do-good things. I don't give myself enough time to explore and fulfill my own needs and pleasures.

I feel mad and guilty when I behave in selfish ways and say "no" to others' demands for my time and attention.

No. I don't ignore my own needs in the process of helping others, but I do help others every day o my life. I work hard and reinforce myself with pla Being happy with who I am, what I have, where I'm working and providing economic protection f loved ones and employees are all choices that adu are free to make wisely, and I feel that I do.

I don't give myself permission to feel down or let anyone bring me down. Negativity makes me feel like I'm losing my mind! I am a risk taker who ca take action in spite of uncertainty or fear. I have a plan, and I work my plan. I don't dwell on misery since misery loves company. I believe in doing go works that last beyond this lifetime. My job is not be a martyr or help others in spite of my own nee for personal growth, peace and serenity. I try to do something positive for people who don't cope well with painful life happenings each and every day.

I realize that I can feel over-responsible at work a thus put more energy into work achievements tha personal emotional intimacy. I feel sad and guilty when I don't meet others' demands for my time a attention. I have trouble expressing how I feel an I'm prone to say what you want to hear. If I don't check in and tell my partner how I feel today, it le the air out of the relationship tires.

I stuff feelings. I've got to tell my partner what's going on in my head more. I feel sorry for people who believe that life dumps a bad deal on them. I am disappointed in people who blame me for the situation. Sometimes I feel like I can't do anythin right. It's draining and irritating, too. I hate feeli disconnected, worthless or alone.

Empathizers and Instigators feel guilty for their approaches to communication and the unintentional difficulties that take place. E-types and I-types want to feel okay, loved, and free to feel enjoyment, not entitlement, free to feel rapture, not rupture, in their interpersonal relationships. All of us have a long way to go to let go of unfair guilt and to grab hold of loving feelings, loving thoughts, loving actions, and loving words.

E-types and I-types want to feel okay, loved, and free to feel enjoyment, not entitlement, free to feel rapture not rupture, in their interpersonal relationships.

EMPATHIZER VS. INSTIGATOR INTERPERSONAL STRENGTHS

1. The emotional brain vs. the logical brain

E-types access and use the Emotional Brain more often, while I-types access and use the Logical Brain more often.

2. Interpersonal sensitivity vs. interpersonal insensitivity

E-types more often use selfless sensitivity to cope in normal, day-to-day, interpersonal interactions, while I-types use selfish insensitivity more often to cope.

3. Behind the scenes vs. star of the show

E-types habitually dislike being the center of attention, while I-types habitually like being the center of attention.

4. Past focus vs. future focus

E-types focus on the past because they want to see where they have been before moving forward, while I-types want to look ahead to where they're going and move beyond or forget about the past.

5. Talking about a problem vs. fixing a problem

E-types typically approach change by trying to *understand* the problem, while I-types typically approach change by trying to *fix* the problem.

6. Interpersonal cooperation vs. interpersonal competition

E-types believe that needs are positively met in a spirit of friendly win-win cooperation but they might not insist on their needs being met, while I-types feel more comfortable insisting that their needs be met even if doing so takes a spirit of winner-take-all competition.

7. Hopelessness vs. helplessness

E-types hate feelings of *interpersonal hopelessness,* while I-types hate feelings of *interpersonal helplessness.*

8. Internally motivated vs. externally motivated

E-types believe motivation comes from inside the self, while I-types believe motivation stems from external reinforcements.

AN ADDITIONAL EXERCISE: RE-SCORE YOUR NICI

For fun, after reading my coaching section and the classic responder comments, go back and rescore your NICI inventory for accuracy. Either way, you probably now have a good feel for which style of communicator you are.

TELLTALE ROAD SIGNS THAT YOUR COMMUNICATOR SKILLS ARE IMPROVING

How will you know when your communicator skills are improving? What are two obvious road signs to guide you?

- *You are heading in a positive direction as an Empathizer communicator when you don't take things so personally or literally.*
- *You are heading in a positive direction as an Instigator communicator when words don't come out of your mouth that you wish to take back.*

I have spent 30 years as a family psychologist studying assertive and positive communication moves that are non-judgmental. If you think about life as a big chess board, the *Talk to Me* approach shows you the black and white moves that can rid your relationship of bad feelings and replace them with positive movement and change.

This communication training is meaty and muscle-packed with new insights about communicating more smoothly and expertly in ways you can repeat on your own. Once you understand the moves, communication will no longer be a hit-and-miss mystery that knocks the breath out of you.

It may not be time quite yet to jump up and down and give high fives, but it is time for your personal trainer to deliver a little help and hope to you during low periods of your relationship.

II

LET'S TALK

To tell you the truth, I disagree that we can agree to disagree.

TRAINING GOAL

To talk deeply about two communicator styles: Empathizer and Instigator

THAT'S SO NARROW

"It's my way or the highway" is a threat that promises to break apart any relationship if you do not understand or agree with your co-communicator's frame of reference.

And as nice as the saying "Why can't we just agree to disagree?" sounds, few among us consistently take action on that sentiment, much less follow through in effective ways, because most people want things *their* way—even at the expense of the relationship.

Ah, how we love to be in control. Worse yet, assassinating the character of someone who disagrees with you, or playing the victim violin to get others to dance to your tune, is a cheap shot that is very costly in terms of relationship satisfaction.

One of my goals in providing these insights is to help you let go of negative controlling behaviors and feel more loving. Don't push, don't hurry or rush through this work. Take your time, and take it slowly, just like the tortoise in the old proverb of the Tortoise and the Hare. The truth is that your communication skills will zoom ahead effortlessly, in fantastic ways, just like the Hare, and you may even feel on fire, with insights bursting like fireworks, if you stick with this material and let it sink in.

And while that sounds dandy and inspirational, I don't want you to turn into a communications zealot, either. The last thing I want *Talk to Me* practitioners to become are fanatics—people who think they're "good" or "right" or "better than" because they're either an Empathizer or Instigator. I want you to be more open-minded, more aware, more autonomous, more spontaneous, more tolerant and more curious about your and your co-communicator's types. Enough of mindless negative labeling that creates mental laziness, interpersonal division and smugness.

Enough of mindless negative labeling that creates mental laziness, interpersonal division and smugness.

In fact, I recommend that you say *"That's so narrow of me!"* to yourself when you get too narrow-minded, deadlocked over good/bad, trapped in right/wrong debating, or start to get negative and inaccurate in your rhetorical beliefs or black-and-white view of the world. The cost of narrow-mindedness—of being so certain that you are right and the other person is wrong—is a lifetime of regrets. When you see only a narrow piece of reality, you won't see the forest for the trees, and you'll be prone to overlooking innovative and easy solutions to complex problems.

The cost of narrow-mindedness—of being so certain that you are right and the other person is wrong—is a lifetime of regrets.

One final achievement I predict for you: You will no longer feel misunderstood, lonely, unsupported or unloved for very long ever again.

THE TORTOISE AND THE HARE

Do you remember the childhood story of the Tortoise and the Hare?

It is one of my all-time favorite fables, one I've told and retold to my children. The storyline underscores a simple message: You and I can influence and control social perception in negative or positive ways, and the choice is up to you and me.

For example, you can paste a negative label on someone—such as "slow" or "fast," or "brilliant" or "dense." And if perhaps you're a decent debater, you can make that label stick. But in reality, the label is a negative power play meant to get your way at the expense of positive communication.

Back to the storyline: As you recall, The Tortoise and the Hare tells the story of a big race, or competition, between a slow-moving turtle and a speedy rabbit. The Hare raced off into the future, leaving the bulky Tortoise moving ahead slowly—but behind in the race by a mile. The Hare got so full of himself that he became lazy and unfocused and stopped to take a few too many luxurious naps. Slowly, but steadily, the Tortoise plodded ahead, eventually to cross the goal line in first place.

The pearl-colored and heavy-shelled Tortoise wins the race because his witty friend, the hurried but frazzled Hare, allowed himself to become distracted by excessive self-esteem. He was too proud, easily distracted and prone to boredom while traveling on a road he seemed to own. He slowed down when the action wasn't hot and allowed self-inflation to derail his race and take him off track. The Turtle, on the other claw, didn't need fanfare and refused to allow despondency to keep him down. . .he kept focusing on doing "first things first." He persisted, while the Hare resisted, and the Tortoise finished the race and enjoyed the fruits of victory.

Perhaps the Tortoise initially fell so far behind because he negatively *thought* the glass of success was half-empty. And perhaps the Hare positively *felt* the success glass was full-to-overflowing because he was so far ahead so early in the race. In reality? The volume of pessimism and optimism in that glass of success was the same, no matter who looked at it. (Not that anyone is counting or measuring how big first and last is. Are they?) Confidence comes less from winning than from demonstrating who you are and what you stand for during difficult and spirit-trying times.

Confidence comes less from winning than from demonstrating who you are and what you stand for during difficult and spirit-trying times.

Stephen and Sean Covey believe that success stems from doing "first things first." Secondly, Dr. Covey knows that success always stems from the Tortoise vs. the Hare philosophy. Namely, *keep going in the right direction because sooner than later, you will arrive there.* In more complex concepts, do not waste your/my time on preventable crises—*do what is important but not necessarily urgent to achieve your positive goals.* Usually, you and I save the best for last when you and I would be wiser to spend our best first.

Keep going in the right direction because sooner than later, you will arrive there.

Many times the big pay-off is more often in the little daily deeds done well. On our positive communications road traveled courageously together, you will *go for love. . .wisdom. . .compassion. . .peace in mind. . .peace in emotion.*

Many times the big pay-off is more often in the little daily deeds done well.

DON'T PLAY THE VICTIM VIOLIN

Now suppose the Tortoise and Hare race had featured a soundtrack. Would you have heard victim violins playing in the background. . . and for whom?

Sure enough, the slower Tortoise crossed the finish line first, while a much faster but frustrated bunny pulled out his own whiskers with self-defeating behaviors.

Think of that context of your own larger questions and issues: Who in your own life plays the victim violin and expects you to feel sorry for them and dance to their tune? And when do you play the victim fiddle in your life and talk negatively like a victim? Or when you use "reverse bragging" to downplay your positive strengths so your co-communicator will try to pick up your spirits with compliments and reassurances.

Who in your own life plays the victim violin and expects you to feel sorry for them and dance to their tune?

Who in your life is harvesting your attention with a "Woe-is-Me-Me-Me" story line that hardly ever changes? Who in your life feels sorry for you, with a "Woe-is-You-You-You" story line and why do you like that type of negative attention?

One dynamic of negative or controlling relationships is that guilt trips, brainwashing, bullying, anger attacks, and other negative paybacks are foisted on others. Visually speaking, the controller lifts the flap that covers your brain and inserts a poisonous disc of crap. Or worse yet, you think negative and inaccurate thoughts about yourself that poison your confidence and interpersonal responsiveness, such as: "I'm fat and ugly." Remember, you and I are co-responsible for co-creating the negative thoughts that lead to the negative outcomes you and I complain so vociferously about.

What's important for you to accept now in small or large measure: You are not a victim but a victor. You are a victim only if you want to be or if you desire to act out/play that role with drama and energy. As a victor, you take joy in mastering communication and creating a positive self-attitude. You are learning how to disallow narrow-minded guilt trippers and emotional bullies from pushing your buttons and making *you* feel their guilt. You decline to participate in blame games because you know in your gut and from a lifetime of experience that "what goes around comes around," including positive paybacks.

You are not a victim but a victor.

You choose to think and do what's positive, because you want positive paybacks to come circling back to you. And there's nothing quite like positive blessings being dropped into your life on a gray day.

That prospect sure beats the proverbial dropping of the other shoe on your skull.

SO WHAT MOTIVATES YOU?

So aren't Empathizers more negative than Instigators because they're so sensitive? That all depends on how you look at it, so let's be very careful and accurate here.

Under relational distress, an E-type's light bulb burns dimmer and dimmer until it (and the person) burns out. Oppositely, under relational distress, an I-type's physical health battery is run down more and more until it's drained and can't start any longer. Which scenario is better and which is worse? Both negative outcomes aren't very positive moves for either, and neither outcome is a good representation of the *"being vs. doing"* communicator behavior that I so dearly cherish and so love to interact with so positively.

In terms of Skinnerian rewards and punishments, E-types shrivel under negative words, disapproval and criticism. In contrast, I-types shiver at the loss of behavioral "add-ons" such as power, mental control, position or status and money. Both E-types and I-types fear interpersonal punishers such as loss of love, control or respect.

Thus, Empathizers are positively motivated when they receive accurate praise and fair criticisms. In contrast, Instigators are positively motivated when they are able to execute accomplishment strategies and subsequently receive timely financial rewards. Neither motivational preference is better or worse—just different. *Thus, E-types typically are emotion and relationship-centered, while their I-type counterparts typically are money and power-centered.* It's just the way it works for the best of all.

E-types typically are emotion and relationship-centered, while their I-type counterparts typically are money and power-centered.

In the world of business, knowing the communicator type you are dealing with makes a world of a difference.

ACCURATE OR INACCURATE THINKING

A word about negative thinking: Negative thoughts (Beliefs or B1-mode) are either accurate or inaccurate. Likewise, positive thoughts are either accurate or inaccurate.

Start now to categorize your thoughts and beliefs as either negative/positive and as either inaccurate/accurate. What about the other three talk quadrants of Emotions, Behaviors and Talks? You can do the same thing. Categorizing your own transactions is a fun emotional/mental exercise that will help you stay interpersonally upbeat, aware and emotionally fit and honest. I suggest you begin by categorizing your thinking.

Categorizing your own transactions is a fun emotional/mental exercise that will help you stay interpersonally upbeat, aware and emotionally fit and honest.

Let's start with a typical thought: "I deserve to get even!" It would best be categorized as a negative thought that is inaccurate. Also, the saying: "The last laugh is on you!" would also best be categorized as a negative thought that is inaccurate. Why do I say that? Because my experience tells me this: When you go for revenge, the last sob is on you!

Because my experience tells me this: When you go for revenge, the last sob is on you!

And you guessed it: Positive thinking can be accurate or inaccurate too.

"I'm the best thing that has ever happened to you!" is a very positive thought (or spoken sentence) that is inaccurate. "I have to make time to read Stephen Covey's 'first things first' time management habit!" is positive thought (or spoken sentence) that is inaccurate because procrastination will intervene.

My dear co-communicator, I don't want you to be extremely negative or extremely positive—I want you to be positive... accurate...realistic most of the time. When you live in that energy place, as Bob Dylan sings: "Things really start to get interesting right about now!"

So strive today to be accurate and positive, or accurate and negative, whenever possible in your thought and speech and in your written words. Realism and factual accuracy are what the world needs more today than ever before.

So strive today to be accurate and positive, or accurate and negative, whenever possible in your thought and speech and in your written words.

You will be amazed at what a positive life difference it will make.

THE MANURE SANDWICH

Empathizers, or positive E-types, can become emotionally sick by being around negative controllers too much. Conversely, Instigators or positive I-types can become physically sick by being around negative controllers.

Empathizers, or positive E-types, can become emotionally sick by being around negative controllers too much. Conversely, Instigators or positive I-types can become physically sick by being around negative controllers.

I use the "manure sandwich" metaphor to explain this energy drain and physical depletion. When either E-types or I-types chomp into a manure sandwich, served up by self or another, they gradually become sicker and sicker because of the toxins. Controllers typically brainwash you into thinking the manure sandwich you're chomping on is a bologna sandwich—but that's pure baloney! Then when you reach your breaking point, you vomit up the whole mess.

Negative control is about negative power and hate. Freud struggled with this concept when he wrote about the "Mortido drive," or death drive, the drive toward darkness and death and self-destruction. He contrasted this with the life-creating drive of lightness and life and self-construction. Negative controllers, of course, will fix you a big manure sandwich and tell you how lucky you are to have plenty of food when people all around the globe are starving! Since you are 50% co-responsible for deciding your life, you have the option to

Controllers typically brainwash you into thinking the manure sandwich you're chomping on is a bologna sandwich—but that's pure baloney!

decline biting into the manure sandwich. I believe that by absorbing positive educational information, you will be far less likely to be "brainwashed."

Why allow anyone to feed you a manure sandwich and then sell you on the inaccurate, parlayed positive belief that it is a bologna sandwich? Inaccurate negative feeling. . .or inaccurate positive thinking. . .alike and equally create unnecessary pain, psychodrama and suffering. By putting aside the manure sandwich, you will improve your positive emotions and actions, your positive thoughts and talks. It's possible to get ahead rapidly in the communication race, without losing focus, and you will. Just stick with me for a while!

You can interact with your emotions to affirm instead of condemn a negative person who wishes to brainwash you and take control of your positive emotional mind. You can also interact with your intellectual mind to stop thinking negatively about a negative person who seeks to manipulate your mind and drive you crazy. Your interpersonal, emotional and intellectual powers are incredible.

Negative people want you to feel one-down and out, but I am going to teach you how you can turn inward. . .send positive energy outward. . .feel compassion about negatives without holding on to them. . .turn away from self-hatred. . .and tune out any thief who is hell-bent on stealing your positive life energy. As long as you hold on to negative and inaccurate guilt trips, you will run yourself down and grind yourself into the ground.

I promise you this: Even when your communication race appears hopeless or lost—you will move ahead ever steadily and many times more rapidly than you ever imagined possible.

I promise you this: Even when your communication race appears hopeless or lost—you will move ahead ever steadily and many times more rapidly than you ever imagined possible. You can count on it. All you have to do is make different moves that count for more.

You are raising your interpersonal skills I.Q. as we speak!

You are becoming a positive talker and a positive thinker. You are raising your interpersonal skills I.Q. as we speak!

THE MANURE SANDWICH AND BODY DYSPHORIA

A strange thing is happening in our young teen women nowadays. They incorrectly think they're fat and ugly!

Research psychologists label the phenomenon something like "body perception disorder," but I think of it as "body dysphoria." It's a manure sandwich of the stinkiest kind any way you cut it, because our young women today are smarter. . .healthier. . .and more beautiful than ever before.

But what you think is what you get. It matters not if it's negative and inaccurate. Chart 2.1 has the negative and inaccurate thinking of a slender but "I'm fat and ugly" negative-thinking female teen:

2.1

Negative Belief (B1-)	Fact
I'm fat.	The fat to muscle ratio is near-perfect.
The scale says I'm fat.	The scale simply gives a numeric value.
I've got to lose weight.	Actual body weight is about perfect.
I can't eat supper tonight.	A healthy meal will promote positive energy and demote binge eating.
I'm so stupid for gaining weight.	One is supposed to gain appropriate weight during puberty.
I am so ugly.	The young woman is physically radiant, emotionally stunning and intellectually beautiful.

Negative Emotion (E-)	Fact
I just hate myself.	The young woman is lovable and loving, honest and sincere.

This inaccurate negative thinking takes a beloved teen downward in a negative spiral from which she feels there is no escape. Then extreme negative emotions come pouring in, adding gasoline to the fire. And parents have the nerve to wonder why female teens are so moody?

My point is this: Parents must teach teens to put down any manure sandwich that anyone tries to feed them, including society, peers, siblings, parents, and especially teens themselves.

Just as I hope *Talk to Me* will help couples, partners, workers, family members and adults adopt better communication skills and behaviors, *Talk to Me* can help teens to think straight in a crooked world—a world so crooked that teens often feel that ineffective beauty power is more preferable and socially influential than effective brainpower and positive interpersonal power. Go figure.

I wish for our teen young women and men to have it all—particularly a healthy love of and for the Self.

I wish for our teen young women and men to have it all—particularly a healthy love of and for the Self.

ACTIVE LISTENING VS. DIRECTIVE QUESTIONING

Almost everyone agrees that effective listening is a pillar of positive communication.

The rule states that you should be able to paraphrase accurately what someone has told you, and you should be able to check with the speaker that you have indeed heard the correct message. Only then are you permitted to go onto the next transaction. Typically, this clarifying question is asked: "Can you repeat back to me what I just told you?" This is a fine transaction, a way to double check if someone is listening to you or simply listening to his/her own internal dialogue. What's clear, however, is that Empathizer and Instigator communicators use very different listening approaches.

Empathizer and Instigator communicators use very different listening approaches.

Let's take the "golden" communication rule of effective listening as a simple example. This rule of positive communication says that your ability to accurately hear and paraphrase back your co-communicator's message is essential to effective communication. Furthermore, when your message is misinterpreted, you experience mounting frustrations that lead to additional miscommunications.

However, what if E-types and I-types listen to information and process it quite differently? Then what should you do?

E-types listen with three ears; they want to understand every nuance before moving forward with problem solving. In contrast, I-types listen with one ear and rapidly want to come up with advice to fix a problem.

For instance, I determined that E-types listen with three ears; they want to understand every nuance before moving forward with problem solving. In contrast, I-types listen with one ear and rapidly want to come up with advice to fix a problem. E-types will peer deep into your eyes, and give you their undivided attention. I-types will multitask and be thinking of something else while you are talking to them, tuning in when they have to.

Either way, the correct turn for you on the communication highway is the wrong turn for your opposite type.

Neither method of listening is right or wrong, they're just different ways. You will become a more effective communicator when you use active listening and ask many open-ended questions with E-types because they will feel heard. In reverse, what I call "directive questioning," or asking close-ended questions, will work best with I-types. Overall, E-types by nature listen inclusively, while I-types are by nature selective listeners.

This one difference makes a world of difference in the universe of communication.

POSITIVE TALKING

So dear reader, begin to think in terms of E-types and I-types in your everyday life.

Begin by asking yourself these important questions:

1. *If I am an E-type or I-type communicator, what exactly might that mean?*
2. *What does that type of communicator do well and what are his or her strengths and weaknesses?*
3. *What vulnerabilities or Achilles heel are typical to that type?*
4. *How can I begin to apply, or experiment with, these new concepts of communication to find out if they really work?*
5. *What positive result will prove to me beyond a shadow of a doubt that this new theory works?*

Remember, you can always go back to your old ways if you find the old patterns work better for you than the new ones. But you deserve to find out factually if you can feel more positive, think, act and talk more positively. You can turn away from negative talk habits and embrace positive talk habits no matter what your age.

You can turn away from negative talk habits and embrace positive talk habits no matter what your age.

In short, my dear E-types, you will learn how to be more insensitive and not to take things so personally. And my dear I-types,

These tools will plug into your mind like a computer chip, allowing your life to take flight as you never dreamed it could.

you are going to learn to be more sensitive and emotion-driven. In all ways, both types win and feel more loved and less guilty for their communication mistakes.

These tools will plug into your mind like a computer chip, allowing your life to take flight as you never dreamed it could.

TAKE IT SLOWLY

Communication itself isn't always easy, but positive talk can be simple when you understand and follow the Talk to Me diagrams that explain the avenues or modes of communications.

Speaking of positive talking roadmaps: Some challenges in life can be simple, but not easy. Good communication is one of them. Communication itself isn't always easy, but positive talk can be simple when you understand and follow the *Talk to Me* diagrams that explain the avenues or modes of communications. If it's true that a picture is worth a thousand words, these diagrams will improve the words that come out of your mouth.

Hey, how simple can this be? Your brain has to hold in it two new communicator types, Empathizer and Instigator, and four communicator modes called Emotions, Beliefs, Behaviors, and Talks. I know you can do this because I've been able to do it. If I can do this, anyone can do it!

My advice is to go easy for now.

My advice is to go easy for now. Trying new skills requires an open mind and the ability to have a good time. As you understand the *Talk to Me* approaches to communication, you'll also begin developing new behaviors and reactions. You'll learn that when someone steps on your toes, or stomps on your foot, you have some choices to make to keep sprinting along on the communication highway instead of veering off or crashing. A sheer act of will won't make the sensation of pain in your foot go away. And you probably won't be able to short-circuit your mental reaction or change your attitude about feeling bad. Nevertheless, you do get to choose with whom and how to talk productively about the pain with your co-communicators.

Talk to Me creates productive communication by helping people understand communication styles and make wise choices about talking and listening.

Talk to Me creates productive communication by helping people understand communication styles and make wise choices about talking and listening. Certain talk paths curtail closeness, while other talk paths will open up new avenues of communication and understanding. Certain moves will lead to success, others to failure and disappointment. You'll learn that there are better ways to talk and better ways of encouraging others by how you listen to them.

Talk to Me training is especially helpful in difficult situations, whether they involve a difficult employer–employee relations or tough emotional issues—those turbulent times when the clock is ticking and what counts most is to remain calm and focused. No one should ever give up because of poor communication.

So how can you "go on easy?" I'll teach you how to let go of negative emotions. I'll teach you how to let go of grudges. I'll teach you how to let go of unrealistic expectations and "go on easy" down the path of life. I'll teach you how to let go of unhappy ways of being. I'll teach you how to let go of the old and embrace the new, how to choose different roads and welcome new adventures, how to abandon outdated ways of thinking that no longer fit your life.

I'll teach you how to let go of negative emotions. I'll teach you how to let go of grudges. I'll teach you how to let go of unrealistic expectations and "go on easy" down the path of life.

So here comes the big question: Which communicator type do you think you are? Are you an Empathizer or an Instigator or both? If your friends were asked which type you are, would they be able to offer a crisp answer? Which communicator style do you have the most trouble comprehending?

EMPATHIZER AND INSTIGATOR COMMUNICATOR STYLES

On the next page is a graphic way to pick a style for yourself and with your nemesis, the co-communicator with whom you're having the most difficulty.

Think of Empathizers and Instigators as the members of two opposing teams.

The Empathizer team wears *blue* uniforms and the Instigator team is suited up in *burnt orange* uniforms. On the chest of each member's jersey is a big circle, divided into quadrants by a horizontal and a vertical line. Each of those quadrants has a certain function that we'll learn later. The entire circle resembles a submarine telescope, a riflescope or what you might see if you peer through a pair of binoculars.

The Empathizers' blue jerseys as shown in Figure 5 assist you to drive serenely along on the two-way communicator highway.

EMPATHIZER Communicator Style

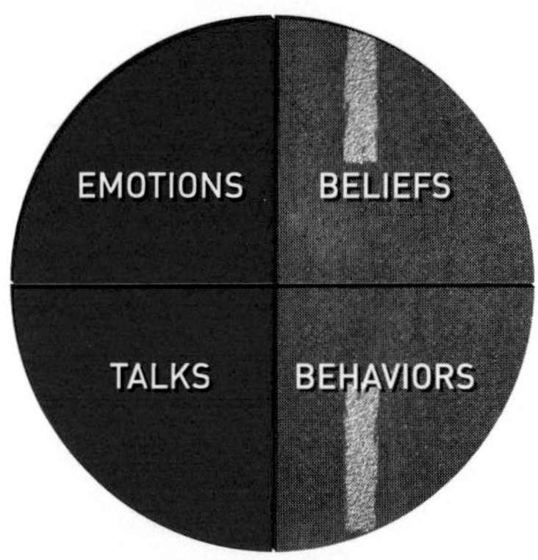

figure **#5**

Team I Empathizer

If you have been told that *you get hurt too easily or get over hurt too slowly,* you probably are an Empathizer.

The core Empathizer strength

The leading strength of an Empathizer is the capacity to give understanding and empathy. You are able to walk in the shoes of others without appearing outlandish or ridiculous. You trust your heart and your gut. Intuition serves you well. You are a relationship expert. You live in an ocean of emotion, and you know love. You are also too shy to speak out and give an opinion.

The leading strength of an Empathizer is the capacity to give understanding and empathy.

The same circle, divided into four quadrants, also is displayed in the middle of each Instigator's burnt orange jerseys, as shown in Figure 6. (By the way, I selected the names for the two communication styles very carefully to avoid any bias or judgmental beliefs. Preconceived notions can cause talks to blow up or communications bridges to fall down. They can lead to blame games and mud/slime-slinging, and none of those behaviors is productive.)

The Instigators' burnt orange jerseys as shown in Figure 6 help you to drive sanely along on the two-way communicator highway.

INSTIGATOR Communicator Style

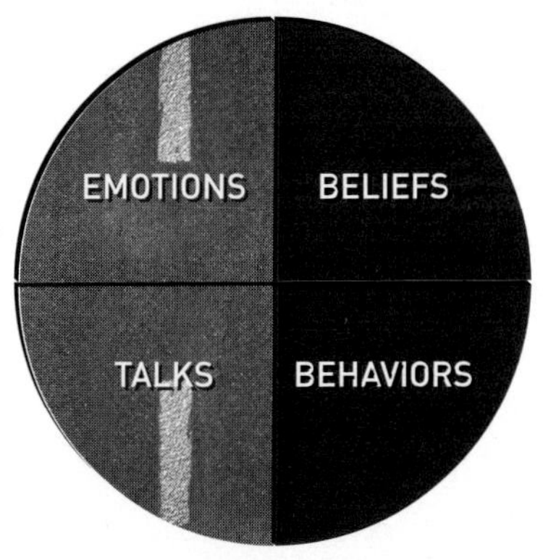

figure **#6**

Team II Instigator

If you have been told that *you're too insensitive or debate how you didn't mean to cause hurt* than probably you are an Instigator.

The core Instigator strength

The leading strength of an Instigator is the capacity to initiate action. Instigators can play above the pain when they are hurting. Instigators have the enormous capacity to make someone feel good or bad by what they say or do. Instigators are both revered and looked down on because they are powerhouses and dynamos. They are also too often the proud, charging bull that crashes through the jewelry store.

The leading strength of an Instigator is the capacity to initiate action.

Case in point: As the father of three young daughters, it's sometimes my duty to call a family powwow. And I often hear the now-famous line: "I didn't do it!" What makes this so funny is that the defensive line usually is spoken faster than my offensive line of inquiry. My Instigator child's impassioned plea is, "If I did it, I didn't do it on purpose." My Empathizer child explains, "I probably did it so I'm sorry."

In my opinion, the term "Instigator" is not any more negative or positive than the term "Empathizer." If you think about communications in terms of sports, members of both teams—the Instigators and the Empathizers—are equal in terms of ability,

In my opinion, the term "Instigator" is not any more negative or positive than the term "Empathizer."

strength and worth. Members of both teams play mind games, and some members have a few characteristics of the members on the opposing team. There are no first- or second-class communicators. The playing field is even, and if one team doesn't show up dressed for the game, there is no play.

But what the two teams have in common in this: both are in the dark about how the other team prefers to perform, and in this case, that means they don't have a clue about how the other team communicates. Empathizers don't "get" the Instigators, and Instigators don't "get" the Empathizers.

But in fact, many Instigators play a key role in your life and are affecting your life every day in every way. Why? Because Instigators have the guts to institute change and to be fearless leaders. The lifeblood that pumps through an Instigator's heart is change and progress. An Instigator pushes for something different to happen.

Either style alone is both a turn-on and a turn-off.

That doesn't mean the Instigator's style is superior or that it demands everyone's obedience. Each style, in fact, can help the other style achieve a new level and lift up spirits. Either style alone is both a turn-on and a turn-off. The key is flexibility—learning to understand both your own style and the opposite team's style so that you become a more flexible communicator.

By answering six of the 12 questions "yes" on the NICI, you've indicated to me that you really are ready to expand your Empathizer or Instigator viewpoints. You're ready to understand the opposing style and spare yourself a great deal of future heartache and pain. Right?

- Do you really intend to stop the hurt by using healing talk?
- Are you willing to learn what makes an Empathizer and Instigator really tick?
- Would you like to stop getting upset and frustrated and choose behaviors that work better in your life?

Then let's start with exercises that teach you the words and ways of playing the talk game that make a difference. Because whether you believe it or not, both Empathizers and Instigators can turn off communication in a split second.

EMPATHIZERS AND INSTIGATORS SIDE BY SIDE ON THE COMMUNICATION PLAYING FIELD

You were born to play and win on the communicator team of either an Empathizer or an Instigator. In my opinion, Mother Nature did not hardwire your brain to be one style or the other. In your family of origin, you learned what to think and feel and how to get along with people. Your family of origin influenced your basic ideas about what to do when communication gets difficult, and that's the team you ended up on.

The Two Communicator Styles placed side by side on the communication field look like this in Figure 7.

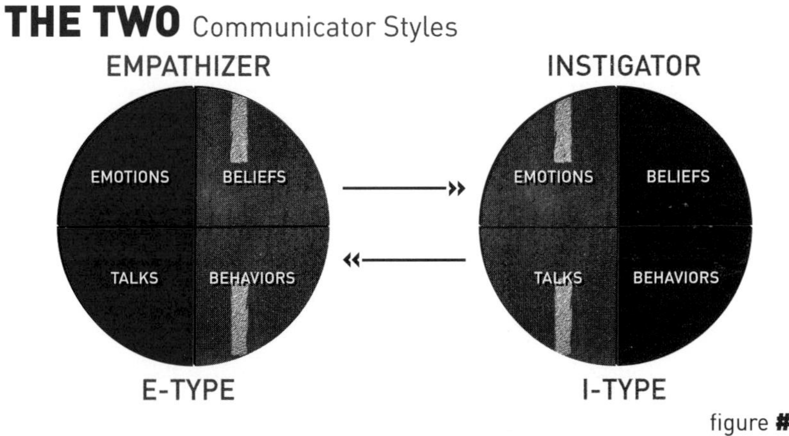

figure **#7**

Here's another way to think about communication styles. You're probably either right-handed or left-handed through a combination of biology/nature and family/nurture. Your preferred handedness, your way of picking up a pencil or using a spoon or throwing a ball, was either supported or denied by your family of origin.

Let's take that analogy one step further. Let's imagine that Empathizers are left-handed while Instigators are right-hand dominant. Neither hand is better off in the world. Neither hand is better for applauding. Your hands don't duke it out over which is better or worse. Instead, they function because of learned behaviors

There is plenty of room for your communication capacities to grow.

that become associated with preferences.

When I was growing up in the 1950s, schools and society in general preferred right-handedness. So if you were a kid who started writing with your left hand, you were "encouraged" to switch the pencil to your right hand and start writing right-handed. I am right-handed, but perhaps I would have been left-handed or both-handed in today's world. My point is this: just as a preference for using your right hand or left hand is a matter of biology and your environment, there is also plenty of room for your communication capacities to grow, no matter what style or mode you've been taught to prefer.

Stop cheering for the belief that someone is bad if they don't believe or do as you do.

And if you understand that about yourself, understand it about others, too. Stop cheering for the belief that someone is bad if they don't believe or do as you do. Stop judging and condemning that which you know so little about. No one grows up in communication limbo. You have developed a preference, a way of doing things, a frame of reference about the world that makes you feel at-ease and comfortable.

You have learned and refined this family identity script through years of feedback and experience to be either an Empathizer-dominant or Instigator-dominant communicator. That does not make you right and the other style of communicator wrong. Of course, when you have to switch to a different communication style, you'll experience discomfort and aggravation, the same as you'd feel a little awkward and foolish if, as a right-handed person, you were asked to write an essay by using only your left hand (it might even be a bit sloppy).

The whole point is this: you never know how it feels on "the other side" unless you try to understand it. If you continue to use your communication style with an opposing communication style, chances are you'll continually miss the mark or continue having trouble connecting, understanding or resolving problems. So your first goal must be to gain empathy for the other style because no single communication style fits all.

When you try the new moves, when you start understanding other people's communication styles, it's like a light goes off in a darkened room.

When you try the new moves, when you start understanding other people's communication styles, it's like a light goes off in a darkened room. Once you know where that light switch is, it's an "aha!" experience. You'll be able to say to yourself, "So *that's* why

I've been having trouble. I wasn't told where the light switch was before. Now I know what better to do and why it works. Eureka!"

In Figure 8, you can see for yourself how your energy flows unimpeded between the four communicator modes to get "the light bulb went on" effect.

FOUR Communicator Modes Transacting

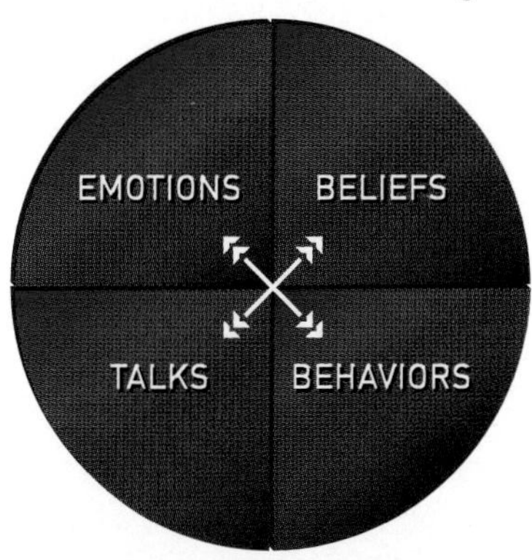

figure **#8**

The first *Talk to Me* exercise, *Unstressing Distressed Relationships* establishes the focus of our work together. My goal as your coach is to help you achieve your goals ethically and quickly.

TALK TO ME EXERCISE: UNSTRESSING DISTRESSED RELATIONSHIPS

This training will sink in faster when you focus the concepts on a few key individuals instead of letting your mind drift or generalize.

I believe that someone currently in your life is causing you concern or to feel confused—someone with whom you have a riled-up relationship. Did someone just pop into your mind?

I believe that someone currently in your life is causing you concern or to feel confused—someone with whom you have a riled-up relationship.

Was it a spouse? A partner? A family member? In-law? Your boss? An employee? A child? These communication concepts apply at home and at work, so it's possible the person (or persons) who came to mind was someone close to you or someone whose relationship has troubled you for some time.

Here are some other ways of determining whether your mood or demeanor toward this person is mangled by missed communication:

- You like the difficult person but you dislike his or her behavior.
- You will stick up for the difficult person even though you dislike how he or she is behaving.
- You feel invested in the relationship as an ongoing concern.
- You feel nervous talking to the person for fear of creating a bigger mess or misunderstanding.
- You think you should probably get over your feelings of being weak or hurt by this person and show tough love instead.
- You mull over the situation in your mind in the morning and at bedtime.
- Your good feelings in the relationship are an exception instead of the rule.

Is there someone in your life with whom you'd like to communicate more flexibly, effectively and responsively in order to feel better and learn faster? In the chart below, write down the name of the person, the relationship and the problem that you perceive to be at the root of your troubled relationship.

Troubled Relationship

Name

Relationship

Problem

A missed message means that even though you feel you've said what you need to say, the other person doesn't pick up on it, doesn't understand it or doesn't know how to provide what you need.

Usually, poor communication results in many mix-ups, misinterpretations and missed messages.

A missed message means that even though you feel you've said what you need to say, the other person doesn't pick up on it, doesn't understand it or doesn't know how to provide what you need. Maybe the other person doesn't really "hear" what you need or doesn't know how to respond. So in turn, you'll shout louder or get more emotional about it. And that still might not work if your co-communicator still doesn't understand your need or your plan for filling that need. Repeated missed messages ground the chances that your relationship will improve.

Repeated missed messages ground the chances that your relationship will improve.

Talk to Me will teach you how to walk the talk that your listeners can hear. You are going to deliver better-targeted messages, stop picking up guilt trips, and sidestep mixed messages. And you will take a long, deep look into the interpersonal world where new frontiers of excitement and intimacy await you.

You can't afford to be a poor communicator. Negative communicators constantly crash and burn, never getting where they want to go, never getting what they need from others—much less giving anything positive to this wonderful world.

SIX SKILLS NEEDED TO CREATE POSITIVE COMMUNICATION CHANGE

When you become embroiled in a communication traffic jam, you can use some of the talents and strengths of the other style so that you can start making progress instead of always falling behind or spinning your wheels.

These are the six skills I need from you now to create positive communication change that's tangible and real:

1. Keep it simple, sweetie

Wrap your mind around the fact that there are two types of communicator. Starting today, begin using the labels "Empathizer" and "Instigator" to begin guessing which types the people in your life are. Although you are a unique individual, you and your co-communicators will fit into the same style or a different one. You and yours don't live in a nowhere-man or nowhere-woman zone; you are either an Empathizer or Instigator.

2. Diagnose your and your opponent's style

It takes a little practice to get the hang of the styles, but your new insights will form quickly. You and your talk opponent—the person with whom communication is most difficult—is either an Empathizer or Instigator. Usually, your opponent's communicator style will be the opposite of yours. If for example, you diagnose yourself as an Empathizer, then your talk opponent is probably an Instigator, and vice versa. With which person in your life is communication most difficult or challenging? Which style do you think that person is?

3. Focus first on understanding your style before trying to understand the opposing style

First, take care of you. Understand your style first before trying to figure out the opposing style. If what you read and comprehend about your style "clicks" with you, that's very good. You will learn best and deepest when you can sift through and relate the material to your own key life experiences. Don't try too hard right now to understand the opposite style. That understanding will take place naturally and completely by focusing first on you. As your communications coach, I will help you get to know how your opposite style believes, feels and behaves.

As your communications coach, I will help you get to know how your opposite style believes, feels and behaves.

4. Refuse to keep score or engage in one-up behavior

Begin now to eliminate bad habits that classify communication exchanges or behaviors as "good" or "bad." Don't keep score. Don't engage in put-downs. Don't try to out-talk your co-communicator with a goal of "winning." If you disagree, don't criticize or call your co-communicator "bad." I believe most people are good, and your primary goal is to understand better what a co-communicator is saying. If you continue to have conflicts with someone whose communication style is opposite of yours, it's because you're engaging in these scoring/one-up behaviors. Adults agree to disagree, sometimes. Right/wrong and good/bad thinking is a mental habit you can break. Who knows, you may learn that your enemy might just be your friend.

Right/wrong and good/bad thinking is a mental habit you can break.

NEGATIVE AND POSITIVE Communicator Modes

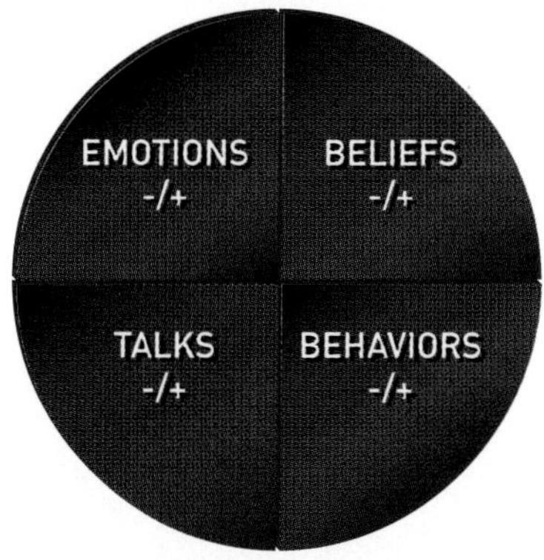

figure **#9**

5. Keep your mind open to the four avenues or modes of communication used by both types of communicators

Empathizers have the same four avenues or modes of communication as Instigators. Again, let's look at the four communicator modes or negative/positive communication quadrants called Emotions, Beliefs, Behaviors and Talks, found in Figure 9.

These four modes are the tools used by every communicator, no matter what his or her type. These four modes shape every communication. You will learn a bunch more about these modes of talking in Look Who's Talking, Chapter 3.

Chart 2.2 shows five quick examples of what the four talk quadrants sound like in actual conversations. These examples cover five common topics: money, age, sex, divorce, and prayer. For each topic, I'll provide a sentence for each communication mode: Emotions, Beliefs, Behaviors, and Talks. Can you guess which topics and transactions are negative or positive?

Chart 2.2 Pages 84–85

A new world of understanding yourself and others will open up when you know more about how the modes work, and in which order. Your talk world will never be the same again.

2.2 Emotions (E)	Beliefs (B1)
Money	
I feel poor.	Money can't buy happiness.
Age	
I feel like I'm over the hill.	I'm too old to be doing this.
Sex	
I feel attractive and sexy.	Sex is best in a loving relationship.
Divorce	
I feel really weak and bad.	I can't stand feeling this bad.
Prayer	
I feel better when I pray.	I believe prayers are answered everyday.

Behaviors (B2)	Talks (T)
I'm working extra hours to make more money.	I'm meeting with my accountant today to go over the numbers.
I don't laugh like I used to.	I made an appointment with my doctor for a checkup to discuss my health.
We acted out this sexual fantasy.	Let's talk about making our sex life better.
I've got to do something to feel better before I go insane.	My parents tell me it's wrong to divorce even when you're in a loveless and sexless marriage.
I pray first thing in the morning.	When I pray, I talk to God and listen for answers.

6. If you get caught in a communication crossfire, don't panic

Growth takes place naturally and steadily but sometimes comes in fits and spurts.

Growth takes place naturally and steadily but sometimes comes in fits and spurts. Feeling stumped but not stymied, or feeling like a failure, is part of succeeding at the communication game. Overall, though, your communicator confidence will increase quite dramatically as your begin to use and assimilate these new skills.

"Using your ideas, Dr. O'Grady, is like taking rocks of resentment out of my backpack. I feel lighter, I have more energy and there's a bounce to my step."

One of my trainees told me, "Using your ideas, Dr. O'Grady, is like taking rocks of resentment out of my backpack. I feel lighter, I have more energy and there's a bounce to my step. I don't feel so lost and alone any more. It's like I have the tools to not only survive but to thrive in the wilderness."

I believe as a family psychologist that fun and closeness, particularly emotional and sexual closeness, are absent in many marriages. I also believe that good talks can heal hurts, and that healing those hurts can build the emotional closeness that generates sexual closeness. It's all related, and you deserve the best of both worlds of intimacy.

The old saying, "It's nothing personal, it's only business!" is a half-truth. Your communication life is all personal and all your business.

TALK TO ME EXERCISE: THIS SHOE DOESN'T FIT!

Your communication style may not match or fit the style of the people you're trying to talk to.

This Shoe Doesn't Fit! is a fun way of acknowledging that your communication style may not match or fit the style of the people you're trying to talk to. It's a quick way to grasp the fact that everyone has their own communication style. Ready?

Right now, imagine taking off one of your shoes and exchanging it with the shoe of someone else in your family, household or workplace. If we were in a seminar, I would actually have you exchange your footwear for the shoe of whoever's sitting next to you.

Do it fast, don't think about it. Just do it!

In my household, my daughters wear children's sizes 10, 8 and 4. My wife is a ladies' 8 1/2, and I'm a men's 12. If we'd all exchange shoes, my foot will be squeezed and my partner will be sloshing around in my large shoe. Recrimination results.

Now imagine exchanging your shoe with your mother's shoe. Or your father's shoe. Try to imagine stuffing your foot into your neighbor's shoe. Chances are, your foot is going to be either too big or too small to fit properly in someone else's shoe.

Now, let's examine briefly a few typical emotional reactions to the shoe exercise and what they tell us about communication.

The Feelings involved with Exchanging Shoes

- Some shoes you try on will be too tight, some too large and some just plain impossible to get on.
- Did you take off your left shoe or your right shoe? Because instructions were vague, right shoes and left shoes are floating in the mix.
- What feelings ran through your mind as you exchanged shoes? Did you feel a tinge of depression, anxiety, anger, revulsion?
- Were you worried that your shoe would stink. . .or that the shoe you were handed would stink, too?
- Were you more concerned about your shoe fitting your neighbor, or your neighbor's shoe fitting you? Were you worried about pleasing the partner who had to wear your shoe. . .or did you focus more on how your neighbor's shoe would fit you?
- Did you luck out and find the right shoe and the right shoe size that comfortably fit you?
- Was your neighbor's shoe an uncomfortable fit for you?

This simple exercise teaches several important concepts. First, one communication size or style doesn't fit all temperaments or personalities. And emotions play a part in every communication exchange.

Why then do you and I believe that talking in our customary style will automatically fit another's style? Could this explain why some people aren't receiving the messages you feel you are so carefully sending? Indeed, it does.

The Beliefs involved with Exchanging Shoes

Communicators discuss beliefs as if they were as obvious as the noses on people's faces. But beliefs are not facts.

"It was the right thing to do" is a common belief that can lead the way to making some pretty good or some pretty bad choices.

"It was the right thing to do" is a common belief that can lead the way to making some pretty good or some pretty bad choices.

- There is no "right or wrong" shoe size, is there? Either the shoe fits and you can wear it, or it doesn't fit and you can't wear it.
- Men's and women's sizes are different. It's a fact. Men and women aren't wrong or right in their styles, but the fact is their feet are different.
- The shoe size you wear is determined by the size of your foot. It's not your fault.
- Shoe size isn't a reason to tease, bully or belittle.
- Old, raggedy-looking shoes don't make their owner an old, raggedy, or bad person.
- An ill-fitting shoe can cause different responses. It'll make some people feel bad. Others will feel extremely irritated. Some will want to do something they wouldn't normally do. But bad feelings don't make you a bad person.
- Bad feelings can also cause different responses. When you feel bad about this ill-fitting shoe, did you want to talk about it with someone or did you hide your feelings?
- When shoes don't fit right and your feet are rubbed raw—the support of a talk partner can really help, right?
- If an ill-fitting shoe makes you say something mean or do something out of exasperation, that reaction doesn't solve the problem of the ill-fitting shoe, does it?
- Blaming the other person or cursing about the shoe, doesn't make the foot fit the shoe any better, does it?

What's the point? Empathizers and Instigators wear different shoes.

I am not telling you to wear a shoe that doesn't fit or go to war over it. I don't want you to wear a shoe that makes your foot hurt. Nor am I advising you to get into a snit and throw a fit or tantrum when you feel frustrated by old, ill-fitting shoes. I'm just saying, "You probably didn't learn perfect communication skills from your family, and now it's time to try a few new tricks. . .find out what it's like to walk in other people's shoes." Otherwise, everyone will continue to walk around feeling the pain of "not fitting" in.

Assigning blame is a distraction from the healing of the pain. What to do about sad, mad, scared and glad feelings is the real issue. When you process painful and uncomfortable feelings instead of pass them around, you gain the freedom to make new choices.

Assigning blame is a distraction from the healing of the pain.

One of my clients today said, "I feel so tired. I am sick and tired of feeling tired." It's easy to feel down or dejected when people whose opinions you value continue to make your journey difficult or nearly impossible on the communications highway. Most of your fatigue stems from blame games that drain your energy and take you nowhere on the communications highway.

EMPATHIZER AND INSTIGATOR: DISTINCT DIFFERENCES

Empathizer communicators agree to pick up negative feelings too easily and Instigator communicators agree to pass along negative feelings too easily without realizing it:

An Empathizer is naturally sensitive and tuned into the feelings of others.
Listening with three ears is typical of Empathizer behavior.

An Instigator is naturally insensitive and tuned into the thoughts of others.
Listening with half an ear, or maybe half an ear on each side of the head, is common among Instigators.

An Empathizer is at his or her best when relationship waters are calm.
Stroking loving bonds, and feeling loving and valuing, are feelings with which Empathizers feel comfortable.

An Instigator is at her or his best when a crisis is burning or brewing.
Keeping a calm head during a blazing crisis is what Instigators do best.

An Empathizer feels sad because he/she fears Instigator anger.
Feeling lonely brings down the mood of an E-type.

An Instigator feels mad because he/she fears Empathizer sadness.
Feeling bored brings down the mood of an I-type.

An Empathizer deals with anxiety by talking about negative issues with a friend.

An Empathizer follows gut feelings and leads with emotions.

An Instigator deals with anxiety by doing something positive with a friend.
An Instigator follows logic and takes the lead away from emotions.

An Empathizer may stuff hurt feelings inside when he/she doesn't get what he/she wants.
An Empathizer, when hurt, can avoid or pull back from relationships.

An Instigator pushes without guilt to get what he/she wants.
An Instigator, when smarting, can be too aggressive about relationships.

An Empathizer prefers to speak by using emotions.
An Empathizer changes more when using the language of beliefs.

An Instigator prefers to speak by using beliefs.
An Instigator changes more when using the language of emotions.

An Empathizer correctly believes the world is one in which humans help each other.
An Empathizer works hard to reduce losses.

An Instigator correctly believes the world is a dog-eat-dog kind of place.
An Instigator works hard at winning.

An Empathizer wants to resolve past issues now, in the present moment.
They prefer relationship problem-solving to improve togetherness.

An Instigator wants to move beyond what's happened in the past.
Fixing things and making strategic future change—plans are what Instigators prefer.

An Empathizer forgets to put on his/her stage makeup.
Sincerity, being loyal and real confidence are everything to an Empathizer.

An Instigator puts on a positive face.

Genuineness, being powerful and projecting confidence are everything to an Instigator.

As Empathizer and Instigator communicators learn to better understand their weaknesses and proactively utilize their respective strengths, then every communicator, couple and family will feel more at ease.

WHAT EXACTLY IS A NEGATIVE COMMUNICATOR?

A negative communicator feels negatively—thinks negatively—acts negatively—talks negatively. Poor communication results from the fear of feeling hurt and the fear of feeling too excited by the changing landscape of life.

Following are the typical *booby traps* of a negative communicator that you must first recognize and then step around to keep yourself traveling steadily on the communications highway.

In short, a negative communicator:

1. Plays blame games

A negative communicator blames you for their projected beliefs and tells you what a bad person you are.

2. Escalates emotions

A negative communicator promotes negative emotions by escalating already tense or difficult situations. It's like pouring gasoline on a brushfire to make it flame up, only negative communicators do it to stoke irrationality and snuff out logic.

3. Loves psychodrama

A negative communicator promotes self-created crises and relationship conflicts in order to alleviate boredom and provide a sense of fleeting intimacy.

4. Recites the "poor me" storyline

A negative, "poor me" communicator snipes and insinuates with one-liners like, "You get what you want and I get nothing, so you owe me and I own you."

5. Stirs the pot

A negative communicator stirs the pot, and stirs up everyone else, to gain a feeling of importance without solving anything important. A pot-stirrer behaves in provocative ways to set off the fireworks of power plays.

6. Snipes

A negative communicator can't get a grip. A negative communicator gripes, grumbles, snaps, snipes and snips like a pair of scissors or some bitter old married couple. One-liners and "zingers" are his/her specialty.

7. Is a guilt albatross

Just when you think you're sailing along smoothly, a negative communicator kills the messenger and the message. The goal is to put you in the middle of a big emotional hurricane.

8. Is a gut-ripper

A negative communicator emotionally guts you to contain the emotions that are spilling out of him/her.

9. Spins your head

A negative communicator will talk circles around you and make your head spin in order to contain his/her painful emotions.

10. Slings manure

A negative communicator slings mud but loses ground. A negative communicator tosses you crap that you ought to flush down the drain and forget.

11. Lectures you

A negative communicator gives the same tired lecture 1,000 times while you look on yet again, bored and angry.

12. Gets even

A negative communicator keeps score and tries to even a hurt score with the warped thinking that "what goes around comes around."

Negative communication stems from the fear of feeling hurt, and the fear of feeling too excited by the changing landscape of life.

A BRIEF INTERLUDE: GRASS

Time for us to have a little fun now. . .and time to take another driver's test.

My 11-year-old daughter wrote the following funny/beautiful poem, *Grass.* I am protecting her privacy by not giving you her name, but she gave her permission to reprint it.

Here is the "mission possible," if you care to accept it: Can you tell from this short poem if the young author is an Empathizer or Instigator communicator? I bet you can! It's as clear as the nose on your face or as blue as azure ocean water.

GRASS
As I looked at the grass
It stared right back
This was very weird in fact
They stared at me with gleaming eyes as if trying to say
"Please don't step on me and make me cry"
I stood on the sidewalk just amazed
Like I was in a dream or I was just crazed
Now that's why I'm so sensitive to grass
I even pray for them at mass.

(I love you, Panda girl. I am guessing, dear one, that you are a true blue Empathizer communicator because you have intuitive powers like Counselor Troy of the hit television show, *Star Trek.* May you live long and prosper, precious soul).

WHAT EXACTLY IS A POSITIVE COMMUNICATOR?

A positive communicator feels positively—thinks positively—acts positively—talks positively. Positive communication results from the hope of feeling emotionally connected and the excitement of enjoying a fulfilling relationship.

Following are the typical characteristics of positive communicators. Unlike negative communicators, positive communicators are like the welcome mats that wipe away the mud of the day from your shoes.

In short, a positive communicator:

1. Knows and practices empathy

A positive communicator seeks first to see a tough situation through the eyes of the speaker in order to de-escalate negative emotions and game playing.

2. Acts as a good listening post

A positive communicator asks a multitude of open-ended questions and shows active interest in the responses.

3. Improves him/herself

A positive communicator pursues personal growth and develops awareness by hiring psychological and spirituality consultants.

4. Engages in dialogue

A positive communicator believes in back-and-forth communication and seeks anyone's opinions, no matter how big or small the role they play in any communication situation.

5. Knows that knowledge is power

A positive communicator makes time to read good books, listens to self-improvement tapes and gets a grip on important new concepts that keep the mind on the right track. A positive communicator is always willing to learn more to better one's self.

6. Is compassionate

A positive communicator knows that good talks are possible when other speakers are treated with compassion and respect in a way that gives them a sense of worth.

7. Focuses on goals

A positive communicator is motivated primarily by an intensive desire to understand other speakers without distractions or interference. Likewise, a goal-focused communicator understands that if frustration and roadblocks occur, more empathy is required.

8. Is gut-reassuring

A positive communicator understands that all people talk with their heads and their guts. But most importantly, a positive communicator understands that balancing head talk with heart talk can be a reassuring force when wild emotions break out of the corral that surrounds the heart-mind.

9. Pursues sane drama

A positive communicator reveals the self instead of concealing or hiding the self. Instead of stirring the pot and making things worse, the positive communicator adds to the pot to make the soup better.

10. Works hard at communication

A positive communicator puts in the hard work necessary to build a healthy relationship. The result is gratitude and personal enrichment for everyone involved in the relationship.

11. Adopts a pattern of healing

A positive communicator doesn't pursue long, drawn-out communication patterns that hurt others, divide others or drive wedges between positive people.

12. Employs a "Can we talk?" attitude

A positive communicator apologizes readily for his or her role in mistaken identity, miscommunications or lame blame games. Excuses and rationalizations ("psycho-excuses," I call them) are not allowed, ever.

"Positive talking" does not come easily, but it *is* very easy to learn. I believe effective positive communication should not be a fluke. Positive talks are a routine part of long-thriving and long-loving relationships.

Long, long ago, you and I were carefully taught by platitude-speaking parents that nothing valuable ever comes easy. What an untruth! Many worthwhile things in life don't require a whole lot of blood, sweat and tears. This training is one of them.

Many worthwhile things in life don't require a whole lot of blood, sweat and tears. This training is one of them.

SNAPSHOT OF AN EMPATHIZER COMMUNICATOR (E-TYPE)

- Is empathetic and open-minded
- Accepts ambiguity
- Has a difficult time pursuing a goal through adversity
- Believes that feelings must match words
- Is warm and dependable
- Is perceived as a weaker personality; is publicly shy but privately outgoing
- Takes things too personally
- Likes tranquility, peace of mind; rarely stirs the pot
- Gets lonely easily, needs regular positive emotional stimulation
- Often acts behind the scenes in a major supportive way
- Requires honesty, relationship management, times to talk
- Follows progressive leaders, dislikes uncomfortable changes
- Is relationship-centered, likes to connect, prefers stability
- Works from this frame of reference: "You have the power—the power's in you, not me!"
- Is perceived as too unselfish, altruistic, indirect
- Doesn't push back in a debate, can be out-talked

- His/her romantic partner feels valued, respected, loved
- Can be emotionally neglectful, negative and forgetful of self
- Feels obliged to talk out feelings and listen carefully
- Doesn't keep score: "I'm trying to reach a compromise here!"
- Routinely deals with emotions and emotional losses
- Possesses moderate to low self-esteem most times, can feel unworthy
- Feels ashamed when pushed hard to have own personal needs met
- Acts from this self-concept: "I'm not as popular as I'd like to be because I'm real."
- Believes in this truth: "I'm far more positive than I look like I am."
- Is agitated in a crisis
- Doesn't have to be the boss, is skilled in following
- Won't say "No" when no is the right answer, gives rewards for compliance
- Uses pessimism as a defense mechanism
- Loves loving feelings, will allow others to force their agenda on them
- Works hard for relationship agenda and interpersonal objectives
- Is very able to get inside others' hearts
- Understands how to listen with three ears, is a pro at relationship healing
- Freely gives positive feedback, feels anxious about conflict
- Uses emotional problem-solving approach
- Is considered a "peace freak"
- Puts self on bottom of "to do" list
- Backs down when talks get heated
- Is a big believer in: "There's no right or wrong emotion!"

SNAPSHOT OF AN INSTIGATOR COMMUNICATOR (I-TYPE)

- Is genuine and blunt
- Is a qualifier and leader by nature
- Is able to shepherd a goal through adversity
- Is convinced that beliefs must match actions or guilt results
- Is dependable; "What you see is what you get!"
- Is perceived as a strong personality by associates and family
- Won't take things too personally
- Likes to stir the pot; enjoys debating and winning a point
- Gets bored easily and needs positive mental stimulation
- Commands the center of attention
- Requires proof, facts, statistics
- Empowers progress, likes change for change's sake
- Power-centered, likes to influence; prefers to be an instigator of change
- Uses self as a frame of reference: "I have the power—it's in me!"
- Is perceived as too selfish, self-absorbed, complex
- Can talk circles around anyone; great debaters
- His/her romantic partner can feel undervalued, disrespected, unloved
- Tends to be emotionally neglectful of long-term romantic partner's needs
- Feels obliged to act on values, frets about what is right or wrong
- Keeps score and likes numbers: "I'm trying to make a point here!"
- Lacks confidence in dealing with emotions and emotional losses
- Has high self-esteem most times, but can feel unlovable
- Is disturbed by insecurity
- Takes pride in pushing hard for own personal needs to be met

- Possesses this self-concept: "No one knows the real me or how I truly feel."
- Accepts as truth: "I'm not as good as I look like I am."
- Remains calm in a crisis
- Possesses Leadership skills aplenty
- Says "no" easily, takes away items to punish noncompliance
- Uses optimism as a defense mechanism
- Loves control, doesn't want others to force their agenda on them
- Works hard for company and global objectives
- Is very adept at getting inside others' heads
- Understands how to listen selectively; is a pro at multitasking
- Freely gives negative feedback, doesn't mind conflict
- Uses strategic problem-solving approach
- Fits the definition of "control freak"
- Puts self on top of "to do" list
- Talks over co-communicator or talks more loudly to get point across
- Is a big believer in: "There's a right way and a wrong way to do this!"

TALKING NEGATIVE EXERCISE: COMMUNICATION INTERRUPTUS

Negative communicators use a large variety of disrupting transactions—behaviors or one-liners—that interrupt direct communication and interpersonal honesty with their co-communicators.

If you are part of a small study group, pick a topic and assign one of these commands to each group member. Each time a speaker gives a paragraph of information, he or she is required to use the interrupting sentence listed below.

If you are working on your own, here are a few typical one-liners to listen for and steer clear of during your day:

- "Excuse me, but I've got to jump in here to set the record straight."

- "I have a point to make here, so listen up."
- "That's not the way I see it."
- "Why don't you ever try to understand where I'm coming from?"
- "Why do you always make a mountain out of a mole hill?"
- "You never try to understand what I'm going through."
- "I don't mean to interrupt you, but I've got to say something here."
- "Let me be perfectly honest with you."
- "I think you've missed the point by a mile."
- "So what do you expect me to do about it now?"
- "You are a control freak."
- "You are negative, negative, negative. Why can't you be more positive?"
- "You're consumed with yourself."
- "What do you expect me to do about it? Get over it."

Talk to Me is not about putting difficult people down or running away from them. Instead, it teaches you to understand key differences in communicator styles that will unlock the door that you, until now, have been ready to kick in.

TALK BACK: CO-COMMUNICATOR COUNTERPOINTS

At the end of each training session are questions many of my trainees and clients often ask:

1. How did you first get the idea for **Talk to Me?**

It was a coincidence born out of a series of questions. I spend 55-plus hours a week in my office as a family psychologist, and I noticed that clients often sought my help because they were feeling bad and wanted to feel better as fast as possible. The starting blocks of *Talk to Me* are rooted in mood management.

2. What does communication have to do with mood?

Well, I started with my clients' bad feelings and then asked them why they were feeling anxious and depressed. Most of them singled out "relationship distress" as the cause of their bad feelings. And when I asked why key relationships at work or home weren't going well, many of them cited poor or no communication. From "I'm feeling bad" to "we can't communicate" was like a long, cross-country race but it helped me understand the dynamics.

3. Are you saying that depression and anxiety stem from miscommunication as much as from biological factors?

Yes, I am absolutely saying that depression, anxiety, anger and other negative emotions are heavily involved in relationship fights, emotional/interpersonal power plays and miscommunication blowouts. If not confronted, the bruises or injuries of miscommunication show up in our doctors' offices to be treated, and that includes depression.

4. How did you come up with the communicator styles of Empathizer and Instigator?

Empathizer was the easy one. In psychotherapy research, "empathy" relates to major positive client changes. Instigator was harder but came to me from childhood instances when my mom would say, "You're trying to instigate something, Denny." Mom was right to accuse me of trying to stir the pot. I do like change. (At one point, I considered using the term "genuine" for Instigators, because as a psychotherapy trait, genuineness also fosters hope and optimism).

5. Are you an Empathizer or Instigator communicator?

I really don't like to answer that question because it takes all the fun out of getting to know you and me by discovery. If I were an Empathizer, though, I would be motivated to rescue people in my communication ambulance after they've been driven off the communications highway. If I were an Instigator, I would be putting energy into this project to help myself out of pain and into pleasure. Either way, you win, I win and we win before we complete our journey.

6. Which way is right: the Instigator or the Empathizer way?

An old Scottish saying says, "You can't walk on both sides of the street at the same time." Although you prefer the side of the street you are used to walking on, you don't get anywhere fast when you judge or condemn the other side of the street for being who and what it is. There is no "right" or "better," only different.

7. Are you saying that each one of us has a preferred system of communication operation, much like a computer has?

Yes, I'm definitely saying that you and I have learned to prefer and rely heavily on one style of communication. Your family environment and upbringing either helped or hindered, refined or squashed that budding talent.

8. Does being an optimist help to communicate better?

No, an optimist believes that he can jump over a communication gap. A super-optimist believes she can fly over a communication gap. The realist or expert communicator brainstorms flexible ways to bridge the gap with the materials at hand without becoming too rose-colored or too cranky.

9. Aren't you implying that women are likely to be Empathizers and men are more likely to be Instigators?

No, gender roles are not the same as communicator roles. Communicator style is not determined or driven by gender, age, race, geography or religion (at least in my experience and clinical studies). In fact, machismo men are more than occasionally E-types, and feminismo women are more than occasionally I-types. So, don't be fooled by sex-role masks. It's not the look, walk or message that counts—your true communicator style does.

10. Aren't we really discussing introverts vs. extroverts?

No, not really, because *Talk to Me* isn't rehashing the very fine Myers-Briggs work—just adding to it. Here's the reverse psychology truth: Empathizers aren't always introverts and Instigators aren't always extroverts, as might be suggested by the descriptions. Empathizers and Instigators are evenly represented in the extrovert and introvert camps, so you never know who's in the bunk beside you.

11. Shouldn't I pray for my antagonist to see the light?

I can't knock prayer because I pray daily. However, I'm not a big believer in turning the other communication cheek. I dislike prayer if it's used to back off from healthy anger or other enlightening emotions. I don't like to hurt people, but sometimes you have to.

12. What question would you like to answer?

I would like to answer this question: "Why do people act stubborn and difficult and why are they their own worst enemies sometimes?" And my answer would be: "People are stubborn, difficult and act in their worst interest sometimes because their emotions get escalated over clear thinking. Also, self-defeating actions happen when people don't feel they are good enough to deserve really happy, juicy lives."

13. Aren't we supposed to learn good communication skills from our mothers?

No, you are supposed to learn good communication skills from whoever can teach them to you in ways you can hear and use. Let's not worship mothers; if they're positive communicators, let's learn from them!

14. I always want to be helpful. Are you suggesting I become more selfish?

Yes, I'm suggesting you try to help yourself in a caring way before you try to help another who doesn't really want your help. Sometimes trying to help too much hurts everyone involved.

Communication problems aren't typically the result of people who are being difficult, stubborn and bullheaded.

It's not family dysfunction or codependency; it's just life. The dysfunction, and extended family puts the "fun" in "dysfunction," if any, is not driven by any particular person. It just occurs as part of the process when we assume that one communication style fits all.

NEXT UP: LOOK WHO'S TALKING

It dawned on me recently that I see so many couples who should have learned basic communication 101 in high school from family psychologists like me! We all need to know how to love and how to communicate when we are feeling unloving and unloved.

With a little bit of coaching and in a short amount of time, you will see so much light instead of the darkness surrounding you. You will feel at peace. You will know what you did to bring about these positive emotional states—and you will choose to do the same again and again.

You can count on me. Next, we will flesh out together the bold emotions and the bold actions of the inner world of Empathizer and Instigator communicators!

III

LOOK WHO'S TALKING!

Instigator Belief: It's nothing personal, it's only business.

Empathizer Belief: It's not only business, it's also very personal.

TRAINING GOAL

To use the four communicator modes to better maneuver the emotional and logical two-way communication highway system

It's an energy thing: Your life battery is filled up or drained by how you think and talk to yourself and others.

YOU DRIVE ME CRAZY!

As a family psychologist, I'm reluctant to use the word "crazy" in a demeaning way. Most psychologists are.

However, "You drive me crazy!" is a cutting belief that's often said in the heat of the moment. Likewise, the sob-story expression "They drove me crazy!" is an attention-getting sentiment meant to express disappointment, worry and exasperation. Both are wrong turns on the communications highway.

What both of these negative statements indicate, though, is that your emotional and mental states are tremendously affected by how negatively or positively your loved ones and work associates talk to you—and how positively or negatively you talk back to them. It's an energy thing: Your life battery is filled up or drained by how you think and talk to yourself and others.

Negative communicators are negative drivers on a one-way communication highway—their way is the only way. Negative communicators (whether Empathizer or Instigator communicators) cynically believe they are always one step ahead of everyone else, always winning the game. The truth: Negative communicators don't feel worthy or good enough to enjoy pleasure or to enjoy the pleasures of loving. They don't consider themselves worthy of being loved. They drain your life battery and can make you feel sick.

In contrast, positive communicators responsively contribute to your feelings of sanity, confidence and independence, whether you are a positive or negative thinker. They don't seek to brainwash you. Positive communicators are optimistic drivers on a two-way communication highway—their way is only one way among many to travel. Positive communicators (whether Empathizer or Instigator communicators) realize that what they feel, think, do and say really matters. They choose to use all four communicator modes in positive ways to make a difference. They prefer to feel well, and choose not to suffer unnecessarily by collusively using soap-opera *psychodrama*.

Positive communicators are optimistic drivers on a two-way communication highway—their way is only one way among many to travel.

Winners don't con others by draining everyone's energy. People who love choose instead to recharge others' life batteries. In this chapter, you'll immerse yourself in the four different modes of communication—Emotions, Beliefs, Behaviors, and Talks—so that you can better understand your own and others' communication styles. The goal is to make sure you're a positive communicator, not an energy-draining negative communicator.

THE POWER OF LOVE

Love is a river. Love is the force. Love is the source.

Love is an invisible energy force. You and I shouldn't shoot love in the gut. Sadly, many of us do just that. Love creates positive feeling and positive thinking. Love thrives in the positive. Love is ever ready to serve you.

You and I shouldn't shoot love in the gut.

You no doubt have heard of the concept of "positive thinking." It works half of the time. I will caringly teach you how to use "positive talking" that works the other half of the time. Additionally, I will also teach you how to do "positive feeling" and "positive behaving," both of which culminate in "positive communicating."

I am not making a judgment call that positive is superior to negative, or negative is safer than positive. You will have to decide how you want to live in your own psychic skin. I would advise you to choose love. After all, true love is the highest positive emotion and is the only thing that lasts—while everything else passes away. Negative is easier.

Positive loving relationships aren't fluked. They require work and smarts. Life happens. A positive communicator chooses to deal with negative life events in positive ways that accentuate the positive and diminish the negative. In a *loving relationship,* (which one-third of us have) both partners prefer to achieve an equal balance

A positive communicator chooses to deal with negative life events in positive ways that accentuate the positive and diminish the negative.

of loving attention-giving.

Being fearful of hurting another's feelings is dishonest.

Love comes with a price. The price is emotional honesty. Being fearful of hurting another's feelings is dishonest. We hurt the feelings of those we love. It should be no other way. Emotional honesty is practiced in reciprocally loving relationships— and insecurity and negative thinking aren't tolerated. Lovers choose instead to believe in the power of love! Almost all of my communications clients prefer to live in loving relationships instead of co-dependent ones.

Positive communicators talk love, act love and make love. A negative thinker says, "Oh, that's too much hard work." In fact, plenty of emotions, feelings, life circumstances, ideas about love, different types of relationships and other factors can influence your communication style. So before I get to the meat of the four communications modes, I want to spend some time talking about those issues.

HATE VS. LOVE

Relationships range from Extremely Negative to Extremely Positive, with Neutral in-between.

Whenever I discuss this concept in front of a crowd, I first move my left hand all the way to the left of my body to indicate Extreme Negative Relationship Energy, and then I move my right hand all the way to the right to indicate Extreme Positive Relationship Energy.

Empathizer communicators are prone to pick up negative or positive emotions from others.

Empathizer communicators are prone to pick up negative or positive emotions from others. On the other hand, *Instigator communicators are prone to incite negative or positive emotions in others.* Both types are quick to find fault or place blame for a communications mishap or accident.

Instigator communicators are prone to incite negative or positive emotions in others.

Hating, hateful words, spiteful actions and revenge motives aren't uncommon in relationships. How does hate impact you? It depends on your communicator type. *E-types lose their sparkle or dry up when they feel unloved.* In contrast, *I-types' physical batteries run down and they can become physically sick.* Hate-filled and conflict-ridden relationships sicken both types of communicators dramatically but differently.

In addition, E-types normally function like finely tuned pianos.

Reject them, and they increasingly sound off and out of tune. Oppositely, I-types are piano tuners. Reject them, and they increasingly don't show up for work because they are sick. Whichever your type: "You have to think like me or I'll take something away from you" or "I'm right and you're wrong" or "You're bad if you feel that way" are three examples of dominance-driven power plays.

Let me put this plainly: negative emotions that are co-created inadvertently or intentionally in the relationship context do impact Empathizer and Instigator communicators negatively but quite differently.

E-types become emotionally drained and emotionally sick from an excess of negative emotions. Over time, they dry up.

1. *E-types become emotionally drained and emotionally sick from an excess of negative emotions. Over time, they dry up.*
2. *I-types become physically drained and physically sick from excessive negative emotions. Over time, they flake out.*

I-types become physically drained and physically sick from excessive negative emotions. Over time, they flake out.

Strained or distressed communicators are never pretty sights to behold.

CONTROL...AND DEFINING LOVE

You believe in positive control. You don't want to exert negative control because you want to live in love.

Power plays are control-centered, not relationship-centered. Here's what people say if they're trying to control what someone thinks: "You're dumb if you think that way!" This power play seeks to dominate another mentally and is driven by hatefulness.

Power plays are control-centered, not relationship-centered.

Here's what people say if they're trying to control what someone does: "You're dumb if you decide to do it that way!" This power play is emotional, manipulative and driven by hatefulness that seeks to dominate the will of another. Either way you cut it, the words stab you and make you bleed with barely a visible wound.

I believe that hate is the opposite of love, and I believe that negative control is letting go of love. In the spirit-freeing works *Conversations with God, Course in Miracles,* and *Love is Letting Go of Fear*—each of these seminal works spoke out in unison that *fear is the opposite emotion of love.* Quite differently, most of my communications clients believe *indifference is the opposite of love.*

I believe that hate is the opposite of love, and I believe that negative control is letting go of love.

Hate and other forms of negative anger are love's opposites.

In the *Talk to Me* communications theory, neither fear nor indifference is love's opposite. *Hate* and other forms of negative anger are love's opposites. Rejection, resentment, and revenge spit in the face of love. Acceptance, affirmation and affection respect love. Perhaps all negative emotions are love's opposite!

In my perspective, angry, negative power plays that strive for domination and control block the loving feelings that people are fully capable of experiencing. As well, since love is the opposite of anger, the ability to heal resentment that's built up in a relationship (whenever possible) is a requirement for that relationship to be positive.

The negative talk habit

Unhealthy anger begets negative communications, which bring on less loving feelings.

The positive talk habit

More compliments. . .More tender touch. . .More inspirational phone mail. . .Making love more. The choice is yours.

Both E-types and I-types receive a "C" in the Course on Anger mostly because of family experiences/ upbringing and religious indoctrination.

Your anger is either healthy or unhealthy. Both E-types and I-types receive a "C" in the Course on Anger mostly because of family experiences/upbringing and religious indoctrination. And E-types and I-types experience anger differently.

E-type irrational anger

I define the interpersonal impact of E-types negative anger as, "The experience of feeling unloved and unloving."

I-type irrational anger

I define the interpersonal impact of I-types negative anger as, "The guilt experience of feeling and believing I am undeserving of love."

You are lucky in love if you are in a relationship where A loves B, and B loves A, and that love is demonstrated about equally every day.

You are lucky in love if you are in a relationship where A loves B, and B loves A, and that love is demonstrated about equally every day.

RELATIONSHIP DISTRESS

While trying to make things better in a relationship, both communicator types often make things worse. The co–communicator feels put off, put down, hurt.

E-types who don't feel important are quiet about asserting their needs but will have no problem making a laundry list of dissatisfactions. I-types, on the other hand, don't check in with their primary partners often enough to find out what compromises need to be made because they fear hurting everyone's feelings.

In terms of communication feedback, when Empathizers receive signs of being disliked, they take that social cue of disapproval personally and alter their relationship behavior. When Instigators are given social cues of disapproval, they don't read the social writing on the wall because being disliked doesn't really matter very much to them at all.

Negative *dysphoria,* or hurt and sadness, are the emotions that Empathizer communicators struggle with the most in negative interpersonal interactions. Anger, guilt-tripping and disappointment are the emotions that Instigator communicators struggle with the most. Either way, we are wise to understand our opposite communicator a whole lot better.

After all, we are all in the same canoe headed downstream to somewhere pleasant. Why whack anyone with your paddle? Remember, what goes around comes around, including negative or positive paybacks.

THE FOUR NEGATIVE EMOTIONS THAT CREATE RELATIONSHIP DISTRESS

Negative communicators co-create negative emotions and mindsets.

In particular, four core negative emotional states act like fog on the communication highway, or they work to create a fogged-up windshield that increases the risk of accidents, clouds your mind and trips you up along the communication highway.

The four negative emotions causing relationship distress are:

1. Dysphoria

Depression, sadness, hurt, feeling down and blue, disappointment, expectations crashes, "If it's worth doing—it's worth doing right" perfectionism, boredom, helplessness and hopelessness, victimization, complaining and loneliness are some members of the emotion family called Dysphoria.

When you feel down, blue, hopeless and isolated in your own inner world, than you can bet you are feeling Dysphoric.

When you feel down, blue, hopeless and isolated in your own inner world, then you can bet you are feeling Dysphoric.

<u>Optimism</u> and <u>enthusiasm</u> are the opposite positive emotions of negative dysphoria.

2. Anxiety

Fear of failure, fear of being abandoned, fear that the other shoe will drop, agitation, feelings of not being good enough, panic attacks, worry, compulsiveness, moodiness, fear of loss, negative thinking spirals, confusion, nagging, finger pointing, controlling, and feeling upset are some of the members of the emotion family called Anxiety.

When you feel edgy, nervous and worried about present events or what the future has in store for you, you can bet that you are experiencing Anxiety. I wrote about overcoming the fear of change and loss in my book, *Taking the Fear out of Changing.*

Excitement and faith-filled contentment are the opposite positive emotions of negative anxiety.

<u>Excitement</u> and <u>faith-filled contentment</u> are the opposite positive emotions of negative anxiety.

3. Anger

Aggravation about little things, nitpicking, irritation, frustration, resentment, rejection, revenge, anger attacks, hate, jealousy, road rage, false pride, criticizing, fault-finding, and judging and bragging are some of the members of the emotion family called Anger.

Anger can be healthy or unhealthy, or positive or negative, as is true of all emotional storms.

Anger can be healthy or unhealthy, or positive or negative, as is true of all emotional storms. I spoke about this intricate emotion in my audio program *No Hard Feelings.*

<u>Love</u> and <u>peace of mind</u> are the opposite positive emotions of negative anger.

4. Guilt

Shame, embarrassment, secret keeping, interpersonal dishonesty, lack of being genuine, holding back praise, feeling selfish or self–centeredness, helping others to the exclusion of yourself, feeling God is watching you critically, being a martyr, resisting success, listening to the gossip grapevine, being sexually uptight are some of the members of the Emotion family called Guilt.

Guilt trips leave your mind open to truckloads of undeserved criticism and character assassinations that fuel self-doubt.

Self-blame (or other-person blame) is the customary mental action that results from feeling guilty. You exaggerate your control and responsibility over negative events when talking with others by thinking: "It's all my fault. Why couldn't I have seen this coming?"

Self-blame (or other-person blame) is the customary mental action that results from feeling guilty.

The Judeo-Christian culture encourages accepting guilt and resisting joyfulness with these two negative beliefs: "Good fortune is hard to enjoy when people less fortunate than me are suffering" and "God is keeping track of the hurtful things people do to one another."

Confidence and high self-esteem are the opposite positive emotions of negative guilt.

LIFE AS A SOB STORY...OR A LOVE STORY

As a positive communicator, you set patterns of positive emotions in motion that make you feel optimism, excitement, love and confidence. Thus, every one of us gets to choose how to experience life: either as a Sob Story or a Love Story.

Every one of us gets to choose how to experience life: either as a Sob Story or a Love Story.

Dysphoria, anxiety, anger and guilt are the four doorways to negative or positive self-created experiences (depending upon your viewpoint) or emotional states that act like a fog. This fog clouds minds and makes driving along the two-way communication highway intimately risky. You shouldn't have to be billed for a costly mistake that you are completely capable of avoiding.

Remember, every emotion is experienced by you as either positive or negative, depending on your frame of reference. Each communicator you talk to will feel more vulnerable to one type of emotion vs. the other types of emotion.

You can get along with anyone—to a degree. It's especially possible when you learn how Empathizers and Instigators both cross the line when they change talk lanes without looking over their shoulders or checking ahead for oncoming traffic.

You can get along with anyone—to a degree.

Negative emotions fuel negative debates that preclude open-minded discussion of sensitive issues. I will show you later in this book how exactly to avoid avoidable talk impasses. Just one example: The fervently held emotional opinions you worship aren't always the communication scientific facts you may think.

Negative emotions fuel negative debates that preclude open-minded discussion of sensitive issues.

I am not saying here that you have to like those you don't want to get along with because you don't have to do anything. Realistically,

I respect your desire to interface responsibly with all emotions, whether they're rated positive or negative by you, to drive smoothly and sanely and to achieve the intense emotional and sexual closeness that comes from deep communication and emotional connecting or connectedness.

Just keep in mind that clinging to the four negative emotions increases the chances that you will be involved in a talk collision or relationship crash that you can better control. Life happens. Why make it any worse?

By better managing these emotions, you will better manage to create and engage in more and more and more positive communication outcomes.

THE THREE TYPES OF RELATIONSHIPS

There are three types of relationships, married or otherwise. In ascending order of maturity, they are: *Controlling, Friendship, and Loving.*

Relationships are grouped according to negative, neutral and positive attributes. The three relationship types also are like the steps of a ladder—each relationship type forming a step or move up to the next most positive level. I like to think of it as a "Love Ladder."

People move forward and progress from a *Controlling Relationship*. . .to a *Friendship Relationship*. . .to a *Loving Relationship.* Now don't be impatient or assume you've already reached the highest rung: Just because you think you are in love, doesn't mean you are really in true *love.* It depends on the type of relationship you're in.

I believe that one-third of Americans are happily married while two-thirds of us are just getting along or are plain downright miserable.

I believe that one-third of Americans are happily married while two-thirds of us are just getting along or are plain downright miserable. The three relationship categories are distinct and separate. And according to my clinical experience, you can't take a partner at one level and grow with him/her to the next level.

For example, you can't turn a *Controlling Relationship* into a *Friendship Relationship* any more than you can make a *Friendship Relationship* transform into a *Loving Relationship* with the same partner. It just can't happen. This is why divorce is often a positive move, especially when divorcing individuals learn from the experience and choose a new partner who's capable of a higher relationship level. Continuous bad luck at relationships probably means that you're picking the same type of communicator and/or the same type of relationship you just moved out of.

In all my years of communications psychology practice, I have not seen anything like today's push for love and loving relationships. More people than ever before expect to live and feel loved in a mutually advantageous, loving relationship. And the fields of psychology and communication have the technology available to make the dream of love come true if we pick a partner wisely and use smart communication moves.

The fields of psychology and communication have the technology available to make the dream of love come true if we pick a partner wisely and use smart communication moves.

Following are fuller descriptions of the three types of relationships from which to choose:

1. The Controlling Relationship

The frame of reference of the *Controlling Relationship* is fairly straightforward and characterized by these types of thoughts and behaviors: "I want to get my way at the expense of a positive relationship." "I will fight unfairly to have my point of view heard or to win debate points." "I shoot razor-sharp arrows at the heart and head of my partner." "I make threats and smear my partner's good reputation, all the while claiming that the blame falls squarely on his/her shoulders because I am not aware of what I'm doing." "Tit-for-tat." "I'm not going to take that from you!"

In a *Controlling Relationship,* spats and squabbles make problem-solving all but impossible.

In a Controlling Relationship, spats and squabbles make problem-solving all but impossible.

Unnecessary psychological crisis fires are set as the couple goes round-and-round the bases of rejection, resentment and revenge. The anger game is played constantly.

In a Controlling Relationship, self-inflicted masochistic conflicts are a form of false intimacy because without conflict, the couple has precious little in common. Sexually, this partnership "makes war, not love."

The co-dependent rationalization says that we only hate those who we truly love—I say we hate whom we hate. So in a controlling relationship, there is no love to it at all. Some people love to hate, but that is not you. You love to feel loved and loving.

The *Controlling Relationship* is the Freudian, unresolved co-dependent mother–son or father–daughter psychological mismatch that overflows with negative and positive anger.

2. The Friendship Relationship

The frame of reference of the *Friendship Relationship* is based on friendship. It's based on a belief that life partners ought to take pride in the fact that they have never had a fight. At the heart of this type of relationship is a belief that you should marry your best friend, since that's the safest way to ensure a long lasting union.

In the world of negative, neutral and positive emotions, this arrangement fosters neutral vanilla emotions and stability. Unfair fighting doesn't occur. Neither does fair fighting, since friends conjointly believe: "Why fight? It's not worth fighting over!" Overall, there is not much spice in this arrangement and the mind-bending experience of passion typically is lacking. Sexually, this partnership "makes sex."

The Friendship Relationship is our cultural darling because it almost eliminates the possibility that anyone will feel hurt, betrayed or let down.

Love here means, "I like and respect you." Friendship-couple types can't become Loving-couple types any more than Controlling-couple types can become Friendship-couple types—even when tons of work and effort are added into the mix. The *Friendship Relationship* is our cultural darling because it almost eliminates the possibility that anyone will feel deeply hurt, betrayed or let down.

The *Friendship Relationship* is the symbolically Jungian brother–sister, sister–sister or brother–brother psychological mismatch that is safe but dispassionate and short on emotional intimacy.

3. The Loving Relationship

The frame of reference of the *Loving Relationship* is that life partners are for life—eternally loved and eternally loving! The loss of a partner is atomic. This relationship is based on the belief that two people should couple up heart-valve to heart-valve. It's a risk-maximized arrangement.

Love is a powerful force that requires the interaction of you and someone you love, who loves you back about equally.

I believe with all my heart, mind and soul that co-communicators speak best when both partners are in love with one another. Love is a powerful force that requires the interaction of you and someone you love, who loves you back about equally.

Love can't grow vigorously when it is one-sided.

Love thrives when you love your co-partner and your co-partner loves you. Love can't grow vigorously when it is one-sided. Contrary to popular thinking, love isn't first and foremost a decision—

nor is love first and foremost an action. Love is an emotion, the most positive emotion that will ever take flight in the human heart. The experience of sexual passion increases over the years spent loving together. Sexually, this partnership "makes love."

Each relationship level is a separate and distinct category requiring a new partner. For example, a *Friendship Relationship* couple may drift apart and watch their relationship collapse over time because of a lack of emotional intensity or if a major purpose for uniting has been accomplished, such as raising children. Once the children are gone and the nest is empty, the remaining couple realizes there's not much left, and this is the reason many long-time couples divorce once the children have left for college, married or moved out on their own.

The experience of sexual passion increases over the years spent loving together.

If you were once in a *Loving Relationship* but have lost your partner—chances are you can and will love another one of your 12 matches again. But breakups are painful: In my case, my partner is not my best friend but my beloved. (My best friends are my best friends!) If my beloved partner and I choose to part, I probably would not choose to continue to be friends, because my own hurt and anger would run too deep.

The *Loving Relationship* is the mature adult–mature adult or the beloved–beloved psychological match-up for the intensely loving, romantic and sexual couple.

TRUE LOVE

Which of the three types of relationship are you in now? My guess is you probably prefer to be in a two-way, loving relationship where problems are resolved and positive feelings lead the way.

In the *Talk to Me* experience, love is the ultimate positive emotion. I have found love in many of the profound books that I have read over my 50-something lifespan. One characteristic I love about love is that two people can't control it, make it happen or buy it at any price.

One characteristic I love about love is that two people can't control it, make it happen or buy it at any price.

I enormously respect and honor Dr. M. Scott Peck's wisdom in his self-help psychology book *The Road Less Traveled* because it taught me so very much—and was such a great source of discussion and inspiration for so many of my clients over the previous three decades.

Likewise, I respect and honor Dr. John Gray's rich ideas found in his landmark book *Men are from Mars and Women are from Venus.* Dr. Gray gave us all permission to be different and unique, and he gave permission for my clients to be stellar communicators.

The new idea that I am adding to our continuing cultural discussion about effective communication is that men and women are not so different, but made different by the co-communicator style that each lives in and experiences.

The new idea that I am adding to our continuing cultural discussion about effective communication is that men and women are not so different, but made different by the co-communicator style that each lives in and experiences. It's not only the road we travel, and not only the planet we were born on—it's the "love talk" we walk and the "love walk" we talk!

Adults also need to teach teenagers about loving relationships and picking a positive match. Adults must teach teens that The Romance Stage lasts from nine months to a year, after which The Power Play Stage commences. We need to teach them not to fear loss and to refuse to settle for less than matching 10 out of 10 top partner traits on their love wish list—and never to stay long in a controlling relationship. Adults need the same knowledge and permission to love fully.

Most of my divorcing clients married for the "wrong" reasons. The couple was mismatched from the get-go, so there wasn't a fair chance to learn how to compromise, meet needs, and fight fairly and so on. These negative beliefs are common: "I knew something was off but I didn't think I could do better—and I didn't want to lose what I had found." "I rationalized that there's no perfect partner and talked myself into it." "I saw the writing on the wall and knew we wouldn't get along because we were so immature but I didn't have the guts to back out and let everyone down." "I thought we should stay together for the kids' sake, but I didn't realize what a bad example we were setting for them."

Love is the most powerful, positive emotion known today.

Love is an emotional force. First, you must love yourself before you can love another. Love is the most powerful, positive emotion known today. The emotion of love is healing, bathing the inner body in positive chemicals. Although it happens aplenty that you can fall in love with someone who isn't good for you—a loving relationship requires the co-equal love of two mature people. I also firmly believe there are 12 suitable love partners for each one of us, so finding the person of your dreams isn't as difficult as many presume and happens every week in my communications psychology practice.

In my opinion, there are no outcasts in the universe of love. All of life ultimately will funnel down to true and everlasting love. All else will pass away. Love is all there is and the rest is child's play. Let me be nit-picky here without confusing you: Love of power is love, but not of the highest order. Love of money is love, but of a temporal kind. Love of winning is love—but of a conditional kind. Sexual love gets close to the top—especially in a loving relationship. But when all is said and done: Unconditional love tops the list in my book.

In my opinion, there are no outcasts in the universe of love.

A recent client shared with me his private definition of love: "Love is when you care about someone else almost as much as you care about yourself." I think that pretty well sums it up.

A recent client shared his private definition of love: "When you care about someone else almost as much as you care about yourself."

POSITIVE TALKS

You choose to talk in either negative or positive ways. There is no Mr. In-Between.

In Figure 10, you see that the four communicator modes are experienced in the skin of an Empathizer communicator as either negative or positive. (So true, too, of the Instigator communicator.) Neutral comes in there too, but it's not worth bothering with.

The key point here: Begin classifying whether you are driving or operating out of a negative or positive frame of mind. Remember, negative or positive, isn't better or worse since accuracy (reality and awareness) matters the most.

EMPATHIZER Communicator Modes

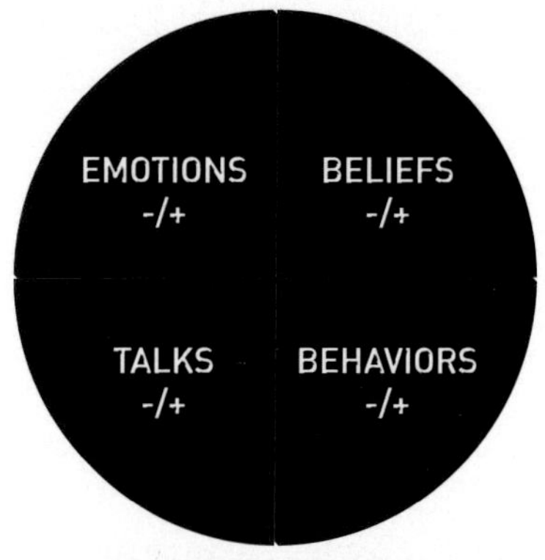

figure **#10**

LET'S TALK ABOUT POSITIVE CHANGE

In visiting my chiropractic physician today, I learned that he is an I-type communicator. While talking about this book, he asked me, "So shouldn't I try harder to be an active listener to get along better with my wife?"

"No," I told him, "As an I-type communicator, you are a selective listener, one who strives very hard to stay calm during a crisis and get the job done."

"Exactly," he replied, "You understand me."

The good doctor's wife was an E-type, so I recommended to my healer-friend that he ask open-ended questions instead of adopting a so-called "active listener" role. Later he told me he was pleased with the better and more positive results he achieved from asking these thought-based, belief-based types of questions: "What do you *think* about your feelings?" "What do you *believe* will fix this challenge?" "What do you *think* about yourself when you're feeling down, inadequate or blue?" I also often hear loud praise when I use this communication theory with family businesses or family business couples: "Wow, after one meeting with you, the light bulb went on! We haven't been this happy in years. We needed specific, black-and-white communication tools to use to get out of our rut and you gave them to us." Additionally, my communications clients report that positive change happens so rapidly that it is a little emotionally and intellectually jarring.

When E-types personally visit the Beliefs mode—change happens! When I-types personally visit the Emotions mode—change happens! Change happens in the funniest of places, namely, the unknown (or opposite, less known) to us. You can and will adopt your opposing co-communicators strengths and avoid your Achilles' Heel.

In my clinical work, I've found change happens so rapidly that teeth rattle.

In Figure 11, you will see that the four communicator modes are also experienced inside the brain of an Instigator communicator as either negative or positive. Negative and positive energy are flip sides of the same life coin. Neutral comes in there too, but it's not worth paying attention to because accuracy is what counts.

When E-types personally visit the Beliefs mode—change happens! When I-types personally visit the Emotions mode—change happens!

In my clinical work, I've found change happens so rapidly that teeth rattle.

INSTIGATOR Communicator Modes

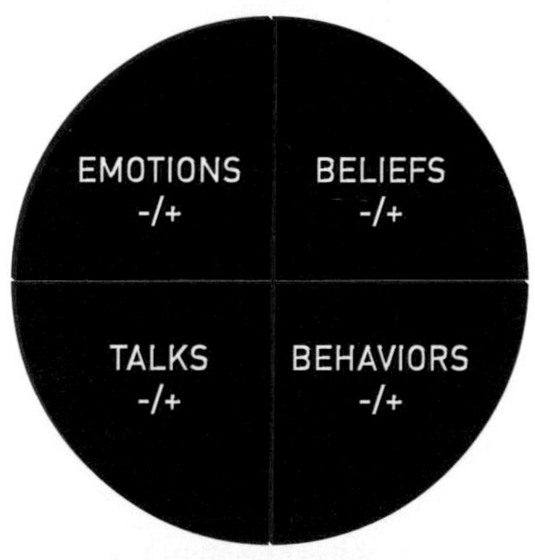

figure **#11**

THE REVENGE CLUB OF NEGATIVE EMOTIONS

Empathizer communicators tend to punish themselves when a conflict arises. Faced with similar conflicts, Instigator communicators tend to punish others who don't comply with their wishes. Thus, E-types blame themselves more often while I-types blame others or the situation more often.

During a conflict, both communicator types coercively and inadvertently stoop to using negative emotions as a club to force a co-communicator into compliance with their respective wants. I call this negative process *Emotional Competition,* and it involves winning the proverbial battle while losing the war. An Emotional Competition is a relationship competition where one competitor wins at the expense of the positive relationship. If you're on the losing end, it means being guilt-tripped and accused of being the "bad person" because of what you feel or think. Dr. Susan Forward wrote adroitly about this process in her superb book *Emotional Blackmail.*

When conflict occurs, Empathizers lose what I call their "sparkle." Energy-wise they feel "like there's a hole in my bucket and I'm being drained dry." E-types, customarily, think too negatively and thus may have self-imposed low self-esteem or LSE. An E-type's coping attitude may be the proverbial negative belief that "the glass is half-

When conflict occurs, Empathizers lose what I call their "sparkle."

empty." Unrealistically negative thoughts can lead to procrastination, poor timing of talks, or sustaining a course of action that should be changed or altered to create positive outcomes.

When conflict occurs, Instigators feel as if they are losing their minds.

When conflict occurs, Instigators feel as if they are losing their minds. Of course, an I-type is as sane as the day is long, but the mind is a prime source of power for them. Conflict drains their energy, leaving them physically empty. I-types, customarily, think too positively and thus may have self–created excessive self-esteem or ESE. An I-type's coping attitude may be the proverbial positive belief that "the glass is half-full to overflowing." Unrealistically positive thoughts can lead to rash actions, harsh words for nonconformers, or uncalled-for drastic action when the current course shouldn't be changed or altered.

Revenge promotes negative conflicts and avoidable crises for both communicator types.

HIGH SELF-ESTEEM

High self-esteem (HSE) or feeling loved and loving while co-creating emotional intimacy is what positive communication is all about.

High self-esteem (HSE) or feeling loved and loving while co-creating emotional intimacy is what positive communication is all about. It means dealing with reality while avoiding emotional power plays, guilt trips, brainwashing or feeding someone a manure sandwich.

Revenge is very sweet—and fattening.

Revenge is very sweet—and fattening. Anything can be used as a revenge club. I've seen children used as revenge clubs in nasty divorces and I've seen control of sex and "making war" used in controlling relationships. Refusing to speak to someone is a negative payback. I've seen disapproval used to put someone down and I've seen manipulative "kissing up" used to socially influence an outcome. All types of emotional manipulation can form patterns or downward cycles that increase negative emotions at the expense of every one.

Emotionally speaking, *E-types more often use negative dysphoria (pain, hurt, sadness) manipulatively to get their way and seize control.* Conversely, *I-types more often use negative anger (rejection, resentment, revenge) to get their way and seize control.* Both E-types and I-types fling guilt trips. To make matters more complex, everyone's emotions can buddy up or live in layers. Thus, if you believe you are a nice person and nice people like you don't get mad, then you will feel anxious about feeling mad—

or fear the anger of a co-communicator and back down.

Pouting, name calling, twisting the facts, lying by omission or commission, throwing a temper tantrum, refusing to talk, turning your back, blowing up, being in a lousy mood, or launching verbal anger attacks are common forms of negative anger. *E-types have the power to make you feel powerless and angry in the interpersonal world.* In reverse, *I-types have the power to make you feel intimidated and afraid in the interrelational world.* Either way, revenge is a form of hate that ends up hurting everyone and spitting in the face of love. Cooperation and compromise work far better.

Revenge is a form of hate that ends up hurting everyone and spitting in the face of love.

Dear reader, I'm not trying to tell you what to feel or think. However, I've said it before and I'll say it again: "what goes around comes around," and that includes positive paybacks. With that in mind, observe what happens, look at the emotional process of communication, and pay attention to how what is communicated is communicated. I am really trying vigorously to steer clear of labels to help you open your eyes to the negative and positive power of the communications process. Using labels will make you lazy instead of forcing you to look at communication in the modes—how people communicate—which is more colorful and complex. And the Emotions mode is one powerful mode!

Technically speaking, there is no such thing as a "good" or a "bad" emotion—emotions just are what they are. You don't have to get bogged down or stuck in them and spin your wheels.

Technically speaking, there is no such thing as a "good" or a "bad" emotion—emotions just are what they are.

THE GUILT ALBATROSS

Guilt is the proverbial albatross that's strung around your neck and bringing you so-called bad luck. Negative guilt drags you down emotionally and contributes mightily to your making poor decisions. Guilt causes you to change something you should not touch with a 10-foot pole and to keep doing something you would be far better off letting go.

Guilt causes you to change something you should not touch with a 10-foot pole and to keep doing something you would be far better off letting go.

Both Empathizer and Instigator communicators suffer from guilt when they play outside the lines of fair-fight communication rules.

Negative guilt affects E-types by making them emotionally hold tight to a relationship or an idea that they should let go.

Conversely, negative guilt affects I-types by making them talk negatively to a co-communicator or hold tight to a negative decision that makes life difficult for everyone.

Relationship expert John Gottman outlines fair fight rules in his book *The Seven Principles for Making Marriage Work.*

Guilt can be rational or irrational, as is true of every single one of your emotions. You can use every emotion, including guilt, in effective ways or ineffective ways. Effective use of guilt creates positive change while irrational guilt makes you feel stuck in the mud. Think of guilt as the potholes on the communication highway that can blow out your tire. Any way you examine it, guilt gets you down and causes regrets about life.

Predictably, many of my divorcing clients feel guilty and think of themselves as "losers," even when the couple was mismatched from the start.

Predictably, many of my divorcing clients feel guilty and think of themselves as "losers," even when the couple was mismatched from the start. "I should have known better," is their feeble cry. I reply, "If you are mismatched from the get-go, or if there is no love or one-sided love, then the relationship should be concluded." Ah, but negative guilt won't hear of love—it wants to hear its own poisonous words shred others' self-esteem one cut at a time. If you're trapped by negative guilt, it will serve as an anchor that will weigh you down and keep your beautiful vessel or ship in a "safe" harbor you despise.

Positive communicators aren't perfect, nor do they ever wish to be placed on a pedestal from which they can fall or be pushed.

Positive co-communicators co-create excitement, high energy, intensity, interpersonal sensitivity, curiosity, open-mindedness, personal and spiritual growth, and acceptance instead of judgment. Positive communicators aren't perfect, nor do they ever wish to be placed on a pedestal from which they can fall or be pushed. Loving communicators don't keep score of who's doing what for them as a gauge to measure whether or not they will behave in caring ways to return the favor. They want to "win" the experience of bathing their inner selves with intensely positive emotions; particularly, Joyfulness.

Positive communicators correctly realize that a pipeline of positive emotions can be tapped for the benefit of all. You do have some choice whether you experience any of the four communicator modes in negative or positive ways as illustrated in Figure 12.

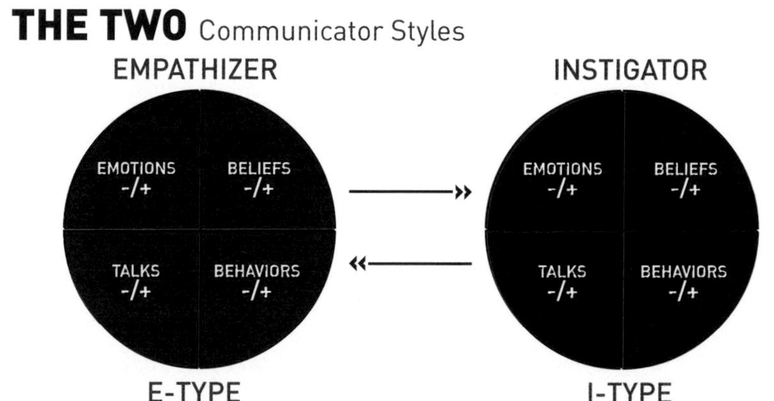

figure **#12**

IT'S YOUR WAY OR THE HIGHWAY?

We began our journey together talking about the communication highway that gets us to the Communication Table where we have a communion of minds.

The Four Communicator Modes I will flesh out for you in this chapter are called the *Emotions* mode (E), *Beliefs* mode (B1), *Behaviors* mode (B2) and *Talks* mode (T). They operate exactly as the American interstate highway system developed in the 1950s. These modes will connect the different parts of the country of your emotions and mind so you can travel more safely and conveniently to locations heretofore made too difficult to reach.

Most conflicts that cause distancing and relationship distress are due to a communicator clash. They occur when two people cut across talk lanes too fast and cause a collision. *When stressed E-types abruptly cross over from the Emotions lane to the Behaviors lane, disaster happens. When stressed I-types abruptly cross over from the Beliefs lane to the Talks lane, disaster happens.* Soon, anger and resentment arrive on the crash scene, and the blame game begins further tearing down positive talks. Positive talks are always a two-way highway. When communication is mutual, no one is threatened nor abandoned with the put-off power play, "It's my way or the highway." Agreeing to disagree, if necessary, is the norm of mature communicators.

Positive talks are always a two-way highway. When communication is mutual, no one is threatened nor abandoned with the put-off power play, "It's my way or the highway."

I am using hypnotic metaphors about cars and communication highways to make this material user-friendly for both the emotional mind of E-types and the logical mind of I-types. Each unique mind is a dazzling triumph. Empathizers prefer emotional metaphors, while Instigators prefer black-and-white "here's what to do and here's how to do it, now go out and do what I told you to do." Neither style is better, just different. In fact, both styles are especially cool when they choose to adopt and accurately use the strengths from the other communicator style.

As you work with this approach, you are going to really feel and see a difference in your positive communication skills, your emotions and your attitude. The two communicator types and four modes of travel you are learning about will really open your mind to new possibilities that can and do come true. So let's carry on and continue with our metaphor. Imagine, again, that there are two colors of cars, blue and burnt orange. Blue automobiles are favored by, and driven exclusively by, Empathizer communicators. Burnt orange automobiles are favored by, and driven exclusively by, Instigator communicators.

Now get ready for a sharp curve in the talk road. A strange thing happened on the way to The Town of Talk. The blue automobiles driven exclusively by Empathizer communicators have the steering wheels on the left side of the car, while the burnt orange automobiles driven exclusively by the Instigator communicators have the steering wheels on the right side of the car. Both styles of vehicle are legally permitted and both are preferred by some (but not all) drivers.

Empathizer communicators love to drive and ride in their blue cars. Empathizer communicators enter their cars from the left side. They throw their duffel bags in the back seat on the left side because it is easy and natural and the way things always are done in their little corner of the world. Empathizers share the highway with Instigator minds but prefer to drive in the left lanes to the city called Sincerity.

Conversely, Instigators love to drive and ride in their burnt orange cars. Instigator communicators enter their cars on the right side, European-style. They throw their duffel bags in the back seat on the right side of the vehicle because it is easy and natural and the way they have always done it. Instigators share the highway with Empathizer emotions but prefer to drive in the right lanes of the highway to the city called Security.

Both communicators get in the groove and become pretty set in their travel habits. Both agree with the sentiment, "Why change what's working?" Both communicators' particular cars harbor many memories that form a life storyline or script. Both communicators have the required sets of keys to get their motors running. No one likes to drive in the "wrong" lane or take a "wrong" turn-off on the communication highway.

Both communicator types want to enjoy the trip. Each one wants to feel good enough to feel love, loving and loved.

E-TYPE AND I-TYPE FACTOIDS

By now, you know there is no victory or sob story attached to being either an Empathizer or an Instigator communicator. Both are okay and needed in this world in order to be a positive communicator. Blue cars and burnt orange cars are equally capable of making any trip.

Knowing your type opens up a positive new change world of exciting possibilities. Being able to quickly diagnose what type of talker your co-communicator happens to be is important to your business and couple success. Especially during tense times of turbulent change, knowing your cohort's talk style will tell you a lot about what to say and do, and what not to say and do, to avoid unnecessary misunderstandings.

Especially during tense times of turbulent change, knowing your cohort's talk style will tell you a lot about what to say and do, and what not to say and do, to avoid unnecessary misunderstandings.

In my clinical studies of couples, coupled co-communicators break down into three categories or thirds. One third of coupled co-communicators are E-E types. One third of coupled co-communicators are E-I types. And one third of coupled co-communicators are I-I types. I really do believe that Mother Nature has made all communicator styles equal—and equal in percentages. At first I believed that I-I types were a 20% club, but then I thought, "Hey, that's just what I-types would want you to think—that they're really special!" Well, of course I-types are unique, just as unique as all those exciting E-types they like to interact with so intensely.

As well, your children and grandchildren will be E-types or I-types. Right away, you're probably estimating correctly that your brother or sister, mother or father are either your same or opposing type. Plus, you're probably correctly guessing the type of the teacher or professor who is teaching you. E-students prefer E-teachers and learn more enjoyably and quickly from them. Many times I-students prefer I-teachers and learn more quickly and enjoyably from them.

And get a load out of this hobby angle: Empathizers seem to prefer to play team sports such as basketball and soccer while Instigators seem to prefer to play individualistic sports like tennis and gymnastics! That's because E-types like to be part of a group while I-types like to be stand-out leaders.

Another fun factoid: Sigmund Freud created the concepts of unconscious vs. conscious minds. His close comrade Carl Jung created the concepts of introversion and extroversion. There was a huge clash of these genius titans and ultimately a very painful falling out. Jung puzzled over the differences between the two culture giants in his 1923 book *Psychological Types.* Then Jung threw up his hands in exasperation and put the project aside. That book gave birth to the Myers-Briggs personality testing movement.

Now get ready for this: I believe that Jung was an E-type (ETI) and Freud was an I-type (ITI) and they had one whale of a talk collision!

SWITCHING GEARS

Switching gears: Your choice of car often reflects a great deal about yourself and how you think about your life. Perhaps your favorite car is a Mazda or Saturn, a Cadillac or Ford, a VW or BMW, a Toyota or a Chevrolet. When it comes to communication, the make of your car does matter a wee little bit. What matters more, though, and what determines a positive talk outcome, is the color of the car in our metaphor.

The blue or burnt orange exterior color of your communicator automobile talking style will determine what will work and what won't work, from a standpoint of talking, and from what frame of mind you will deliver the best results in talking. The blue or burnt orange exterior color of your co-communicators' automobile style will determine how and from what frame of mind you will get the best talk results from them. Be excited, because life is going to become a whole lot easier from here on out!

Have you caught on to the American vs. European distinction

between E-types and I-types? Did you catch on to which side of the car the steering column is on for E-types and I-types? Even though it seems like an itty-bitty variation, the placement of that steering wheel in your communicator vehicle makes a huge difference for this particular metaphor—far more than the size of the engine or the intricacy of the accessories.

Why? If you are an Empathizer communicator, or E-type, you drive from the left side of your blue car American-style and prefer to drive in the two left lanes in the communication chart of Emotions and Talks. If you are an Instigator communicator, or I-type, on the other hand, you drive from the right side of your burnt orange car European-style and prefer to drive in the two right lanes in the communication chart of Beliefs and Behaviors.

Until now, no one much has been able to observe or describe this appreciable and highly encouraging communicator difference to you. By absorbing this material, you are going from the horse and buggy era to riding a rocket ship. And culturally, all of us will make one giant, collective stride in our positive communication attitudes and abilities.

By absorbing this material, you are going from the horse and buggy era to riding a rocket ship.

In sum, if you are emotional and sensitive, then you are an E-type. If you use logic and reasoning to cope with life, then you are an I-type. If your feelings are easily hurt and you have trouble getting beyond the past, then you are probably an E-type. If you get mad, tell it like it is and then get over it but are caught off guard when others are still stinging from your words, then, of course, you are an Instigator communicator. It matters not if you are boy or girl, straight or gay, young or elder, generation X or generation Y. What matters is your communicator type.

Until this work, most experts incompletely thought that gender alone was the deciding difference during talks, communication breakdown and blame games.

I'LL TELL YOU WHAT'S CRAZY

I'll tell you what's crazy. It is crazy to assume automatically that someone feels and believes the same way you do. It's even nuttier to think that everyone uses all four communicator modes an equal amount of the time. But no longer, because this is the first time you've learned about the four modes of communication that every communicator has access to.

I'll tell you what's crazy. It is crazy to assume automatically that someone feels and believes the same way you do.

By now, it's sinking in and registering in your mind that *E-types drive in the modes called Emotions (E) and Talks (T) much of the time.* It is also sinking in and registering in your emotions that *I-types drive in the Beliefs (B1) and Behaviors (B2) modes much of the time.* It feels more comfortable for E-types to drive in the Emotions (E) mode. Likewise, it feels more logical for I-types to drive first in the Beliefs (B1) mode much of the time.

Attitudinally, you probably consider it pure crazy to get into a car and drive on the opposite side than your customary way. Why, where you come from, and according to how you were raised and taught to feel and believe, it's just plain unnatural and ridiculous to drive on the other side of the car, right? Your way is the right way! It's your way on the highway. Right? Wrong.

The plain fact is there are two communicator types and four modes to travel in down the communication highway.

The plain fact is there are two communicator types and four modes to travel in down the communication highway. The plain fact is that probably half of all men and women are Empathizer communicators, and half of all men and women are Instigator communicators, which creates some exciting and frustrating business, parenting, teaching and romantic relationships, just to mention a few.

Macho-acting men you relate to are half of the time E-type communicators. Feminine-acting women you relate to are half of the time I-type communicators.

Don't be fooled, though. Listen carefully to your co-communicators to diagnose their E-type or I-type style. Macho-acting men you relate to are half of the time E-type communicators. Feminine-acting women you relate to are half of the time I-type communicators. Don't be fooled by pretty looks, poetic words or social persona.

The style of communicator says it all—and it is not in the way they kiss but in the words they speak. *For coping E-types, new positive actions speak louder than words. For coping I-types, new positive words speak louder than actions.*

Is the next question you want to ask me this one: "Will I be better off matched with the same style communicator type that I am so we can get along more easily at work or home?" Well, that depends. Although there are challenges of communication between all types, sometimes matching to the same type may work out better depending on your circumstances. Overall, though, the presence of co-equal love is more important than communicator type.
Do the numbers: At this time in the evolution of modern relation-

ships, communicator types match up equally two-thirds (E-E, I-I) of the time.

For now, though, own the freeing idea that other communication, feeling, behaving and thinking styles exist. Where you come from and how you prefer your talks with others to be packaged, how you feel and think, and how you drive are not the way it's done all over the town. So get ready to get your motor running and drive in all four talk modes.

God did create, I believe, communicators to be different but equal. The sooner you and I can accept this fact of communication reality and communicator nature, the better off you and I will be, and the fewer communication walls and accidents you and I will inadvertently run blindly into.

It is simply nutty and crazy to talk and behave like everyone around you feels and thinks like you do.

TYPECASTING Empathizer and Instigator Communicators

EMPATHIZER TYPE INTROVERT (ETI)	INSTIGATOR TYPE INTROVERT (ITI)
EMPATHIZER TYPE EXTROVERT (ETE)	INSTIGATOR TYPE EXTROVERT (ITE)

figure **#13**

CLINICAL CASE STUDY OF COMMUNICATOR PERCENTAGES BY TYPE/PERSONALITY/GENDER

In a groundbreaking clinical study, I typecast all of my communications clients from April 2005, to June 2005. Moreover, I figured that the method would give me some valid "real-life" data. Thus, I "typecast" all of my communications clients (160 in all) by communicator type, personality type (introversion/extroversion) and gender to obtain some comparative data. I jointly determined their communicator type through interview and through administering the NICI. Conveniently, about half of my clients are women and half are men.

WHAT IS YOUR COMMUNICATOR TYPE?

You and everyone around you fall into one of four groups. Ultimately, you feel and know where you and your fellow co-communicators stand. Here are the four new communicator/ personality subtypes.

I. Empathizer-Type Introvert (ETI)

II. Empathizer-Type Extrovert (ETE)

III. Instigator-Type Introvert (ITI)

IV. Instigator-Type Extrovert (ITE)

The total number of responders were 160, with 45% of them being female and 55% being male.

PERCENTAGES BY COMMUNICATOR/ PERSONALITY TYPE

Empathizer (E-type)

40% are Empathizer-type
23% are Empathizer-type Introvert (ETI)
17% are Empathizer-type Extrovert (ETE)

Instigator (I-type)

60% are Instigator-type
31% are Instigator-type Introvert (ITI)
29% are Instigator-type Extrovert (ITE)

My middle daughter, because of her grade school experience, predicted the ratio would be 40% Empathizer communicators to 60% Instigator communicators in the world. And as you know, I predicted a 50/50 split. I was off. Way to be, my child!

PERCENTAGE BREAKDOWN OF FEMALE VS. MALE EMPATHIZER COMMUNICATORS (ETI/ETE)

Female Empathizer Communicators Represent 23% of Sample Population

14% are Female ETI's
9% are Female ETE's

Male Empathizer Communicators Represent 18% of Sample Population

9% are Male ETI's
9% are Male ETE's

Take a minute to find yourself in the sample population. How do you feel (proud?) about where you stand?

PERCENTAGE BREAKDOWN OF FEMALE VS. MALE INSTIGATOR COMMUNICATORS (ITI/ITE)

Female Instigator Communicators Represent 22% of Sample Population

11% Female ITI's
11% Female ITE's

Male Instigator Communicators Represent 37% of Sample Population

19% Male ITI's
18% Male ITE's

CO-COMMUNICATOR PREDICTIONS

40% are Empathizer (E-type) co-communicators
60% are Instigator (I-type) co-communicators

Which are you? You know who you are!

My point here is to add to your awareness that communicator type is separate and distinct from gender, personality variables, age, generational, family/work role and many other factors. No co-communicator type is superior to another. Each partner, couple and business arrangement encounters mix-ups in communication and anxiety–arousing conflicts that need to be aired fairly and discussed in reasonable ways. The relationships you now seek are loving and respectful positive co-communicator relationships replete with loving emotions, ideas, actions and heart-to-heart talks.

Say it and it will be so. Believe it, and you will see it materialize, as Dr. Wayne Dyer has shown.

2005 DAYTON LEADERSHIP STUDY RESULTS

With the help of the Dayton Development Coalition, I used the NICI and the NICI-Leadership Scale to test the communicator types of a sample group of 32 proven and effective entrepreneurial leaders in our region. Together, they are responsible for 65% of the jobs in our area. What a blast this "blind study" turned out to be!

Would you be surprised to find out that Instigator communicators led the pack to the tune of 75% of our leaders, many of whom are extroverts? I wasn't! A leader typically has to have a thick hide to shrug off the rejections and failures required to climb to the top.

Here are the results of this dynamic look inside the "real" communicator world of leaders.

LEADERSHIP COMMUNICATOR TYPE BY PERCENTAGE

Empathizer Leaders (E-type)

25% are Empathizer communicator Leaders

Instigator Leaders (I-type)

75% are Instigator communicator Leaders

PERCENTAGE BREAKDOWN OF LEADERSHIP COMMUNICATOR TYPE VS. PERSONALITY TYPE

ETI Leaders

12.5% are Empathizer Introvert Leaders

ETE Leaders

12.5% are Empathizer Extrovert Leaders

ITI Leaders

15.6% are Instigator Introvert Leaders

ITE Leaders

59.4% are Instigator Extrovert Leaders

Leader Extroverts = 72%
Leader Introverts = 28%

The total number of respondents was 32, with 27 males and 5 females, all Caucasian. In total, 50 leaders (including African Americans) received queries to participate in this study.

CO-COMMUNICATOR RESULTS

62% of Leader Partners are Empathizers
38% of Leader Partners are Instigators

Don't you find it fascinating that a majority of the life partners in the Dayton Leadership Study are the opposite or opposing communicator style? That's why adopting the strengths of your opposing communicator style helps you to travel more enjoyably and effectively down the two-way communicator highway—at work and home—and avoid many "talk crashes."

THE FOUR COMMUNICATOR MODES

When I look out my office windows on I-675 in Dayton, Ohio, I see two highways. There are four lanes total, two lanes each traveling in two opposite directions. This highway structure is common in America.

The noise of the highway is ever-present, a sound that speaks to me of progress and commerce. One of the two-lane highways is looping around our fair city going west. The other matching two-lane highway stretches out like a snake, going east. The black asphalt is a palette of gray textures caused by the aging effects of sun, snow and salt in the Midwest.

Figure 14 shows us the four communicator modes alongside their abbreviations and negative/positive valences. They are spray-painted orange stripes on the background of gray asphalt on the highways of life you travel everyday.

These are the four avenues of communication that are to be expected and respected:

Negative And Positive Communicator Modes

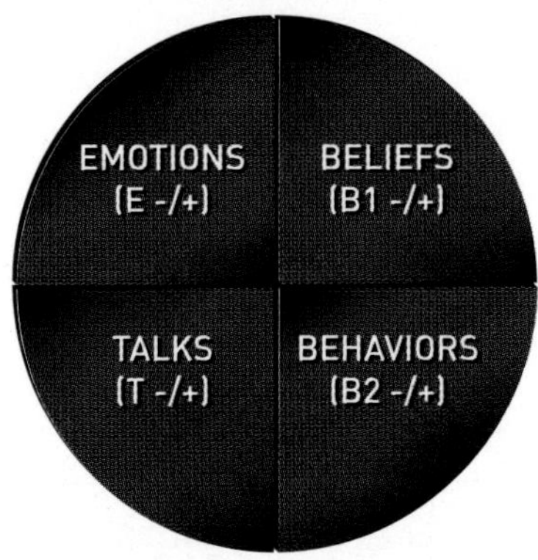

figure **#14**

The communication chart divides a circle into four equal quadrants or portions. As you know, not everyone prefers the same slice of pie or the same lane to drive on the road.

I want you to memorize the modes in a particular order for them to best interact with both your emotional and logical minds.

Start in the upper left side quadrant, or Emotions mode, and move clockwise with enthusiasm. As you memorize the circle of communication, keep in mind:

- **In the upper left quadrant of the communication chart is the *Emotions mode or (E) mode.***
- **In the upper right quadrant of the communication chart is the *Beliefs mode or (B1) mode.***
- **In the lower right quadrant of the communication chart is the *Behaviors mode or (B2) mode.***
- **In the lower left quadrant of the communication chart is the *Talks mode or (T) mode.***

Let me give you some concrete examples of the four communicator modes in action during conversation. Words and sentences from each mode are either positive or negative as indicated in Chart 3.1.

Chart 3.1 Pages 136–137

Now you have a budding awareness of what the four communicator modes are, and how to tell them apart. Soon you will find out which mode you can choose to use in talks when you want to co-create positive outcomes with a co-communicator. Dark times are behind you, brighter times of light and new insights are in front of you! As a recent communications client told me: "I've got my happy back!"

Inspirational teasing aside, *Empathizer communicators generally spend a majority of their talk time in the Emotions mode.* In contrast, *Instigator communicators spend a majority of their talk time in the Beliefs mode.* That's not always terribly helpful to the communication process, you zany E-types and I-types, but that is what is customarily done out of ignorance.

Empathizer communicators generally spend a majority of their talk time in the Emotions mode. In contrast, Instigator communicators spend a majority of their talk time in the Beliefs mode.

Again, please encourage your two minds, emotional and logical, to endorse and accept that much of the time *E-types prefer to use the two left side communicator quadrants, namely Emotions (E) and Talks (T).* And please invite your two minds to realize and accept that much of the time *I-types prefer to use the two right side communicator quadrants, namely Beliefs (B1) and Behaviors (B2).* Soon you will be learning that you are free to use the common talk methods of your opposite communicator style.

In summary, E-types prefer to use the two left side quadrants, namely Emotions and Talks, to discuss the emotional reasons behind their choices, while I-types prefer to use the two right side quadrants, namely Beliefs and Behaviors, to discuss the logic behind their plans to do something.

Now something big is really happening here!

UNDERSTANDING THE MODES

You will be prepared to drive down the communication highway when you are able to recite these four quadrants in your sleep in clockwise fashion beginning with the Emotions mode. You need to understand them verbatim without any outside help, and see them in visual format in your mind—and feel them in your gut for best results.

You will be prepared to drive down the communication highway when you are able to recite these four quadrants in your sleep in clockwise fashion beginning with the Emotions mode.

3.1 Talk Modes In Action

Emotions (E)	Beliefs (B1)
Time Talk	
I feel frustrated when people aren't on time. (E-)	I think it is disrespectful to be late. (B1-)
Career Talk	
I feel excited by my work and really enjoy it. (E+)	I've got the best customers and clients in the world. (B1+)
Divorce Talk	
I feel stabbed in the back. (E-)	I won't ever be able to love and trust again. (B1-)
Beloved Talk	
I get turned on just thinking about my partner. (E+)	I feel more in love with my partner today than ever before. (B1+)
Person Of Your Dreams Talk	
I found out the hard way you can't trust men/women. (E-)	All the good ones are taken. (B1-)
Finding The Person Of Your Dreams Talk	
I feel positive that there are 12 love partners or soul mates currently available to me. (E+)	I use my mind as a broadcasting system to attract one of my beloveds to me now. (B1+)

Behaviors (B2)	Talks (T)
I give a cold shoulder to anyone who can't get their act together and show up on time. (B2-)	You can talk until you're blue in the face but people who are chronically late won't change. (T-)
I greet my customers with a warm smile and my complete attention. (B2+)	I'm going to give sincere encouragement or compliments to everyone I come into contact with during the day. (T+)
I've been shouting at the kids because I've been so upset and moody. (B2-)	I'll lose everything I've accumulated in this divorce. (T-)
I hug my partner tight for 15 seconds when we reconnect at home after work. (B2+)	I'm not embarrassed to share my emotions with my partner. I know that I am accepted unconditionally. (T+)
I'm not going to take risks and get hurt again. (B2-)	I try and I try but I keep attracting real losers. (T-)
I have made a top-ten list of all the key traits I must have to have a perfect match. (B2+)	I will be emotionally honest when I meet new people and talk positively and lovingly. (T+)

Negative speak is a choice, neither right nor wrong.

So far, I hope you are building in your mind and your gut the very real notion that you get to choose, to quite a large extent, whether you feel/think/act/talk negatively or positively. Negative speak is a choice, neither right nor wrong. Now, however, is the time to contrast the negative news article about teens in the Daily Talk newspaper, with the positive news article about teens in the New Insights newspaper. Which way of thinking increases your positive energy?

What do you think about teens today, and how to talk to teenagers? The positive thoughts represented in Chart 3.2 are my "heart thoughts," or what I feel and think in my heart and my mind as the father of two girls—and the very proud father of one very positive fourteen-year-old teen young woman.

3.2

Negative Parent-Teen Talk (T-)	Positive Parent-Teen Talk (T+)
Emotions (–) Mode	Emotions (+) Mode
I could wring my teen's neck, I feel so mad.	I really love teenagers. They're so honest, genuine and real with a positive lifetime ahead of them.
Beliefs (–) Mode	Beliefs (+) Mode
I believe that—for parents—the teenage years are the worst years of parenthood. Just you wait and see!	I believe the teenage years are terrific opportunities to undo negative thinking patterns of youth and help youth to come into their own identity and power as young adults.
Behaviors (–) Mode	Behaviors (+) Mode
I've got to be consistent in my punishment and take away their computer time for breaking curfew.	Teens don't need parent consistency as much as they need parent reasonableness, encouragement, flexibility, attitude guidance and open-mindedness.
Talks (–) Mode	Talks (+) Mode
Teens act like they know everything.	Teens need to be listened to and heard and supported as they find out why and how they don't know everything. They need to learn to speak effectively about all of their emotions, especially disappointment and discouragement.

Always remember that Empathizer communicators habitually drive almost exclusively in the modes of Emotions and Talks, and Instigator communicators habitually drive almost exclusively in the Beliefs mode and the Behaviors mode. Nonetheless, whatever mode you're currently in, you still have easy access to the remaining three modes. For instance, imagine standing at the midpoint of the intersecting lines in the communication chart. You can dash into any mode equally easily!

It is the rule of the road. It is the way we are. It is only natural to like the person you are and the way you drive. I believe (Belief mode or B1+) that both E-types and I-types are truly lovable and logical!

> *Mode:* 1. A way or manner in which something occurs or is experienced, expressed, or done: *"His preferred mode of travel was a kayak."* 2. Differences between language modes, namely speech and writing.

TALKING IN THE FOUR COMMUNICATOR MODES

Your mind is ever busy.

Empathizer and Instigator drivers all have access to the same four communicator modes at any time, awake or asleep. Interestingly, the modes are also in operation silently or in your "skull talk," as I call it, even when you aren't actually verbally relating to the outside world. As Dr. Phil McGraw discussed in *Self Matters*—83% of your daily communication doesn't involve externally spoken words at all! That's a large percentage. As a thinker with a will, you are free to choose, to some extent, whether your inner world of emotions and thoughts are positive or negative.

Empathizer and Instigator drivers all have access to the same four communicator modes at any time awake or asleep.

83% of your daily communication doesn't involve externally spoken words at all!

Again, the Empathizer talker will spend most of his or her talk time in the left two lanes of the communication chart—namely hanging out in the Emotions mode and in the Talks mode. E-types love to feel connected via chat. An Instigator talker spends most of her or his talk time in the right two lanes of the communication chart—namely hanging out in the Beliefs mode and

E-types love to feel connected via chat.

I-types love to feel connected via logic.

in the Behaviors mode. I-types love to feel connected via logic. Also, these early preferences were either reinforced or diminished in the family of origin.

The communication chart looks simple, but it is wonderfully rich and complex. Mark the diagram on your emotional mind, and make the diagram part of your everyday life. Intentionally and purposely driving in the four communicator modes will help enormously to co-create positive communication outcomes that improve both your mood and your mind. Use any memorization tricks to plant the modes in the fertile field of your two minds. (When I memorized the modes, I thought of them as four seating areas in my automobile. I also thought of the standard four-on-the-floor, gear-shifting pattern in my Mazda RX8). Thinking of the natural elements of Earth, Wind, Fire and Water helps, too. E-types are Water-Earth while I-types are Fire-Wind.

E-types are Water-Earth while I-types are Fire-Wind.

To reinforce my own learning and memorization, I also drew the communication chart circle with the initials of the modes or E, B1, B2 and T in the quadrants and looked at the graph while listening to a client speaking. During business meetings, I would draw the communicator circle chart and try to psyche out the mode the talker was using. I began to hear and understand things I had never before comprehended. I love the experience of intense listening or listening with three ears.

It took me a while to be able to keep the names in my mind while I actively listened to my psychology clients. Talking about the modes to others helps a great deal too. When you can cite the modes in order of Emotions, Beliefs, Behaviors and Talks—you are nearing your home destination. The modes interact with your mind, and flip on your headlamps to make driving easier, more fun and emotionally enriching in the pitch dark of tough relationship times.

When you can cite the modes in order of Emotions, Beliefs, Behaviors and Talks—you are nearing your home destination.

The modes are the doors you must go through to reach intense emotional intimacy.

The modes are the doors you must go through to reach intense emotional intimacy.

USING THE MODES TO TALK POSITIVELY

Modes can be used to talk either negatively or positively—sometimes neutrally. However, now you get to choose what mode you use and how you come across in negative or positive words.

Let me give you both black-and-white descriptive language and colorful concepts to help you more easily and accurately remember the four communicator modes for talking positively:

EMOTIONS (E) MODE

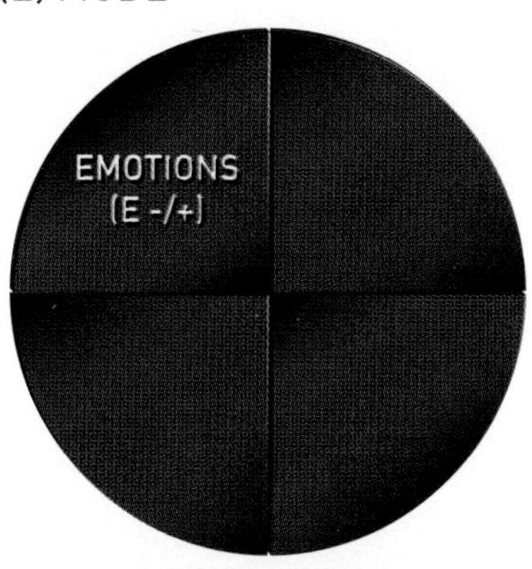

figure **#15**

Emotions (E)

Emotions constitute internal or external verbal or non-verbal transactions coming from the upper left-side quadrant of the communicator chart that involves *feeling. The positive intent of Emotions is to encourage you to take bold new positive action.*

The positive intent of Emotions is to encourage you to take bold new positive action.

This is the mode Empathizers lead from and prefer to use when relationship tensions arise. E-types also can become stuck in negative emotions ("I feel like I'm going to explode!") and ground down from negative thinking and negative self-talk. The Emotions mode is the place where Instigators develop the powerful emotional self and create amazing and lasting positive changes.

The Emotions mode is the place where Instigators develop the powerful emotional self and create amazing and lasting positive changes.

It is also the steering column that Empathizer drivers turn to during power plays when communication breaks down.

BELIEFS (B1) MODE

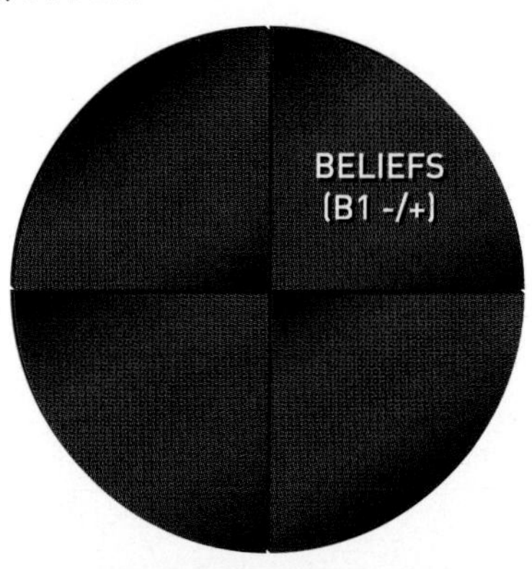

figure **#16**

Beliefs (B1)

Beliefs constitute internal or external verbal or non-verbal transactions coming from the upper right-side quadrant of the communicator chart that involves *thinking. The positive intent of Beliefs is to encourage you to speak positively about new opportunities.*

The positive intent of Beliefs is to encourage you to speak positively about new opportunities.

This is the mode Instigators lead from and prefer to use when relationship tensions arise. I-types also can become stuck in negative thinking (close-minded beliefs) and physically drained due to negative feelings and negative behaviors. The Beliefs mode is the place where Empathizers develop the powerful intellectual self and create amazing and lasting positive changes.

The Beliefs mode is the place where Empathizers develop the powerful intellectual self and create amazing and lasting positive changes.

It is also the steering column of Instigator drivers during power plays when communication breaks down.

BEHAVIORS (B2) MODE

figure **#17**

Behaviors (B2)

Behaviors constitute internal or external verbal or non-verbal transactions coming from the lower-right side quadrant of the communicator chart that involves <u>*doing.*</u> *The positive intent of Behaviors is to encourage you to do the new.*

It is also the right-side back seat of the Instigator car, the place where I-types toss their big duffel bags stuffed full of relationship resentments. It is from negative Talks (negative words spoken) and from negative Behaviors (negative actions taken) that I-types unintentionally pursue self-defeating actions that unravel love.

The positive intent of Behaviors is to encourage you to do the new.

During negative relationship Behaviors, such as power-plays, put-downs or put offs, *I-types typically feel powerless to do anything to improve the mood of the relationship.*

I-types typically feel powerless to do anything to improve the mood of the relationship.

TALKS (T) MODE

figure **#18**

Talks (T)

Talks constitute internal or external verbal or nonverbal transactions coming from the lower left-side quadrant of the communicator chart that involves <u>*speaking.*</u> *The positive intent of Talks is to encourage you to speak positively about your allied strengths.*

The positive intent of talks is to encourage you to speak positively about your allied strengths.

It is also the left-side back seat of the Empathizer car where E-types toss their big duffel bags chocked full of relationship resentments. It is from negative Talks (unloving beliefs spoken), and negative Behaviors (unloving thoughts acted upon), that *E-types typically pursue self-defeating actions that unravel love and bring down the mood of the relationship.*

E-types typically feel dominated by I-types' over-abundant rhetorical skills.

During negative relationship Talks, such as power-plays, put-downs or put-offs, *E-types typically feel dominated by I-types' over-abundant rhetorical skills.* After all, a typical Instigator communicator can talk circles around an Empathizer.

Overall, Empathizer communicators prefer to use the left side front and back seat of the talking automobile. Conversely, Instigator communicators prefer to use the right side front and back seat of the talking automobile.

You will be fully on your wonder-filled journey to emotional freedom and closer, joyful relationships when you are truly able to choose, on purpose, the talk mode/side you want to ride on, side on and use to the benefit of all.

From now on, accept and remember that each driver of the blue and burnt orange vehicles has four communicator modes to use when they drive on the two-way communications highway. Each time they open their mouths, they use one of the modes, whether they're conscious of it or not. From now, on, however, you will have a new level of consciousness and skill.

Sadly, many fender-benders or big crashes occur when a talking driver isn't schooled in the positive talk modes or hasn't been licensed to drive down the fast-moving, lovely, two-way communication highway.

TALK MODES—MODE TALKS

Following is a testimonial from an elder E-type client who benefited from working through the four talk modes.

"My anger is coming under my control. I feel stronger and more able to stand on my own two feet and make the decisions I want to. I don't second-guess my decisions any more like I used to and doubt myself. I make the changes I want to, and I feel more self-assurance due to my communications and emotions coaching with you. I've learned that I can be happy again. I've learned that I feel supported by others. I feel that who I am is right! It's the first time in my life that I've never doubted myself. All of these positive changes slowly developed in me and grew together like vines on a fencepost. When I first came to you, I believed that life never turns out all right. Now, I firmly believe that life always turns out all right. I really like my life!"

"When I first came to you, I believed that life never turns out all right. Now, I firmly believe that life always turns out all right. I really like my life!"

You're tapping into your positive power now, too.

NEGATIVE POWER PLAYS

Speaking negative thoughts out loud or in your skull can drive you crazy. It also bathes your body in undesirable chemicals.

Speaking negative thoughts out loud or in your skull can drive you crazy. It also bathes your body in undesirable chemicals.

Below are the actual transactions (one-sided speaker) of a negative power play in real life that a communications client shared with me recently. First, can you tell me if this next communicator is an Empathizer or an Instigator communicator? Second, can you guess what the issue or dispute is all about?

I promise you that you will find out what all the fuss is about in the final transaction. Do you agree or disagree with the modes I have selected? Why or why not? Also, do you agree or disagree with the negative or positive emotional valences I have selected? Don't try to be perfect, because good enough will work splendidly.

Remember, again, that any transaction can come only from one talk mode at a time. The transaction can be either negative or positive and can come only from one of these four communicator modes: Emotions (E)—Beliefs (B1)—Behaviors (B2)—Talks (T). In the following transcript, the transactions were verbal and made without the other negative power player being present in the room except in spirit.

(B1-) I'm not fighting and arguing with you anymore
(B1-) You're not being reasonable
(B1-) You're making no sense whatever
(B1-) You're so stubborn! Why won't you negotiate with me?
(B1-) You're driving me crazy!
(B1-) You don't choose your battles wisely
(B1-) I can't control your decisions
(B1-) Who says I'm over-reacting?
(B1-) I can't figure you out
(E-) I feel really bad about this
(B1-) I'm trying to be fair
(E+) I'm proud of myself for taking a stand
(B1-) I'm the one doing you a favor here!
(B1-) You don't respect me and I won't stand for it
(B1-) Why do I have to do all the bending and changing
(B1-) You're a control freak!
(B1-) You should be more logical about this issue
(B1-) You think I'm stupid!
(B1-) Why don't you believe a word I say?
(E-) This power play depresses me
(B1-) I'm too smart for my own good sometimes
(B1-) Why don't you trust me?
(B1-) You don't know everything!
(B1-) When are you going to start thinking for yourself?
(B1-) You're making this more difficult than it has to be!
(B1-) You're trying to make me feel sorry for you

(B1-) Why can't you get it?
(B1-) Let's just stick to the black-and-white facts here
(B1-) You only do what you want to do
(B1-) What favors have you done for me lately?
(B1-) You don't care what I think
(B1-) Maybe you could thank me once in a while for a change
(B1-) You like to use threats to intimidate me
(B1-) Why are you always trying to screw with my mind?
(B1-) Why can't one thing be easy in this relationship?
(B1-) I'm done talking to you
(B1-) *You know you get to me when you use the kids as a revenge club!*

TUG-OF-WAR

Negative power plays are like tug-of-war.

It takes two to play the anger game. If you decide to let go of your end of the rope, the expected power play peters out.

Negative power plays involve many inaccurate and negative beliefs, accusations and statements. Watch out for them! In fact, the transactions above came from an ongoing feud between two divorced partners who still have co-parenting responsibilities and need to work out shuttling the kids between two different households. Nonetheless, this could have been a negative talk between a parent and teenager, a controlling relationship couple, two siblings in strife or any common encounter between two people.

Which communicator type did the speaker occupy fully in the negative power play? Of course, the speaker was an Instigator communicator, in the tug-of-war power play, in this case with an Instigator co-communicator. When I-types fight, it's a clash of the talk titans! During conflict, and during normal times, I-types resort almost exclusively to the Beliefs (B1) mode in either negative or positive ways. You knew that, right?

Some of the transactions were a little tricky, weren't they? For example, a spoken transaction may sound like an emotion, but will actually be a negative belief. Plus, a negative belief may have emotional energy surrounding it. Anger was hidden in the transactions above, but negative anger for I-types is a "safe" emotion that isn't terribly helpful. Lastly, dozens of times each day, the female partner in this relationship silently said these negative beliefs to herself in

Negative power plays are like tug-of-war.

It takes two to play the anger game. If you decide to let go of your end of the rope, the expected power play peters out.

the skull talk zone, depressing her, bathing her inner body in negative chemicals.

To what end? I'm not going to relay to you here what I said to create positive change. After all, our positive goal right now is to invite you to observe, feel and think in the four communicator modes. The good news, though, is that this client quickly decided to get an "emotional divorce" from her ex-husband who was inappropriately using her love for the kids as an Achilles Heel to hurt her.

This client let loose of her end of the tug-of-war rope, realizing that she was 50% co-responsible for co-creating negative or positive relational outcomes with anyone. Then when the co-communicator yanked and tugged hard on the rope the next time around, he fell flat on his back in the mud because my client was no longer holding onto her end of the rope.

It was a better outcome for everyone.

CORE POSITIVE BELIEFS (B1+) OF INSTIGATOR COMMUNICATORS

Okay, let's be perfectly fair and accurate here.

From the *frame of reference* of an Instigator communicator, the following beliefs, rules and standards of conduct are a routine part of life:

- Values protecting loved ones
- Values love of country, company, profession, religion
- Thinks big and bigger and biggest
- Talks confidently and persuasively
- Prefers being in control, anxious when loses control
- Enjoys making change and progress happen
- Operates in extremes of pleasure/displeasure
- Gives self huge challenges on regular basis
- Dislikes hurting others
- Believes in rapid consequences, rewards, take-away punishers
- May stress out loved ones when intensely focused
- Hates to be bored

- Energy burns bright like the orange sun
- Can be an introvert type or extrovert type
- Drives the mood of the household or office for better or for worse
- Likes to operate in black-and-white thinking
- When negative, is extremely negative; if positive, is extremely positive
- Relies on the mind and intellectual powers as prime driving forces
- Considers a handshake better than legal contracts
- Requires respect to feel up to best
- Takes pride in accomplishments—doing is better than being
- Is suspicious of emotions and knee-jerk reactions
- Enjoys excitement and drama, putting out fires, cool under pressure
- Is prone to Excessive Self-Esteem (ESE) but can feel insecure
- Tends to be a hard and smart worker
- Is achievement-centered throughout life
- Exudes a fast tempo, perceived as "Type A" personalities
- Is a natural-born leader, willing and able to take charge any time
- Adopts a "The buck stops here but don't play blame games with me!" philosophy
- Uses an interpersonal approach: "Since I apologized for my mistake, let's move on and get on down the road."
- Figures that words matter as much as actions do

EMPATHIZERS NEGATIVE THINKING (B1-) ABOUT INSTIGATORS

As John Gray, the author of *Men are from Mars and Women are from Venus* challenges: "Would you rather be right, or would you rather be loved?" Of course, being the witty human beings we are, the honest response would be this one: "I would rather be right *and* be loved!" There is everything right about you wanting it all!

Are you ready to rumble, my dear I-types? The I-types I know love to keep score, since I-types prefer to know exactly how far away they are from diving into the end zone to score. Nonetheless, especially during tense times of conflict, Empathizers negatively perceive and experience the words and behaviors of Instigator communicators to indicate that I-types are:

- Emotionally cool
- Not good at listening
- Unmindful of stomping on toes
- Moody, distant, put up walls
- Hard-driving and demanding: "It's my way or the highway!"
- Energy drainers
- Riding the mood roller coaster of highs and lows
- Unable to handle guilt, so they shy away from discussing emotions openly
- Valuing of tradition, policies and laws but ultimately do what they want
- Exacting of revenge and they pout to get their way
- Rationalizing and excuse-making, thus fending off fair criticism
- Nit-pickers who complain about trivial matters
- Self-flattering, narcissistic, high-maintenance types
- People-users when hot on the pursuit of specific personal goals
- Close-minded, narrow-minded, one-minded when miffed
- Biased, stubborn, harsh punishers of disobedience
- Fearful of being vulnerable, erecting walls to protect self from hurt
- Shunning of emotional accountability, likely to lop off heads when mad
- Likely to use revenge as a payback; users of put-downs, put-offs
- Emotionally stunted, won't put much work into relationship matters
- Lazy communicators

- Insensitive, critical parent types
- Negative thinkers: "It's a human-eat-human world out there!"
- Coaches/talkers of a good game but don't follow through in actions
- Great debaters, talk circles around anyone
- Needy for tons of positive and negative attention
- Hateful when the word "No" is spoken
- Inpatient and easily irritated
- Harsh to those who don't tow line
- Pot stirrers, excluders
- Avoiders of emotional intimacy and emotional honesty
- Irresponsible keepers of relationship commitments
- Finger pointers, likely call the kettle black
- Conflict lovers who come alive during strife
- Grumpy, moody people who motivate via crises
- Changers of what shouldn't be changed
- Social perception influencers who omit key facts
- Emotionally opinionated: "Don't be so sensitive!"
- Optimizers who seek to feel good during bad times
- Deaf to partner/customer complaints
- Able to brainwash co-communicators easily
- Average to below average Emotional I.Q.
- Selfish: Thinks of the world in terms of "What have you done for me lately?"

In the next chapter, I will share with you, my beloved E-types, the negative thoughts that I-types harbor against you during tense times of conflict. The sharp and keen knife cuts both ways, you know.

Are the accusations stated above true or false? How much truth is there in these criticisms of the Instigator communicator *frame of reference?* You decide, but do not judge—and do not label. You have the choice to think negatively, neutrally or positively about the mindset of Instigator communicators as well as Empathizer communicators. You decide.

In my world, I choose to think positively about both communicator types and deliberately choose to take on and adopt the strengths of Empathizers and Instigators alike. What could be more fun and enriching?

EMPATHIZER Communicator Style

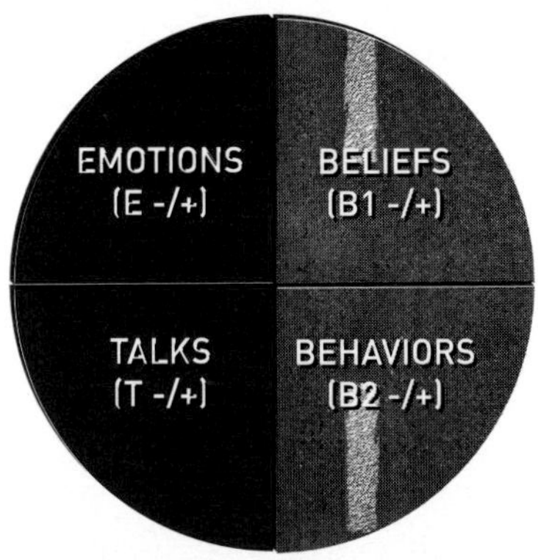

figure **#19**

EMPATHIZER DRIVER COMMUNICATOR MODES

Empathizers and Instigators alike really want to learn what their opposing talk type is like.

Empathizers feel strongly they are right-on communicators because their steering columns are on the left side of the vehicle. However, Instigators believe firmly they are right-on communicators because their steering columns are on the right side of the vehicle. Which frame of reference is right?

Figure 19 shows the communication and driving world according to Empathizers.

Until now, a well-kept secret was that Empathizers, those drivers of the blue cars with steering columns on the left side of the car prefer to feel with you from the Emotions and Talks modes.

INSTIGATOR Communicator Style

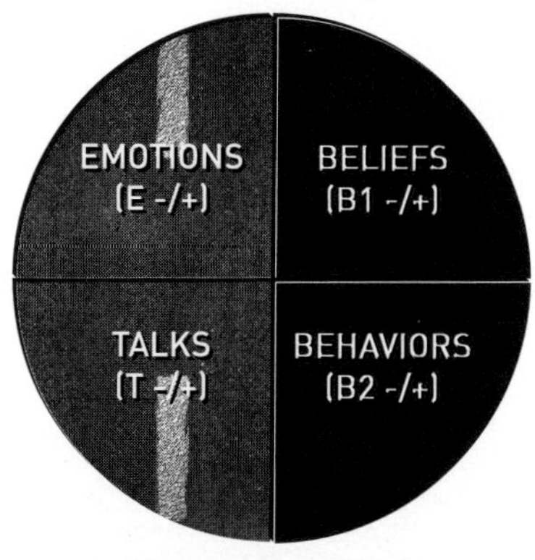

figure **#20**

INSTIGATOR DRIVER COMMUNICATOR MODES

As well, until now, a well-kept secret was that Instigators, those drivers of the burnt orange cars with steering columns on the right side of the vehicle prefer to think with you from the Beliefs and Behaviors modes.

Instigators believe strongly that the true way to get the communication car rolling along properly is to develop plans of action based on logical reasons. Of course, I-types and E-types have all four communicator modes at their disposal every second.

Figure 20 shows the communication and driving world according to Instigators.

Neither way of driving is superior, just different. So don't be prejudiced and don't label one type "good" and the other type "bad."

All four communicator modes are available equally to every communicator. It's just that you grew up preferring to travel the two-way communicator highway a certain way.

COMMUNICATION AIMED AT EMPATHIZER AND INSTIGATOR DRIVERS

Your attitude about how positive a communicator you are determines the effort you will expend to become a great communicator. You absolutely deserve to use peak communication skills that make you feel emotionally empowered and an intellectual powerhouse.

These are four negative talk attitudes that you are wise to let go of today:

- "I can be too sensitive and hard on myself sometimes." (E-types)
- "I can be too insensitive and hard on others sometimes." (I-types)
- "I feel about as positive a communicator as a swimmer with no arms." (E-types)
- "I am positive if I ignore problems; in time, things usually get better." (I-types)

You have acquired many basic and advanced communication skills. However, my communications program will require you to use your skills in a slightly different way and in a new order to achieve superior results. Tweaking the system will net you huge profits.

When I coach you to use a new communication move, you might feel awkward at first, and that is to be expected. The move, idea or motion might not fit your customary feelings, beliefs, actions or words. That is perfectly okay. A new move isn't supposed to feel quite right at first. Persevere, a wee bit. Stick with the communication move at hand for a few weeks, keep an open mind, let your style change a little bit and don't worry about making a mistake or losing points.

Are you beginning to hear the difference in talk styles coming out of the different talk modes? I bet you are.

Memorize the four communicator modes and listen to them internally and interpersonally as you go through your day. Here are the four modes that E-types and I-types share in common and use to

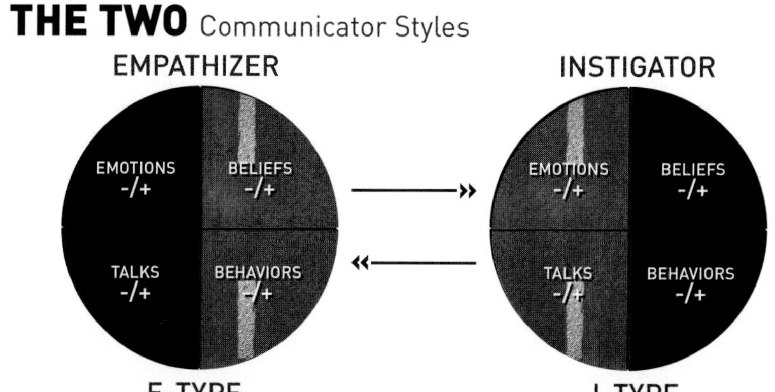

figure **#21**

communicate everyday: If you have two whole brains—Emotional and Logical—and I guarantee you that you do, then you can and will live and drive well in the four talk quadrants. Learn them well, and they will treat you as well or even better.

EMPATHIZER AND INSTIGATOR STYLES OF DRIVING

What type of communicator driver are you? What kind of mood are you in when you drive? What do you say or do when you are in a bad mood? Knowing the answers to those questions makes all the difference between the highway and the ditch.

Driver style I: Empathizer

Empathizer is the communicator style that naturally focuses on *Emotions* and *Talks* but uses all four communicator modes. An Empathizer's steering wheel is on the left side of the blue vehicle.

Talk Driver Style: The Empathizer driver magnifies issues through the lens of *feelings.*

Interpersonal Emotional Encounter: The E-type talk style can come across very colorfully and intensely.

The E-type talk style can come across very colorfully and intensely.

Driver style II: Instigator

Instigator is the communicator style that naturally focuses on *Beliefs* and *Behaviors* but uses all four communicator modes. The Instigator's steering wheel is on the right side of the burnt orange vehicle.

Talk Driver Style: The Instigator driver magnifies issues through the lens of ***thinking.***

The I-type talk style can come across very black-and-white and cold.

Interpersonal Intellectual Encounter: The I-type talk style can come across very black-and-white and cold.

Being an Empathizer communicator indicates you listen well, have good intuitive skills, put a high value on productive relationships and prefer to know what makes others tick. Unfortunately, an Instigator can tick you off.

Being an Instigator communicator indicates you lead well, do not fear change, like to fix things and engineer solutions, and put a high value on positive-pleasurable relationships. You understand what makes others motivated or miffed. Unfortunately, an Empathizer can make you feel sad and powerless.

Good communication is a process of carefully maneuvering the on-ramps and off-ramps on the two-way communication freeway. It is all about verbal and non-verbal inputs and outputs that are messages and signposts. Your mind, body and emotions will be far better off because of positive communications. Accepting and nurturing differences in communicator styles will move you around more smoothly and effortlessly on the two-way communication highway.

After all, why risk a crash and have an air bag explode in your face?

E/I: YOU 2 CAN'T MERGE

Let's not qualify. Let's not hedge. Let's come to truth.

You can't merge the E-type and I-type communicator types or personas into some kind of blended, more flexible, more perfect communicator style called E/I. I just don't think that happens! You may think you can, but you can't. You are what you are—so take pride in that fact! However, you can adopt the strengths of your opposite communicator type. You bet you can!

My communication theory essentially links together and builds a bridge between your Emotional Brain and Logical Brain.

You also can change and adopt more strengths of your own talk style. As beloved boxer Muhammad Ali was fond of saying: "Float like a butterfly and sting like a bee!" My communication theory essentially links together and builds a bridge between your Emotional Brain and Logical Brain. So I say to you that you will float, sting, heal and soar!

Your brain is certainly up to the task! The human brain is the most complex system in the universe. Your brain is a "three-pound universe" in which 100 million cells talk to 10,000 neighboring cells every second. Consider this: If you look at a microscopic picture of brain cells, they look like white solar systems in outer space.

Daniel Goleman, author of *Working With Emotional Intelligence,* describes how a brain shrinks when in depression, and how stress and depression shrink us emotionally. Better news: Your emotional and intellectual brains are like clay—still malleable at any age. Old dogs can, indeed, learn new tricks and young leopards can still change their spots. So, now hear this: You, too, can change any second of any day! By working with this material in positive ways, your brain(s) will give you new options. Believe you me!

Your emotional and intellectual brains are like clay—still malleable at any age.

I challenge you to initiate change by replacing hate with hope… pessimism with optimism…depression with faith–filled excitement…anger with joy…in order to completely love and embrace your life fully.

Now this is some very good news.

TALK BACK: CO-COMMUNICATOR COUNTERPOINTS

Prepare yourself again for a few more terrifically insightful questions that beget world-helpful answers:

1. I've heard it reported in the media that only 17% of our communication is verbal communication. What's happening during the rest of the time?

Great question: Where is your mind when you are in the inner, silent, non-verbal world of the four talk quadrants? Well, you are spending 83% of your time in the four non-verbal communicator modes of *Emotions, Beliefs (B1), Behaviors (B2)* and *Talks.* It is hard to know exactly how much time anyone is spending in each mode. However, if you are an E-type, you prefer to hang out in the Emotions and Talks modes. Oppositely, if you are an I-type, you prefer living in the Beliefs (B1) and Behaviors (B2) modes. Thus, E-types are *feeling* and *talking* in themselves but they aren't crazy! I-types, on the other hand, are *thinking* and *planning* in themselves but they aren't crazy either! Although 83% of communication is non-verbal, communication is hardly a silent phenomenon.

2. In your opinion, what is happening inside my co-communicator when he/she isn't talking?

The very same thing, and by the way, very well done. Your thinking is right on the money. Your co-communicator is silently (to your observation) walking around in his/her mind in the four communicator modes of *Emotions, Beliefs (B1), Behaviors (B2)* and *Talks*. As you also know, your co-communicator will be exuding negative, neutral or positive energy. Thus, if your co-communicator is a silent E-type, or a combative I-type, he/she is having intense feelings and thinking to the self about the event that caused the intense feelings in either negative or positive ways.

3. The E-type and I-type communicator differentiation reminds me of Type A and Type B stress responders. Are they the same?

No, although I believe you are onto something here. Type A personalities are described as hard drivers and heavy hitters so you could incorrectly associate Type A's with Instigator communicators. Type B personalities are more easy-going and patient so you could incorrectly associate Type B's with Empathizer communicators. I believe E-types and I-types have less to do with personal tempo than they do with communicator temperament.

4. Do attitudes about change differ significantly between Empathizer and Instigator communicators?

I've thought a lot about the possibility that E-types and I-types have different attitudes about change, but I don't think so. The three types of changers I have written about before are: *Change Resisters, Change Experts* and *Change Compulsives*. Resisters are people who change too little, while Experts change just enough and Compulsives change too much. It is, of course, tempting to say that Empathizers resist change. It is equally tempting to say Instigators embrace change too much. Nonetheless, I think the more likely scenario is that Empathizer and Instigator communicator types deal with change about equally.

5. Do E-types and I-types handle anger differently?

Yes, E-types are prone to suppress anger or take anger out on the self. In reverse, I-types are prone to taking anger out on others. Paradoxically, E-types are afraid of their healthy or positive anger, while I-types are afraid of their healthy or positive sadness. The purpose of positive anger is to push for positive change, while the purpose of negative fear is to constrict positive change. Both E- and I-types prefer to feel positive, satisfied and happy. Always remember, emotions are two-faced or double-sided; one side is negative while the other side is positive.

6. Why do I feel confused during emotional storms?

Your emotional brain and your logical brain make it possible for you to talk to yourself, process how you feel about your potential actions, and even think about your thoughts. It is a very rich space you live in when you are living in your mind(s). In short, thoughts travel along your neuronal network like cars on a highway. You feel confused due to the negative emotional intensity or volume. If you lighten the emotional stress load by downsizing or clarifying expectations, you will think more clearly.

7. Why are there only four talk modes or quadrants? Aren't there many more you aren't telling us about?

There are only four talk quadrants, in my opinion, in our communicator brain. When vacationing in Cabo San Lucas, Mexico, recently I bought a piece of artwork that is a circle cut in four equal parts which represent the four elements of Earth, Wind, Fire, and Water. The four inner and outer world talk modes are the four elements of *Emotions, Beliefs (B1), Behaviors (B2)* and *Talks.* To me, it feels true, like the four elements of life, but who really knows? Always remember, you use these same four avenues when you talk to yourself, talk to another or tell yourself what you wish you would've/could've/should've said.

8. I believe you're saying I would be better off choosing to be a positive person and a positive thinker. Is there hope for me?

Absolutely, but I believe you are the best person to decide which way of living you would prefer at this time. Negative isn't bad and positive isn't necessarily always good; that's extreme thinking.
I believe positive communication skills hold the possibility to work better than pills for many people and just as fast. I am not

anti-medication, as some of my staunchest professional allies are psychiatrists. However, positive talk habits create positive relationships and empower co-communicators to heal lingering relationship resentments, mend fences that have been broken down by blame games, and rebuild broken bridges of communication. I believe that a major cause of dysphoria, anxiety and anger is negative communication that shoots down high hopes. Positive communication causes a positive mood, and people who communicate positively sleep better, eat better and feel better, thereby flooding their chemical bodies with positive physiology.

9. Why doesn't my partner listen to me? If couple satisfaction is related to empathetic listening, why can't my message be heard without debating, fault-finding or criticizing?

"Listen unto others as they would like you to listen unto them!" is a fine commitment to make. Let me explain: E-types and I-types don't just speak differently—they listen differently. E-types listen inclusively: They want to hear and understand every bit of the message, including non-verbal cues. I-types listen selectively: They want to hear and understand only the part of the message that will help them fix a problem or address something specific. Thus, asking broad, open-ended questions to E-types works better with E-types. Oppositely, asking narrowly focused or close-ended questions that lead somewhere specific works better with I-types. You will also notice that E-types look you in the face more often during talks, while I-types look around the room or into space more often. "Active listening" is not a cure-all for all communication ailments; one listening size does not fit E- and I-types equally well. Frankly, I put more stock in "active questioning" and "assertive summarizing" techniques. I will teach you these tools and more in future chapters so you can be a more flexible listener and questioner.

10. What is the difference between sadness and dysphoria and depression?

First, there is a *scale of severity* from less intense to more intense. Think of a 1–10 rating scale that encompasses a spectrum of feelings that include sadness. . .dysphoria. . .depression. Second, how *pervasively* your life is affected is another indicator. For example, if you are dissatisfied with your career, plus your financial life, plus your personal relationships, plus your health life, plus your parenting life, etc. then the more *negatively impacted by mood* you are. Over 6 million older adults suffer from depression. I believe all of our moods are wacky due to negative communication. Depression causes loss of sleep, decreased energy, changed appetite, psychomotor slowness or agitation, and diurnal mood variation.

Overall, think of your communication style as not being set in stone but more like moldable clay. The magnificent being you are today cannot be summed up as a mere bumping together of childhood conditioning and chemical reactions slopping around in a skin bag.

Overall, think of your communication style as not being set in stone but more like moldable clay.

You have innocently made talking errors in the past because you didn't know about this new communication theory—one based on two communicator types and four communicator modes.

No worries: You will learn these new communication skills in 30 days, not years. Your brain is an ever-expanding universe and an ever-busy message center with a stream of thoughts and feelings leading to an ocean of positive actions. It always wishes to be at disposal to your best interests. Trust me on this!

No worries: You will learn these new communication skills in 30 days, not years.

NEXT UP: CAN WE TALK?

Chapter 4, titled "Can We Talk?" is dedicated to talk show host Joan Rivers. My answer is, you and I can talk whenever and wherever we so care to.

Life is so much more fun, sizzling and scintillating that way! Just like a flash of light during a time of darkness, positive communication is a warm breeze and a blast of joy during a snowy winter storm.

IV

CAN WE TALK?

E-types think: "Actions speak louder than words!"

I-types feel: "Words speak louder than actions!"

Positive communicators know: Positive words...positive actions...positive thoughts say it all—especially when you're swamped by negative emotions.

TRAINING GOAL

To acknowledge how Empathizer and Instigator communicators are unique and vulnerable without casting stones

Being a flexible communicator works best for all parties and all situations, whether negative or positive.

THE TWO COMMUNICATOR TYPES— THE FOUR COMMUNICATOR MODES— AND THE MIRACLE OF POSITIVE CHANGE

To review briefly, the two communicator types are named Empathizer and Instigator, and they comprise two opposing life viewpoints. Each is able to operate effectively and efficiently in the four communicator modes *(Emotions, Beliefs, Behaviors, Talks).*

Being a flexible communicator works best for all parties and all situations, whether negative or positive. Even if you're in a stress swamp filled with big, medium and small alligators— you might not be able to remain calm but you can make change miracles happen!

The Empathizer or E-type life viewpoint of what matters most, namely the Emotions mode and Talks mode, is visually depicted in Figure 22.

EMPATHIZER Viewpoint

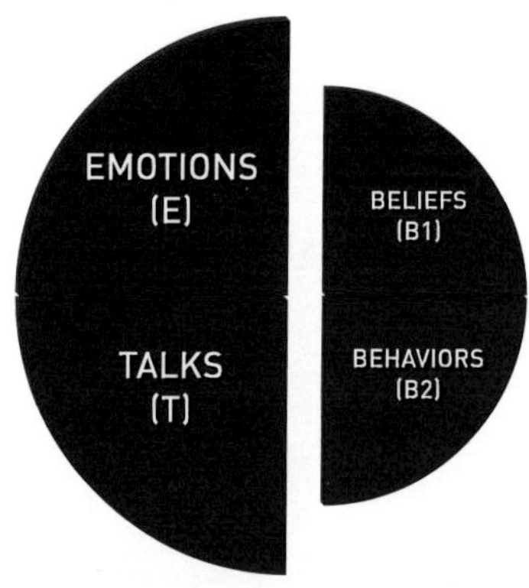

figure **#22**

Empathizers naturally prefer to relate to you (whatever your type) through the modes of *accurate* positive Emotions (E+) and accurate positive Talks (T+).

When E-types change or convert negative Beliefs (B1-) to positive Beliefs (B1+) change happens!

Instigators, on the other hand, naturally prefer to relate to you (whatever your type) through the modes of *accurate* positive Beliefs (B1+) and accurate positive Behaviors (B2+).

When I-types change or convert negative Emotions (E-) to positive Emotions (E+) change happens!

The Instigator or I-type life viewpoint of what matters most, namely the Beliefs mode and the Behaviors mode, is visually depicted in Figure 23.

INSTIGATOR Viewpoint

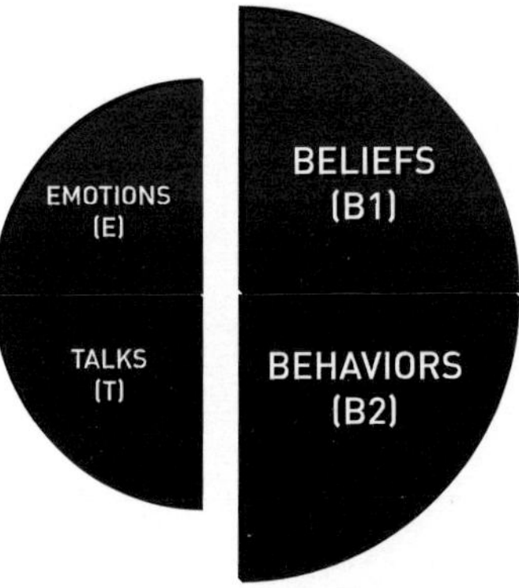

figure **#23**

Thus, Empathizer and Instigator communicators have dramatically different and diametrically opposed life viewpoints. Our beloved E-types and I-types are looking at the world from totally opposite directions!

You are a positive person today, aren't you? *I challenge you today to feel, think, act and speak in ways that mirror exactly your opposing communicator style as you live out your positive goals.* If you can do that, you will not only understand what it's like to walk in your opposing communicator's shoes, you will also be able to adopt into your life the strengths of your opposite communicator style. It will change your life forever.

Which two modes would you be wise to use more often in Figure 24? If you are an E-type, you will want to drive in the Beliefs and Behaviors lanes on the two-way communicator highway more often. Likewise, if you are an I-type, you will benefit immensely when you drive in the Emotions and Talks lanes on the two-way communicator highway more often.

EMPATHIZER VS. INSTIGATOR Viewpoint

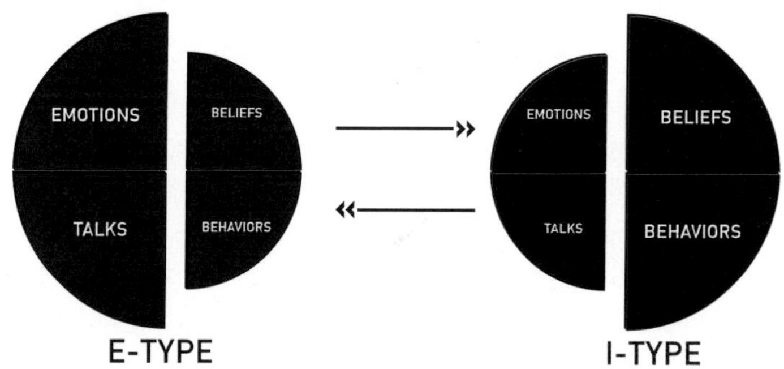

figure **#24**

It's such great fun and I promise you that you will enjoy becoming a multiple (multiplied/synergized/upsized) personality!

MOUTH CONTROL

I've studied positive communication tools for 30 years, yet many times in my own communication life, I still have "out-of-mouth" experiences. I bet you do, too.

"Out-of-mouth" experiences occur when your feelings run away with you and words come out of your mouth that you would give a million bucks to take back. Most people want to get along better and not alienate each other, yet harsh words can fuel that alienation. And alienation causes negative feelings of separation and apartness that contribute to isolation and loneliness in your loving relationships and in your extended family support systems.

Empathizers, or E-types, and Instigators, or I-types, are different as night and day when it comes to interpersonal relations and self-expression. E-types strive to please others and stuff their own feelings, so they bite holes in their tongues to avoid saying something negative or regrettable. I-types, on the other hand, strive to be genuine and aren't afraid of losing love so they just let their real thoughts roll out of their mouths without much censoring.

E-types strive to please others and stuff their own feelings, so they bite holes in their tongues to avoid saying something negative or regrettable. I-types, on the other hand, strive to be genuine and aren't afraid of losing love so they just let their real thoughts roll out of their mouths without much censoring.

Neither style is right or wrong. E-types, however, can stockpile resentments while believing that their co-communicator is mistreating or ignoring them. I-types, on the other hand, can toss resentment rocks around like hand grenades when they feel mistreated and rejected. Both E-types and I-types go down hard when they're hit in the head by someone else's sharp rocks of resentment. Yet neither E- or I-types are "mules" meant to carry heavy resentment packs across great distances in the desert.

E-types correctly believe that mental health suffers when negative feelings are squelched or squandered. In comparison, I-types correctly feel that physical health improves when negative thoughts and feelings are released into the open. Both E- and I-types function best when they know who they are dealing with and how to deal with them. To this end, a fantastic tool that you will soon be learning is *Directive Questioning.*

Whether I *feel* misunderstood (E-type) or whether I *think* you are misunderstanding me (I-type)—I am going to feel grumpy and not very happy. Compassion stems from comprehending what your co-communicator might be experiencing but not openly telling you. Both communicator types are vulnerable if they're trapped in an emotional swamp. . .surrounded by alligators, without a map and bug spray. Not a good recipe for escaping intact, is it?

THE STRENGTH OF VULNERABILITY

When stuck and sweating in an emotionally challenging swamp, an Empathizer's biggest vulnerability is *to do* something stupid from the negative Behaviors (B-) mode.

An Empathizer's biggest vulnerability is to do something stupid.

E-TYPE Talk Collision

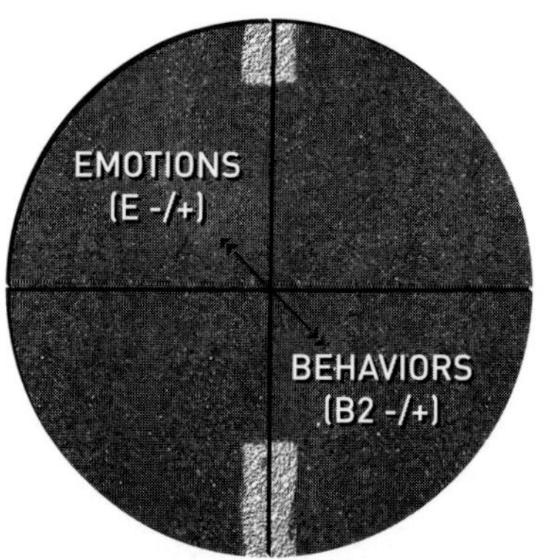

figure **#25**

Sweating it out in the same swamp, an Instigator's biggest vulnerability is *to say* something stupid from the negative Talks (T-) mode (Figure 26).

I-TYPE Talk Collision

figure **#26**

Thus, when E-types are distressed they pull a fast one and abruptly change lanes from Emotions (E-) to Behaviors (B-). In reverse, when I-types are distressed they pull a fast one and abruptly change lanes from Beliefs (B1-) to Talks (T-). This is how talk collisions occur!

E-TYPE AND I-TYPE Talk Collision

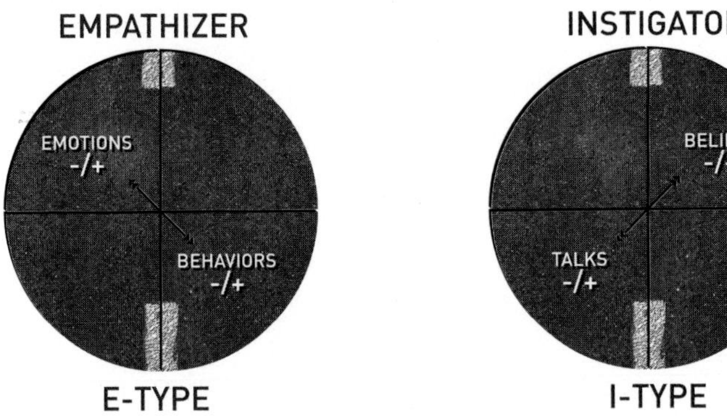

figure **#27**

Actually, the best route to create rapid, lasting positive change and to avoid accidents is for Empathizers to move from the negative Emotions mode to the positive Beliefs mode (E- to B1+). Likewise, what works far more constructively and safely for Instigators is to move from the negative Beliefs mode to the positive Emotions mode (B- to E+). Of course, accuracy counts for much because whether you are inaccurate and negative or inaccurate and positive, you are going to make mistakes you regret.

These communication insights will help you wrestle the big alligators and then march out of the emotional swamp.

CONFLICT AND LEADERSHIP STYLES

Empathizer and Instigator communicators have almost completely different frames of reference or life viewpoints about communication etiquette.

For example, use this helpful rule of thumb: *E-types typically withdraw or back away during a conflict, while I-types typically advance or push forward in a conflict.* Neither type has the corner on the communications market, for sure. Enjoy the ride and talk positively as you more fully appreciate the different lanes in which E-types and I-types prefer to drive.

In general, E-types feel better whenever they take a leadership role in their inner-personal life by striving toward positive "I-love-ME" personal goals. Likewise, I-types feel better whenever they take a leadership role in their relationship life striving toward "We-love-US" interpersonal goals.

When you spontaneously "tweak" my talk approaches, you will add immensely to your positive feelings of joy and contentedness. You are about to discover that more often times than not, the big pay-off really is in the little deeds done well. A client told me recently, "It's spooky, Dr. O'Grady. I tell you a little about my wife and you know exactly how she thinks and even what she told me. I swear you must be talking to her by phone."

You are about to discover that more often times than not, the big pay-off really is in the little deeds done well.

What a compliment about this communications theory—and no I hadn't ever met his wife (by phone or otherwise). What I did know was this: my married male client was an Instigator-type extrovert (ITE) while his beloved wife was an Empathizer-type introvert (ETI). Talk about opposites attracting! These two types come at life from opposite corners of the globe. For example, the more explaining he did as an ITE from the Talks mode (T-) the more negatively his ETI partner came at him from the Behaviors (B-) mode. And that's one very stinky swamp!

In general, a common Empathizer relationship problem involves infusing their mood in other people. In contrast, Instigators commonly run into problems by trying to impose their thoughts on other people. *Relationship life is far sweeter between E- and I-types when E-types are mindful not to automatically infuse their moods in other people when feeling bad, while I-types are sensitive not to impose their thoughts on other people when feeling off-kilter.*

Relationship life is far sweeter between E- and I-types when E-types are mindful not to automatically infuse their moods in other people when feeling bad, while I-types are sensitive not to impose their thoughts on other people when feeling off-kilter.

> *Frame of reference:* 1. The negative and positive beliefs (and talk habits) learned in the childhood family of origin that are repeated and recreated in adult interpersonal relationships. 2. Customary and comfortable ways of interacting.

IN THE EMOTIONAL SWAMP, WRESTLE THE BIGGEST ALLIGATORS FIRST

When I'm under great stress, I'm fond of thinking to myself: "Stick to wrestling the biggest alligators in the swamp." Otherwise, it's so easy to become distracted by how many alligators (small, medium, large) lurk there, just below the surface. And those nasty bugs swarming around my head and chomping on my face don't help much either!

When I'm under great stress, I'm fond of thinking to myself: "Stick to wrestling the biggest alligators in the swamp."

I like the swamp analogy to describe unpleasant and painful emotions. Negative emotions can feel dark, isolating, consuming. The swamp has quicksand pits to sludge and trudge through. And it's easy to get turned around and lost in the swamp, going around and around repeatedly in the same self-denying circle when civilization is just a stone's throw away. If only you had a bird's eye view!

The negative emotional swamp, as you know, is extremely hot and exhausting. Trekking through the never-ending bog, while inhaling the dark stenches of wretchedness, quickly wears down and tears at the heart of even the strongest mind, body and spirit. You are familiar with that old sinking feeling that you're going to be stuck in that swamp forever—and that no one is going to come to your aid or rescue. The fear: Only your chewed bones will remain to speak of your existence. As you sink into a depressive pit, you wonder if you will ever have the strength to pull yourself out of it.

When you feel attacked by your partner or co-communicator, especially in a loving relationship, you're going to get that old familiar painful sinking feeling of the swamp, regardless of your communicator type. Negative emotions take unfair snipes at love: pain-filling and pain-compelling jealousy, mistrust, resentment, ridicule, shame, guilt are just a few. You go crazy; irrational!

Love is strong, but sometimes even love feels like moving out of this relationship town.

HAVE A MELTDOWN

"I'm having an emotional meltdown!" may be one of the most courageous and accurate negative admissions ever spoken by you. Empathizers and Instigators, of course, melt down differently but just as completely negatively. A mood meltdown is not a sight that is very pretty to behold.

Look at Figure 28 to see why Empathizer vs. Instigator meltdowns produce similar pains for both:

EMPATHIZER VS. INSTIGATOR Meltdown

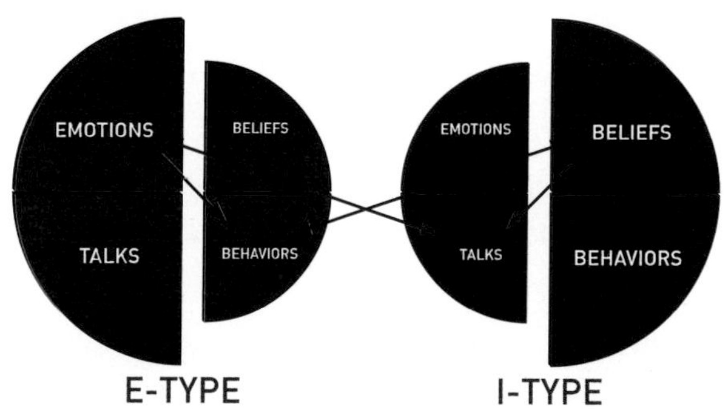

figure **#28**

Okay, this is advanced theory so let's go on easy right now. I am completely confident that you are ready to take these new communication moves on one adult step at a time.

I. An Empathizer (E-type) Meltdown

- Intensely disturbing *negative emotions* (E-) for an E-type
- Can lead to surprisingly disturbing *negative interpersonal actions* (B2-)
- That co-create *negative beliefs* (B1-) in an I-type partner or co-communicator

II. An Instigator (I-type) Meltdown

- Intensely disturbing *negative thoughts* (B1-) for an I-type
- Can lead to surprisingly disturbing *negative interrelational words* (T-)
- That co-create *negative feelings* (E-) in an E-type partner or co-communicator

So let's put the pieces of this intricate communication puzzle together for a change:

- *Under stress, Empathizers (E-types) blast away at I-types beliefs, convictions, rationale, morals, precepts, cherished ideas, values, norms, principles, etc.*

- *Comparatively, under stress, Instigators (I-types) blast away at E-types emotions, feelings, self-concept, comfort level, privacy zone, security, sense of trust, faith, belief in "love never fails."*

But meltdowns can create new life if you allow them to.

EMOTIONAL ESCALATIONS

In the swamp, everyone feels fearful and overwhelmed. But everyone also needs to remain as calm as possible and not make matters any worse.

When you snap at your fellow swamp mate, negative emotional escalations occur when you and your exhausted co-communicator:

1. *React as close-minded, narrow-minded, a 'know-it-all'*
2. *Confuse the small alligators with the big alligators in the swamp of negative emotions, meaning you wrestle with the wrong or incorrect issues*
3. *Don't answer questions completely or honestly*
4. *Fail to stick to the topic at hand*
5. *Hold grudges in your mind for a long time*
6. *Inaccurately mishear the truth that is implied or vocalized*
7. *Allow yourself and your co-communicator to feel attacked, closed-off, shut out, shut down*
8. *Feel guilty for being anxious, and end up acting or talking negatively*

Being responsive vs. being reactive helps you and I survive the swamp (and the bugs and critters, oh my!). Being responsive also eliminates unnecessary pain and grief, even though you may feel panicky in the negative emotional swamp. When you're responsive, you consciously react instead of automatically going on autopilot and flying on a fight-or-flight interpersonal relationship disaster course.

You can and do keep a positive mindset as you panic. In this way, you team up or *meld together your mood and your mind in positive intentions.* I positively believe (B1+): Upon death, it's not the person with the most toys who wins. *It's the E-type or I-type person with the most joys, and the most toys, who wins!*

Actually, I was just playing with your mind there for a moment. Perhaps the person with the most tears shed—because of the most love shown—wins.

That person can and should be you.

Upon death, it's not the person with the most toys who wins. Perhaps the person with the most tears shed—because of the most love shown—wins.

EMOTIONAL DE-ESCALATIONS

When you support your fellow swamp mate, you de-escalate downward-spiraling negative emotional cycles. This spares your and your exhausted co-communicator's precious reserves and much-needed energy. Things may be out of control, but at least you have the power to decide which alligators you'll wrestle with first!

Even though you and your co-communicator are still very vulnerable, still are unnerved, and still feel scared that you don't have a map, at least you're working together. You have the same frame of reference, which is: "We're in this emotional swamp together and we'll get out of this emotional swamp together." That's when change happens.

When you and your co-communicator are seething in an emotional bog, rely on these common-sense methods to become unstuck:

1. *Be open-minded, think big-minded, be a 'know-a-little'*
2. *Clearly separate the big alligators in the swamp of negative emotions from the little alligators. Wrestle the big ones first.*
3. *Ask and answer questions as completely and honestly as possible*
4. *Stick to the topic at hand*
5. *Hold compliments in your heart and speak of them on a daily basis*
6. *Accurately hear the truth that is implied or vocalized through the use of Directive Questioning*
7. *Allow you and your co-communicator to feel affirmed, included, valued, opened-up*
8. *Be okay about being anxious but think positively, act positively and speak positively!*

Be okay about being anxious but think positively, act positively and speak positively!

In other words, when you feel mad, bad, guilt-drenched and deserving of punishers—breathe in those ugly feelings (Buddhist nun Pema Chodron's *Awakening Compassion* style teaches us how to) and don't do (B2-) or say anything (T-) too crazy (E-), stupid (B1-) or lazy (B2-).

You move on down the Road of Life best by going on easy, by staying centered and by going in the correct and right direction... just like the proverbial Tortoise.

HEALING RELATIONAL WOUNDS

You can feel and think as One.

With the help of this communications training, you can deal with the arousal of negative emotions (E-) by simultaneously arousing your positive awareness and thoughts (B1+). In reverse, when your negative thoughts (B1-) are aroused, you will simultaneously arouse your Emotional I.Q. (E+).

- *When you use negative emotions (E-) to activate positive awareness (B1+), miracles of change happen.*
- *When you use positive awareness (B1+) to activate positive emotions (E+), miracles of change happen.*

Positive change always happens when you use the four communicator modes positively and effectively. Can it get any better than this? I'm betting you have now linked together the Emotional and Logical Brains as ONE entity. *In other words, you won't stay hurt for long.* Thus, you won't dwell on or obsess about the small alligators in your negative emotional swamp, because you realize they amount to much of nothing or of little of importance.

Together, E-types and I-types can band together to accomplish great things collaboratively.

- *Instead of Empathizers staying wounded by the negative words (T-) shot at them by Instigators—they move beyond the past.*
- *Likewise, instead of Instigators going to war because of negative behaviors (B2-) launched at them by Empathizers—they move beyond the present so both can get on down the change road of miracles.*

For sure, all human beings are imperfect to varying degrees, and everyone does their fair share of time in the emotional swamp.

This work gives you a sense of what the swamp is about and an accurate map for getting out of it. Now, Empathizers and Instigators alike can escape from the swamp—and do so sporting a new alligator purse or wallet and a new pair of alligator shoes or boots.

And once they're out, they can book some Joy time in the luxury-hotel Jacuzzi overlooking Mother Nature. Just you count on it!

DIRECTIVE QUESTIONING VS. ACTIVE/REFLECTIVE LISTENING

One of the powerful new communication tools I want you to begin using is called "Directive Questioning."

If you think reflective listening and parroting back a summary of what's been said is cool, wait until you get a load of the results of Directive Questioning. Directive Questioning quickly brings a deeper understanding, comprehension and empathy toward the issues on the communication table. It acknowledges your communicator strengths and awareness of them. It also divines solutions if they are nearby but hidden.

Reflective listening essentially means you clear your mind to listen neutrally and sincerely to the speaker. The intent is to "Seek first to understand, then to be understood" (it's Habit 5 in Stephen and Sean Covey's heart-full books, *The 7 Habits of Highly Effective People/Teens*). It's a wonderful tool. Instead of talking louder or over the sentences of a co-communicator, instead of interrupting the speaker with a point you've been constructing in your mind while only half-listening—you devote your entire attention to what the speaker is saying.

Instead of talking louder or over the sentences of a co-communicator, instead of interrupting the speaker with a point you've been constructing in your mind while only half-listening—you devote your entire attention to what the speaker is saying.

Active or reflective listening also includes waiting until the speaker is finished and then summarizing or parroting back what the speaker has said—only you do so in your language style. This is hard to do because the mind races a mile a minute with proposed solutions to the speaker's problems. You're not even supposed to give advice—not a single drop! The positive goal is to understand and have the speaker to feel understood. When learning this tool, speakers are thrown off because most people are not used to talking openly about their feelings, much less have someone listen completely to their sentiments. But when you accomplish it, it's a wonderful tool that I recommend you enjoy using.

In contrast to Active Listening, I have developed Directive Questioning. It's better to have both skill sets in your toolbox—

Reflective and Directive—when the need arises. Although I believe Empathizers prefer Active Listening and Instigators prefer Directive Questioning, I've found that Directive Questioning works just as well or even better with E-types when the approach is used caringly and softly.

Directive Questioning by design opens your creative mind to being inquisitive instead of being an interrogator.

Directive Questioning by design opens your creative mind to being inquisitive instead of being an interrogator. The positive intent of Directive Questioning is to better understand your co-communicator's functional frame of reference. Understanding does not mean you must agree with the beliefs and sentiments of your talk partner—it only means you have acquired empathy for that person's unique viewpoint, one that probably involves pain.

Directive Questioning puts an early and easy kibosh on unfair fights that cause both inner-personal wounds and interpersonal scars.

Directive Questioning puts an early and easy kibosh on unfair fights that cause both inner-personal wounds and interpersonal scars. Always remind yourself that inaccurate and guilt-laden hate is the quickest way to plop yourself smack dab in the middle of an emotional swamp, one that's teeming with more and more alligators.

The choice is yours: Draw emotionally together with your co-communicator in positive ways during good times and bad times—or fall apart.

IN A WORLD OF GUILT

Being in a world of hurt is unpleasant, but being in a world of guilt brings bad happenings. Let me explain.

The primal negative beliefs, typically inaccurate, of the strong-willed guilt carrier are:

- I am a bad person
- I need to make up for being a bad person
- Bad things happen to bad people like me
- I deserve to be judged as "less than"
- Other people can push my guilt buttons
- I'm found guilty by a judge and jury every day of my life
- I need to convince my partner/peers/parents/children that I'm good
- Why should I feel good when I am bad?

- I am a bad person who should suffer
- I can't get past being bad or feeling bad
- I don't deserve to have a very good life
- IT (bad things happening to *me*) never ends

Empathizers and Instigators alike go for the guilt. Having an affair is one emotionally loaded example. In our Judeo-Christian culture, affairs are laden with an enormous amount of negative rhetoric. "Affairs are *always* bad and immoral." However, aren't there ever times when the opposite might be true: "Affairs can be good and moral?" You know me: I sure don't want to live in a glass house and throw stones, especially during the winter! And I will be making a case in short order why love affairs can be spiritually uplifting!

Empathizers and Instigators alike go for the guilt.

You know me: i sure don't want to live in a glass house and throw stones, especially during the winter!

In the meantime, when I attend church services I often wonder what the main message of the Maker is. Is it to follow the Commandments verbatim? Is it to follow the wise advice of the Rabbi? Is it to attain the attitude of a *bodhisattva* or the fully awakened person? It is *all* of these, in my opinion.

In my 50-plus years of life, all of the Commandments and ancient teachings seem combined in a unified voice to say to me, *"Love is the way—not hate."* Trust this fact! And love requires we all feel all of our feelings—negative and positive alike—and process them through the four communicator modes. I also believe: "Love is all that lasts—all else passes away and fails to last." Love doesn't fail. Love doesn't fail, you nor me, not now, not any time.

Love is the way—not hate.

Now can we talk about why we don't talk?

THE "DON'T TALK ABOUT FEELINGS" RULES

Have you ever heard a co-communicator say: "You've just got to get over it!" Chances are you have, and perhaps you have even uttered those words yourself. Whether you've heard them or said them, the message is clear: "Change the (emotional) subject."

Or how about this one: "You need to quit dwelling on it!" Both of these one-liners shut down the process of talking deeply about *accurate negative emotions* and *accurate positive emotions.* Lack of honest emotional dialogue co-creates emotional distancing and lack of emotional intimacy and sexual intimacy.

Adding negative to negative, we could say this: "You've got to get over it—quit dwelling on it!" Oh, my, the places we go when we judge.

The "Don't Talk to Me About Your Accurate Feelings!" Rules are absolute relationship killers that steal the self-love of Empathizers and Instigators alike. These, then, are the "Don't Talk About Feelings" Rules:

1. Don't *Talk*

2. Don't Talk About *Your* Feelings

3. Don't Talk About *My* Feelings

4. Don't Talk About *Our* Feelings

5. Don't Talk *Accurately* About *Your or My Negative or Positive* Feelings

Of course, if you don't talk accurately about your negative and positive feelings, you can't be close. The cost of admission to the show of emotional intimacy is talking openly, privately and compassionately about negative and positive emotions alike.

The cost of admission to the show of emotional intimacy is talking openly, privately and compassionately about negative and positive emotions alike.

Now let's learn about the opposite, the "Let's Do Talk About Feelings" Rules.

THE "LET'S DO TALK ABOUT FEELINGS" RULES

Can we talk? Make an agreement with your co-communicator that you vow to keep any past or present painful experiences strictly private between the two of you. There will be *no* sharing of this confidential information with extended family members. That way, you both avoid having it posted on the gossip grapevine.

By respecting confidences, you will immediately tap into these five intimacies: Emotional intimacy, intellectual intimacy, sexual intimacy, physical intimacy and spiritual intimacy. You want to be happy, right? You deserve to feel joyful alongside the parts of life that you experience as painful.

Let's together embrace the "Let's Do Talk Rules" right now:

1. Let's Do *Talk*

2. Let's Do Talk About *Your* Feelings

3. Let's Do Talk About *My* Feelings

4. Let's Do Talk About *Our* Feelings

5. Let's Do Talk *Accurately* About *Your and My Negative or Positive* Feelings

In my estimation, both Empathizer and Instigator communicators would be wise to adopt positive talk rules to achieve the results of joy, tight bonding and the intense positive sexuality they seek.

Am I serious about this? I am as serious as "a heart quake." *Positive communicators do quit dwelling on feelings to start dwelling in feelings.*

Am I serious about this? I am as serious as "a heart quake." Positive communicators do quit dwelling on feelings to start dwelling in feelings.

THE "LET'S DO TALK ABOUT EMOTIONS AND BELIEFS" RULES

By respecting what you think positively, you will immediately drive on new avenues of change.

There are five ways of thinking about thinking: Emotional I.Q., Intellectual I.Q., Interpersonal I.Q., Sexual I.Q. and Entrepreneurial I.Q. You deserve to have it all! Do you have passion for the all?

Let's together embrace the "Let's Do Talk About Emotions and Beliefs Rules" right now:

1. Let's Do *Talk*
2. Let's Do Talk About *Your* Emotions [E-/+] And Your Beliefs [B1-/+]
3. Let's Do Talk About *My* Emotions [E-/+] And My Beliefs [B1-/+]
4. Let's Do Talk Together About *Our* Negative And Positive Emotions [E-/+] And Our Negative And Positive Beliefs [B1-/+]
5. Let's Do Talk Together *Accurately* About *Your And My Negative Or Positive Emotions [E-/+] And Beliefs [B-/+]*

Empathizer and Instigator communicators, in my opinion, are wise to think positively while doing positive deeds and talking positive intentions.

BLAME GAMES AS EMOTIONAL DISTRACTIONS...AND THE POWER TO CHANGE

One sneaky reason that unfair fights occur is because an unfair fight is a strategy to distract both people from talking effectively about painful emotions in non-blaming ways. We are all in collusion to avoid emotions some of the time!

One sneaky reason that unfair fights occur is because an unfair fight is a strategy to distract both people from talking effectively about painful emotions in non-blaming ways.

So who should change? You and I are at our best when we accept and celebrate the five emotional stages of change. Stage 5 in my change theory (showcased in *Taking the Fear out of Changing*) involves *Joy and Integration.*

Overall, Empathizers believe the power to change (blame games) resides outside the Self or in the other person or situation. Since the Empathizer perceives the locus of control to be outside of the Empathizer self/feeling-world, E-types have difficulty coping because they can and do become stuck in a bog of inaccurate negative emotions (E-). When they can't take it any more, Empathizers sharply cut across talk lanes from emotions (E-) into negative behaviors (B2-), stunning their co-communicator and wounding or damaging the relationship—sometimes fatally.

In reverse, Instigators believe the power to change resides primarily within the Self (in the power of the mind) and not in the other person nor in the situation. Coping-wise, since the Instigator perceives the locus of control to be inside of the Instigator self/mind-world, I-types have difficulty coping because they can and do become stuck in a bog of inaccurate positive thinking (B1+), stunning their co-communicator and wounding or damaging the relationship—sometimes fatally.

Now you will know how to make far more positive than negative talk moves, and you'll free up the restrictions on your inner-personal and interpersonal relationships.

Don't get me wrong, though. Joy is highly oversold. Staying present in emotions of all kinds is saintly.

Don't get me wrong, though. Joy is highly oversold. Staying present in emotions (E-/+) of all kinds is saintly. In my theory about change, the Joy Stage is just one of the five wild frontier places on the ride through change.

Modus Vivendi: 1. An arrangement or agreement allowing conflicting parties to coexist peacefully, either indefinitely or until a final settlement is reached.

LOVE IS ALL THAT LASTS

Oprah Winfrey, the nation's beloved cultural shaper and helper, has explained how a positive relationship "brings joy—not just some of the time but most of the time." It was the subject of a column titled "What I Know For Sure" in the February 2005 issue of *Oprah* magazine.

Oprah went on to say, *"I know for sure* that in the final analysis of our lives—when the to-do lists are no more, when the frenzy is finished, when our e-mail boxes are empty—*the only thing that will have any lasting value is whether we've loved others and whether they've loved us."* (*Oprah* Magazine, February 2005, page 234.)

I couldn't agree more energetically with Ms. Winfrey's appraisal of love in relationships. But who am I to say for sure?

This is because I believe that Love is all that lasts. I could be all wrong, but isn't love supposed to be the highest form of positive energy, one that extends beyond time and place? Come now and think with me a minute about what Love just might exponentially (2x2x2x2x2=32) be up to in your life.

Give me your insights into these nonjudgmental, philosophical questions:

- What is love?
- What do you consider to constitute a "negative affair"?
- What do you suppose the definition of "power sex" is?
- Who qualifies in your life as a true, heartfelt, full-blown "Love Affair"?
- Might you be having a full-blown "Love Affair" with your mate?
- What might the phrase, "In-love sex-making activity" actually mean?
- Is that idea different or distinct from "Out-of-love sex-making activity?"
- Are you involved in a Love Affair that includes "sexual love" represented by "In-love sex-making activity?"

Who qualifies in your life as a true, heartfelt, full-blown "Love Affair"?

What on Earth is going on here?!

Emotionally and intellectually, I'm trying to distinguish love from hate, sex from love, joy from anger, healthy anger from unhealthy anger, "good" feelings and ideas about yourself from "bad" ideas and feelings about yourself in order to help you create emotional responsibility and intellectual honesty in your communications life.

Dear Reader: You too can count on love if you care to.

IS IT SEX? IS IT LOVE? IS IT SEXUAL-LOVE?

If the assumption is correct that love is all that matters, then sexual activities take a back seat to love. I'm okay with that.

If the assumption is correct that actions mean as much as words, than sexual love is one of the better ways to express love in action vs. love in words. Emotional intimacy is supposed to lead to sexual intimacy. Positive talking is the way to arrive at both destinations with a smile on your face.

Emotional intimacy is supposed to lead to sexual intimacy. Positive talking is the way to arrive at both destinations with a smile on your face.

If the assumption is correct that the sexual embrace demonstrates love, then the loving sexual embrace ought to spiritualize love through any avenue, either homosexual or heterosexual. Boy loves girl, girl loves boy, boy loves boy, girl loves girl, girls and boys alike love each other about equally. Love is about mutuality and equality and telling the truth.

So let's keep it simple here: What if there were only three types of affairs (of course there are nine more) and we named them thusly:

1. Power Affairs

Sexual encounters that seek to exert interpersonal power over the will of another in order to prove one's attractiveness. Ego-advancement: "I feel attractive, powerful and wanted."

2. Sex Affairs

Sexual encounters that seek to find and discover the genuine self through sexual behavior. Independence-advancement: "I am in control of my own destiny."

3. Love Affairs

Sexual encounters that seek to equally mix loving-tender feelings with sexual actions to access broader spiritual powers. Co-independent actions that declare, "I believe in love!"

To last a lifetime, true love requires a perfect match-up on the "Top 10 Trait List" and sincere feelings. I created the "Top Ten List" so you can absolutely know for sure what makes you feel loved and loving. Nine out of 10 matches on the "what you need most from love" list is plenty good, but it isn't good enough for long-term romance. Love has its mind made up: 10 out of 10 pretty-exact matches are what you deserve in order to receive love and to give love to your beloved each and every day.

Which category of love do you judge as good vs. bad? Everyone draws a line somewhere and tries not to step over it, but what definitions and guidelines do they use? If sex were a game of tennis, which balls do you judge in bounds, out of bounds or smack on the white line?

Let's interact with the third category, Love Affairs, a wee little bit more. Don't we all want to love a little bit more and a whole lot more if we care to?

I'm betting you want to go for the gold of love, instead of the rust of resentment.

I'm betting you want to go for the gold of love, instead of the rust of resentment.

ONLY ONE-THIRD OF COUPLED CO-COMMUNICATORS ARE IN LOVE?

Nowadays, many "good" women and men shouldn't wed or gather together. Staying together with someone who is "nice" isn't very nice at all.

I assume that two-thirds of coupled co-communicators aren't in love but are, at the very best, "in like." As I've said previously, Friendship Relationships are the current cultural darlings.

So let me take a poll and ask for your honest opinion: Are couples, unmarried or married, who are *not* in love, but who are having sex on an occasional basis to relieve physical tensions—are they behaving "morally" in your opinion? In other words, is sex without love a good or a bad thing?

Let's put it another way: Are married couples who stay together for the children, people who are having sex without love—are they practicing some kind of a virtue? When living on a two-way love street, (and assuming that the couple is making sex once in awhile) if their arrangement is namely a Sex Affair, is it right/wrong or good/bad and should anyone feel terrible guilt if they're currently in such a loveless marriage?

Are married couples who stay together for the children, people who are having sex without love—are they practicing some kind of a virtue?

It seems to me that loveless relationships and marriages are endorsed by our cultural mindset, church-think and society. Friendship marriages are the current cultural darlings because people think to themselves, "Why should I leave this relationship because he/she is such a nice person?" However, is a relationship of convenience really healthy? Of course not—not for E-types or for I-types, and certainly not in our current era of love enlightenment. These days being a "good" boy/girl/Jew/Catholic/Buddhist is wearing thin.

Who's to say, really? If you remain married to someone you hate for 50+ years, and who hates you, is that what God/Goddess want for you and me? Is this as good as it gets for you and yours? Are you and I so bad and guilty that we deserve to have super-bad things happen to us over and over again—things that are outside of our control?

I don't think so. There's no need to walk through life with a two-ton albatross of guilt, resentment or un-love hanging around your neck. You deserve to be loved.

THE RABBI, THE PRIEST AND THE MONK IN THE STADIUM OF HUMAN AFFAIRS

Let me courageously focus on negative guilt trips that steal joy and love and contentment. If you must shoot arrows at me, please miss your target!

In my workshops, I use this metaphor: Imagine we have a whole stadium full of regular people like you and me. The sky is blue, and the strands of white clouds are drifting overhead, it's about 65 degrees and there's no humidity. It's a near-perfect day. Now imagine this.

You are in the stadium with a hundred thousand other souls just like you. Everyone looks at the stage and podium. On the stage are seated three world-renowned dignitaries: the Rabbi, the Priest and the Monk. You admire them all, but you have a favorite.

No, this is not a hoax. The Three Big Leaders of conventional and spiritual wisdom are presiding over this gathering of love. Three spiritual dignitaries are seated on center stage. You are enjoying yourself in the stands, and you're very glad that you took time to come here today. Do you get the image?

Also, imagine that the audience members will be asked questions about their love lives and sexual practices. Additionally, imagine that because you have chosen to be in this stadium today, you are under loving scrutiny. Slowly, you feel your blood pressure rise and your cheeks turn red because this is getting awfully personal. Finally, imagine God is overseeing the event, and you must follow instructions and answer every question honestly. No lying, cheating, self-foolery, stealing or other chicanery is allowed. When the questions are posed, you must automatically respond in absolute truth.

TRUTH OR DARE: IS IT LOVE OR IS IT SEX?

Ready? Your only choice is to answer the questions honestly and follow the instructions exactly. A symbolic magic wand is waved over the throng and the event begins.

The Rabbi, the Priest and the Monk ask the following questions:

The Rabbi asks: "Whosoever has had a "Power Affair" *to feel attractive and wanted* while single, married or divorced, please rise."

(Of course, if you are among this group, you rise to your feet without being able to stop yourself. As you look around, you realize that you're not alone.)

Then the audience members take their seats again.

Secondly, the Priest says, "Whosoever has had a "Sex Affair" *to explore the sensual self* while single, married or divorced, please stand up."

(Of course, if you are among this group you rise to your feet without being able to stop yourself. As you look around, you realize that you're hardly alone.)

Again, the audience members take their seats.

Then, the Buddhist Monk says, "Whosoever has had a "Love Affair" *that encounters the heart-mind-body* with your current romantic partner, married or otherwise, please stand up NOW."

(Of course, only you can know for sure if your answers are true or false. Now, if you're lucky to be among the group who is having a Love Affair with your current partner—you rise to your feet perhaps for the third time! As you look around, you realize that you are in the company of ethical others. Are you having a Love Affair with your partner today? Moreover, what might it mean that only one-third of the stadium audience is now standing?)

For a third time, the audience members return to their seats.

Now as you look around the huge stadium, you realize that people of all ages and walks of life are milling around, while many people you know and had expected to be in love have remained stuck fast to their seats. You muse, "BUT they looked like they were *SO* in love!" You wonder silently to yourself what next might happen.
And in a mini-second, your question is answered.

God says, "All of you who could love more deeply and more completely, whether single/married/divorced/separated, please stand up."

Whoops! Almost every behind is airborne, with everyone leaping off the bleachers in a hurry.

You now get God's message—one that urges everyone to stand for love anyway they can.

Then God kids, "By the way, look to the stage where our beloved dignitaries are seated—the Rabbi, the Priest and the Buddhist Monk."

"Do they stand up for love? Do YOU?"

(The three dignitaries are now standing, and you know what that's supposed to mean. You stretch and breathe deep of the fresh air that stands for LOVE.)

The audience in unison hoots and applauds!

BE NOT SO QUICK TO JUDGE OTHERS

When any relationship ends, many people automatically use a common "blame game" to explain the breakup.

The point of this exercise: Be not so quick to judge others.

There is so much condemnation about why relationships finish or end, and much of the discussion is usually negative and hate-filled. I'm asking you, the reader, to distinguish between sex, love, religion and judgmental stone-casting—a task that requires a big leap on your part. I'm asking a lot of you. I'm asking you not to judge, but to be full of caring.

When any relationship ends, many people automatically use a common "blame game" to explain the breakup. And usually, they blame the ending or conclusion of a relationship on the misdeeds or psychological sins of the opposing party. An affair is judged to be a common misdeed. Maybe it's the only way out? I believe that relationships have a natural ending point or time line of conclusion, one that's driven by forces of love.

I believe that relationships have a natural ending point or time line of conclusion, one that's driven by forces of love.

But in reality, there are many co-responsible reasons for a break-up or for the end of a relationship. Maybe both people were mismatched from the very beginning. Maybe one of the people fell in love with the idea of being in love rather than actually feeling the loving emotions that are required to sustain love. Maybe controlling power plays ran amok. Maybe the relationship was marred by unfair fighting or one partner's attempts to dominate the other's self-image. There are many other reasons. Assume, as I do, that only one-third of established couples are in love, which means two-thirds of us are engaging in *sex for power, sex for attention, sex for physical release.* Pretty thought-provoking, isn't it?

And in the context of communications, think of what that means. This communications training is a practice in deepening the loving self. The goal is to help you experience the change from a "doing/fixing" mindset to a "being/loving" frame of mind. Recall vividly, E-types feel vulnerable (hopeless) when they can't have their "feelings heard." I-types feel vulnerable (powerless) when they can't "fix" things.

Power Affairs, Sex Affairs and Love Affairs are equally condemned. I go on record as positively believing in Love Affairs, preferably, with your present partner.

I go on record as positively believing in Love Affairs, preferably, with your present partner.

It doesn't get any better than having a decades-long Love Affair with your partner of choice. Does it?

Whether our beloved sages...the Rabbi...Priest...Monk...are seated or standing—they all stand for *love!*

BEHAVING CIVILLY WHEN YOU'RE RAGING INSIDE

De-escalating negative, emotional, downward cycles means you do your best to remain civil when you are raging inside. It means you do the little kindnesses, such as apologizing for your 50% of the mess you're now in. Always remember, both you and your partner are in the emotional swamp surrounded by ancient-looking alligators and everyone is scared out of their minds. Plus, those gigantic mosquitoes and other bugs keep swarming around your head, making it very difficult to see well, much less think straight.

The first rule of swamp survival is this: Don't make matters any worse by what you say or do.

The first rule of swamp survival is this: Don't make matters any worse by what you say or do. The point of escaping isn't to drain the swamp and relocate the alligators. The point is to move through the swamp as carefully as you can in an accurate and functional way so that you can get out of the swamp and put yourself in a luxurious hotel Jacuzzi that overlooks the ocean. Sometimes, you have to get through pain to get to the joy that awaits. Feeling swamped by negative emotions lends your mind to making hasty and ill-thought decisions that can cost you and yours dearly.

The first survival skill of loving your co-communicators is to sit down and get grounded! Second, as you sit down together to take a deep breath, you exchange accurate negative feelings. Accurate negative feelings like these: "I'm petrified…I hate swamps…I'm phobic of alligators…We're going to die and our bones will never be found!" Well, you get the point: Don't run headlong into a quicksand bog because you're terrified of alligators…get your emotional bearings first.

Then take positive action to move toward your positive goals.

CHARACTER ASSASSINATION

Character assassination is the first and last big mistake of the little person.

Personally disparaging a talk partner's logic, emotional reactions, masculinity or femininity, toughness or softness, sexuality or sexual preferences are common character assassination ploys.

Character assassination is the first and last big mistake of the little person.

Personally disparaging a talk partner's logic, emotional reactions, masculinity or femininity, toughness or softness, sexuality or sexual preferences are common character assassination ploys. To spell out the word "assassination," you have to put two asses in a row. I know you don't like to stand behind a rear end—nor be one.

"You are what you say," I say.

"You are what you say," I say. You can't wound another without harming yourself. You can't put yourself down without putting down someone else you care for. Punishing paybacks are not swell but Hell. And they always result from stalled communication tactics that could have gone decently.

Power plays to avoid when your temper is high and your mouth is running away with your mind are:

- *Back off from verbal blame games*

- *Don't engage in kitchen-sinking (thinking of every nasty thing you can from the person's past and throwing it at them)*
- *Do not "throw in the towel" and walk away or pout*
- *Beware of using threats to win a debate*
- *Remember the impact of Revenge Boomerangs (they always come back to smack you!)*
- *Say "no" to negative paybacks*
- *Say "yes" to positive paybacks, written and verbal*

Staying flexible in your roles is another good way to keep unhealthy debates from spiraling out of control. Instigators can try to be more intuitive, reflective and receptive, and admit how much they need and want to get along with their talk partner. Empathizers can be more assertive, goal-oriented and independent, and admit how well they can take care of themselves during a pinch.

And Instigators need to be reminded that Empathizers are much stronger than anyone might believe.

PSYCHOANALYTICAL CRITIQUES EMPATHIZERS VS. INSTIGATORS STYLE

When you are fearful, angry or down, chances go up that you will become an inaccurate communicator. Plus, chances are your co-communicator is going to feel irritated with how well or not well the talk is going.

When you are fearful, angry or down, chances go up that you will become an inaccurate communicator.

When your co-communicator's hurt feelings mount, then verbal garbage is dumped on the front lawn of your relationship. Have you heard, or heard yourself say any judgmental statements when you're mad at your co-communicator? I bet you have. And now you know which side of the debate you're on.

I'm going to make the going a tad easier for you. On the left side of Chart 4.1 are common criticisms of E-types that I-types make. And, on the right side of the chart are criticisms of I-type communicator's weaknesses that E-types make.

Chart 4.1 Pages 190–191

The chart of examples of criticisms, fair or unfair, fact or fancy, can wound or create anxiety in a co-communicator who happens to be an E-type or an I-type communicator style—one who is mad and talking negatively.

4.1 Critique of E-types by I-types	Critique of I-types by E-types
You are too sensitive.	*You are too insensitive.*
You are too generous.	*You are too selfish.*
You are too passive.	*You are too aggressive.*
You are too codependent.	*You are too independent.*
You are too conforming.	*You are too rebellious.*
You worry too much.	*You don't worry about anything.*
You are too frigid.	*You are too free with your sexuality.*
You are too depressed.	*You are too hyper-optimistic.*
You don't take very good care of yourself.	*You care only for yourself.*
You talk too much.	*You don't speak about feelings enough.*
You are too shy.	*You are too outgoing.*
You nag too much.	*You don't let anything much get under your skin.*
You are too laid back.	*You are too driven.*
You are too easygoing.	*You are too hurried.*
You are too prudent.	*You are too impudent.*
You are a perfectionist.	*You are a workaholic.*
You are too wishy-washy.	*You are stubborn as a mule.*
You are too needy.	*You don't need anybody.*
You are too down.	*You don't feel anything.*

Critique of E-types by I-types	Critique of I-types by E-types
You are too demanding.	*You don't care.*
You pout like a big baby.	*You don't get mad, you get even.*
You can't stand being alone.	*You are a loner.*
You are as dumb as a rock.	*You are too smart for your own good.*
You can't get along with the opposite sex.	*You are addicted to the opposite sex.*
You don't know what you want.	*You think only about your wants.*
You can't ever be satisfied.	*You ought to be satisfied with what you've got.*
You can't let go of fear and relax.	*You're mad too much of the time.*
You beat up on yourself.	*I'm not your whipping post.*
When you're hurt you shut down.	*When you're mad you can't think straight.*
You're too good for your own good.	*You think I'm bad when you're mad.*
You're drug down by guilt.	*You don't feel guilty enough.*
You don't let anything go.	*You want to throw in the towel.*
You're too patient.	*You're too impatient.*
You're afraid of success.	*You're afraid of failure.*
You're a martyr who suffers.	*You're a persecutor who makes others suffer.*
You're afraid of conflict.	*You love conflict.*
You think God is against joy.	*You think joy is God.*
You can't stand being happy.	***You can't buy happiness.***

The traits on the left side of the column are frequent criticisms levied at Empathizers during a heated argument. The traits on the right side of the column are frequent criticisms that E-types think or hurl at Instigator communicators.

Use the lists and concepts above to connect the dots between your head and your heart. In some of your tensest relationship moments, leading with your heart will work, while in other situations, leading with your head will work. You will know which way to go by the time we finish our training together.

In some of your tensest relationship moments, leading with your heart will work, while in other situations, leading with your head will work.

ASKING DIRECTIVE QUESTIONS

As I've previously mentioned, asking Directive Questions that create teamwork is often more important than listening open-mindedly and calmly.

Asking Directive Questions that create teamwork is often more important than listening open-mindedly and calmly.

What I have named "Directive Questions" have clinically proven to work extremely well with both Empathizer and Instigator communicators who are in a communication bind. The intention of these adult-to-adult questions is to co-create communicator responsiveness and flexibility in such a way that each person shares 50% of the responsibility.

Directive Questions respect not only the speaker, who is speaking either negatively or positively, but directive questions also respect the listener. As well, directive questions protect the interpersonal communication process. Your relationship, after all, is in your hands and it is going to end up being either negative or positive and accurate or inaccurate.

I want your so-called "primary" relationship to be positive, positively physically intimate, emotionally enriching and intellectually engaging. You deserve it all!

WHO DOESN'T LIKE "TO DO" CHORES?

"My kid doesn't like to do chores," is a refrain I hear constantly from distressed co-parents or single parents.

I typically reply, "I don't like to do chores, either." Truthfully, I also dislike doing paperwork, paying taxes, buying car insurance, paying dental bills, enduring cold weather in the Midwest, getting stuck behind slow drivers, and dealing with people who don't return your phone calls. Sometimes, I also dislike myself, people who complain more than I do, lazy workers, employees who work too hard, and work in general. I can hate it all while playing the victim violin and stage-acting the martyr role.

Why talk positive or positively together? Here's an example of two co-parents discussing why chores aren't being done equally by their early teen children, the oldest a boy and the youngest a girl.

This Talk Exercise will help you execute the perfect comeback directive question that kicks the speaker off the Royal Throne, also known as the Pity Pot:

Co-Communicator Transaction: What are we going to do about the chore situation?
Directive Question: What is the situation that you are referring to, as you see it?

Co-Communicator Transaction: The chores around here aren't ever being done on some kind of regular basis.
Directive Question: What do you define as a "regular" basis?

Co-Communicator Transaction: Well, it means on a daily basis. The chores ought to be done around here every day without our begging and pleading.
Directive Question: How often, or what percentage of the time are chores not done around here on a regular basis in our home, in your opinion?

Co-Communicator Transaction: Not often enough, that's for sure. I'd say maybe half the time. Our girl is much better than our boy about doing chores without being asked to.
Directive Question: What chores aren't being done on a daily basis?

Co-Communicator Transaction: Well, the boy doesn't make his bed or pick up his room—he only does what he's supposed to when you ride him. The girl does her chores, but you have to remind her to.

Directive Question: Why do you think our girl is better at doing her chores than our boy is at doing his chores?

Co-Communicator Transaction: You let the boy get away with murder. You don't dare ask him to do his chores because you know he doesn't like to do chores.
Directive Question: Do you think I'm being unfair to our girl by giving unfair preferential treatment to our boy?

Co-Communicator Transaction: No, I'm not saying that. You seem to let the boy put you off, but you don't take any guff from our girl. I know you love both of them equally. I'm confused as to why all of this conflict is happening.
Directive Question: Is there something you think I could say or do to make the situation better and run more smoothly for all of us?

Co-Communicator Transaction: Yes, you could ask for my input more often. I realize that you are super-independent but you could include me more often, and tell me what you feel more often. I feel left out, left out in the cold, as if I'm outside this family, looking in.
Directive Question: So, if I ask for your advice more often and listen to you, are you saying that might help ease the tension around here a bunch?

Co-Communicator Transaction: That's exactly what I've been saying for years now!
Directive Question: Okay, I'd like to ask your advice right now about a tough issue. Do you think we ought to pay an allowance to the boy and the girl for doing their chores?

Co-Communicator Transaction: No, we shouldn't pay to have chores done. We assign chores to teach responsibility. The value of chores is to teach how to be part of a family and that family always pulls together. We have chores because we simply have chores!
Directive Question: Should we post the chores on the refrigerator so the boy and girl know what to do right and what they shouldn't do wrong?

Co-Communicator Transaction: Let's put it in black-and-white so every family member is reading from the same page and following the same dictates.
Directive Question: What percentage are we, as co-parents, co-responsible for making the chore situation happen positively?

Co-Communicator Transaction: You are the mother, so you are 70% responsible for the positive or negative outcome that takes place about the chores.
Directive Question: So you as father are only 30% co-responsible for chores being done or not being done?

Well, you get the idea. You listen to the co-communicator transaction and try to pin him/her down with a directive question. You are trying to compassionately link into the other person's private emotion or belief system in order to create positive change.

It's not awkward when you ask polite questions; in fact, the answers to the questions will enlighten you. You are *not* trying to trap your co-communicator, trick them or lure them into a trap. You simply, and only, completely wish to understand the other person's frame of reference. But you aren't going to take inaccurate negative feeling, thinking and talking casually, either.

Understanding is all we're left with after the smoke of talk wars, and negative power plays, disperses into thin air. Isn't it?

You are not trying to trap your co-communicator, trick them or lure them into a trap. You simply, and only, completely wish to understand the other person's frame of reference.

DIRECTIVE QUESTIONING: "YOU DON'T LOVE ME ANYMORE"

Power struggles drain the power of love while intending to drain the swamp of hate. It's no use to drain the swamp. It won't work to go 'round and 'round the swamp in a negative circle with no end.

If you choose to fulfill relationship obligations, you will empower your relationship to live out its fullest potential.

Here are the dual transactions of a couple in trouble who are trying to find their way out of the swamp of negative emotions using the directive questioning communications approach I advise:

Co-Communicator Transaction: Whatever I do isn't ever right or good enough, according to your standards.
Directive Question: What do you do that you think isn't ever good enough by me?

Co-Communicator Transaction: Let's move on, let's not think about it, let's change the subject.
Directive Question: Are you saying that we suffer too much and purposely cause our relationship much unnecessary pain?

Co-Communicator Transaction: Well, we always do too much rehashing. Why can't we let go of past painful events?
Directive Question: What past painful events, in your opinion, do we need to let go of that we can and should stop speaking about obsessively?

Co-Communicator Transaction: I have regrets.
Directive Question: What regrets are you thinking of?

Co-Communicator Transaction: The problems keep rolling in.
Directive Question: I'm not sure what your point is here. Would you tell me?

Co-Communicator Transaction: You act depressed and upset when you don't get your way.
Directive Question: Do you think I usually am being unfair and controlling?

Co-Communicator Transaction: No, I'm not saying that. But you've got to admit you're not happy being with me.
Directive Question: What makes you think I am unhappy being with you?

Co-Communicator Transaction: You love your work more than you love me.
Directive Question: So, if I work too hard you believe I'm ignoring you?

Co-Communicator Transaction: That's exactly what I've told you for years—you can't love your work and hate me at the same time.
Directive Question: Okay. Are you saying I'm withdrawing from you because I don't love you—much less don't like you?

Co-Communicator Transaction: Of course not. I know you love me, but you have strange ways of showing me lately.
Directive Question: Are you saying that we aren't communicating very well lately?

Co-Communicator Transaction: Let me put it this way. I don't think you love me.
Directive Question: What makes you think I don't love you?

Co-Communicator Transaction: You haven't listened to me this way in years.
Directive Question: Would you mind if I listen to you this intensely, and positively, from now on?

It's all downhill or up-mood from this moment already. Be ready! It's high time for a little positive change.

RELATIONSHIP RULES

You and I learn relationship rules from our early family experience. We also learn ways to talk about emotional topics respectfully. Rarely, however, do we put our expectations in black-and-white.

How closely do you follow the 10 relationship rules for emotional honesty and accountability below? Do you put time and energy into maintaining a positive relationship "bridge" or energy by using these positive behaviors (B2+)? Or are you prone to taking care of your needs first and the relationship last, if ever?

There is interpersonal power and then there is inner-personal power. Do you balance giving care to the relationship with the care you give to yourself?

Both Empathizers and Instigators are capable of being exquisitely tuned in (or tuned out) to relationship dynamics. There is *interpersonal power* and then there is *inner-personal power.* Do you balance giving care to the relationship with the care you give to yourself?

Do you agree, or disagree, with the following 10 talk intentions? Are these the behaviors of someone who's truly interested in helping others in loving ways? Do you believe these behaviors come more naturally to Empathizer or Instigator communicators? You decide.

1. **If you need to talk, I will listen.**
2. **If you are emotionally upset, I will try to make you feel better without bringing myself down.**
3. **If you are under severe stress, you can count on me to try and not make matters any worse.**
4. **I will fill in, help you out, and be helpful without being asked when you are doing well or when you feel bad.**
5. **I will give you advice and suggest new directions for change only when you ask me to.**
6. **I will reassure you that you aren't bad when you feel mad at those you love.**
7. **I promise I won't say "no" to you or turn my back on you as a power play or to punish you.**

8. **I will do my utmost not to take on the bad mood of another, when I can.**
9. **I won't pick on you to avoid my own negative emotions.**
10. **I will respect my/your emotions and viewpoints about equally and put equal effort into making this relationship a positive one.**

The wacky truth is that you are first responsible for your own happiness and then responsible second for the positive energy in your relationships. Believe it!

ENTREPRENEURIAL LEADERS ARE INSTIGATOR COMMUNICATORS

Most entrepreneurial leaders are Instigator communicators.

Entrepreneurial leaders have more than their share of failures, because they also have far more successes than the average gal or guy. I-types can take it on the chin and still grin. I-type entrepreneurs are either introverts or extroverts because neither style is better or worse for the purposes of business.

I've found out that entrepreneurial leaders, be they *Start-Up Leaders* or *Go-Forward Leaders,* agonize over failures that turn out to be the seeds of their biggest successes. Anxiety, dysphoria and "riding the mood rollercoaster" are common to genius entrepreneurial leaders. I-type entrepreneurs, female and male, are the backbone of our country's future growth, progress and change.

I truly admire and deeply respect entrepreneurial spirits. Thus, I want to use the Case of the Anxious Entrepreneur to walk you through the four talk modes again. By now, you are able to hear and see the modes in motion and sense how to flip negative sentences around, or turn inaccurate negative transactions into accurate positive transactions. With those skills becoming second nature, you can achieve superior results in your mood and achieve your positive goals.

So don't get over-focused on what the entrepreneur says (because this talk took place in the slimy, slippery and short-lived dark pit of swampy emotions). Instead, focus on the mode from which the words were spoken. Instigator communicators change most when

When I-types encounter their emotions and move through negative and positive emotions, miracles happen. In contrast, when E-types focus on positive logic and positive thinking in order to counteract their negative emotions, miracles happen.

they move through negative emotions without getting lost in the emotional swamp or bog. *When I-types encounter their emotions and move through negative and positive emotions, miracles happen. In contrast, when E-types focus on positive logic and positive thinking in order to counteract their negative emotions, miracles happen.*

However, Instigators are such *strong personalities* that they can lug around a big bagful of emotional rocks that are quite unnecessary. I-types also set the mood in their family of origin, and probably in their household today. Instigators follow strict emotional rules such as "Don't let your feelings get you down." "Don't express sensitive emotions publicly." "Strong people put their mind over their emotions." If you are an Instigator communicator, chances are you are in a leadership position, leading a family, leading a church group, leading an office, leading caregiving for an elder, etc. I-types are natural born leaders!

The upside of Instigator insensitivity is that I-types (either introverted or extroverted) can reduce feelings of rejection, not take things too personally and can shrug off rejections to accomplish tough business goals.

IS IT TRUE THAT INSTIGATOR COMMUNICATORS (I-TYPES) ARE LEADERS BY NATURE?

I propose that Instigator communicators are primarily leadership-types and Empathizer communicators are primarily follower-types or teammates, but not always. Thus, Instigator communicators will make up a large majority of entrepreneurial business owners and leaders—and leaders in general.

I further propose that by using 12 communicator dimensions, leaders can be identified reliably using the New Insights Communication Inventory—Leadership Scale or NICI-LS. Also, an Instigator leader can be highly effective in the pursuit of either ethical or unethical goals.

In working with business, family, church and community leaders, I would say the following 15 categories often seem to fit leaders:

1. Leaders are <u>strong personality types</u> or *I-types*.

2. **Leaders subscribe to a "glass is half-full" mindset.**
3. **Leaders are charismatic.**
4. **Leaders half-listen with a goal in mind.**
5. **Leaders are strategic planners.**
6. **Leaders set the mood in their family/ families of origin.**
7. **Leaders are either effective or ineffective.**
8. **Leaders who are effective do what's important first.**
9. **Leaders who are ineffective do what's important last.**
10. **Bored leaders are self-defeating.**
11. **Leaders dislike working for a boss.**
12. **Leaders are either ethical or unethical.**
13. **Ethical leaders are unselectively frank.**
14. **Unethical leaders are selectively evasive.**
15. **Positive leaders are effective and ethical.**

Don't take me wrong: Empathizer communicators make fine leaders, too. In fact, our future may depend upon more E-types leading the way by adopting the strengths of I-types—while avoiding both types' Achilles Heel. Again, a leader (I-type or E-type) can be highly effective in the pursuit of either ethical or unethical goals. In my opinion, positive leaders are both effective and ethical.

Let's turn now to our story about a distressed leader so we can learn how the modes work marvelously in negative and/or positive ways.

CASE OF THE ANXIOUS ENTREPRENEUR

An Instigator-type, extroverted female entrepreneur in a start-up business told me: "I've hit the wall, I just can't do it anymore."

She was in the Crisis Stage of change. I began recording her sentences and categorized her quotes by talk mode, negative/positive.

Can you decide if the quotes are accurate or inaccurate? It's a little difficult when you don't know the individual, but this businesswoman is plenty sharp, savvy and skilled. Hitting the communication wall is a good metaphor when people go off the road and crash into an immovable object that won't change. The communicator feels unhappy, pressured to live up to the image of the perfect person. Big pressures come from family and spouse.

In her personal life, this Instigator-type extrovert (ITE) is paired with an Instigator-type extrovert (ITE) business partner. Two of a kind should get along just fine, right? That depends entirely on the type of their relationship: If the relationship is a controlling or a friendship one—stagnation and distress will occur. If the relationship is a loving relationship—growth and positive change will occur. By now, you know that each of our two co-communicating Instigator-type extroverts, or ITE's always prefer to drive in their favored modes of Beliefs (B1-/+) and Behaviors (B2-/+).

If both Instigator co-communicator drivers are negative believers and negative talkers—whoa! A verbal clash of the titans is ready to happen in that vehicle.

THE FOUR Communicator Modes Inner-Personally and Inter-Personally

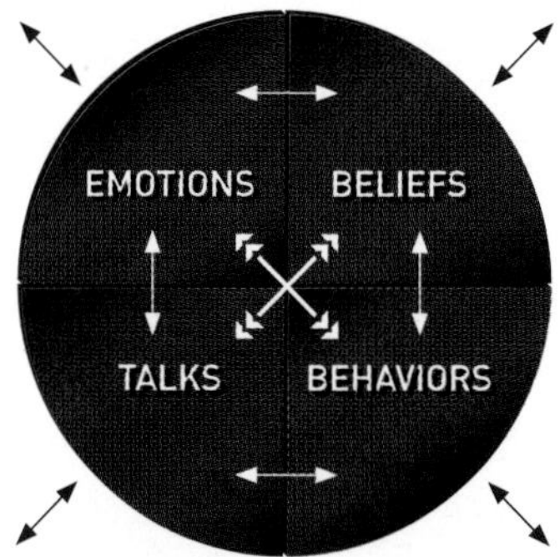

figure **#29**

LEADING THE FOUR COMMUNICATOR MODES—EMOTIONS (E) BELIEFS (B1), BEHAVIORS (B2) AND TALKS (T)

Negative Emotions (E-) mode: How do you **feel** about it?

(E-) I feel anxious.
(E-) I've just lost it.
(E-) I've been depressed and despairing for more than a year now.
(E-) I've lost my motivation and achievement drive.
(E-) I'm so uninspired that I've stopped working out at the gym.
(E-) My mood is in the toilet all the time.
(E-) I'm not having any fun. Even sex is boring.
(E-) I feel guilty for everything and I don't forgive myself ever.
(E-) I'm expecting the worse to happen.
(E-) I've lost sight of my dreams and I feel powerless and helpless.
(E-) I feel totally confused about who I am and where I'm headed.
(E-) I've never been a quitter, *but* I can give up and quit.
(E-) I feel so disappointed in myself.
(E-) *I despise feeling so anxious, down and overwhelmed.*

Negative Beliefs mode (B1-): What do you **think** about it?

(B1-) Well, I don't like how things are going in my company and my career.
(B1-) I'd like to run away.
(B1-) So many employees are depending on me to pull this out of the fire.
(B1-) I'm personally on the line to the bank, which could take everything.
(B1-) I have dreams of doing something else.
(B1-) I hate where I live but I can't leave and do something else.
(B1-) I'm super-strong but I'm getting worn down and emotionally thin.
(B1-) I feel like I'm presiding over a funeral at my own company.
(B1-) I come back positive and optimistic the next day but nothing changes.
(B1-) Bad feelings can't make me quit when I'm behind.
(B1-) I'm not sure what I would do with the rest of my life.

(B1-) All the experts are trying to help but they're dead wrong.
(B1-) My family pulls me up so that I can forget about all this strain.
(B1-) Why is this happening to me?
(B1-) *My anxiety takes my confidence away.*

Positive Behaviors mode (B2+): Is there anything you can **do** about it that works?

(B2+) I need to walk and carry myself confidently—smile—lead again.
(B2+) I must keep a positive attitude especially when negative things keep coming.
(B2+) I know I'm so anxious I could work around the clock now, but I won't.
(B2+) I must look at my awards to remember how time after time I've driven this company down new and better roads.
(B2+) I might find a creative solution to the problem by going out and having some fun.
(B2+) I'm not going to worry myself sick about this. . .I'll eat well and sleep as best as I can.
(B2+) What recharges me is having fun time with my kids and grandkids.
(B2+) I'm taking extra vitamins and taking time to pray.
(B2+) I'm not going to put on a good front while I'm sinking in a cesspool of sludge, even while I'm clutching an anchor.
(B2+) Time to call up that communications psychologist!
(B2+) I won't pull down the people who care for me if I'm down once in awhile.
(B2+) Staying busy helps a bunch right now.
(B2+) I feel open to receiving new unexpected answers to old problems.
(B2+) I am 50% co-responsible for passing on the negatives and picking up the positives.
(B2+) *My anxiety can't make me hold on to an anchor when I'm drowning in an ocean of emotion.*

I am 50% co-responsible for passing on the negatives and picking up the positives.

Positive Talks mode (T+): Does **positive talking** about the challenge make things better?

(T+) I feel at my best when I brainstorm options.
(T+) I like being structured and organized.

(T+) Taking risks doesn't bother me.
(T+) I don't complain about what others won't change.
(T+) I depend on the advice of my close inner circle of advisors.
(T+) I'm always able to come up with positive solutions to negative problems.
(T+) I'm going to look after my physical health better.
(T+) I like people and I like making a big splash in the community pool.
(T+) I feel happier when I set and pursue positive change goals.
(T+) My partner doesn't nag me when I get pensive and quiet.
(T+) I'm stronger and wiser today than I was yesterday.
(T+) I don't think this is going to be a major problem.
(T+) I'm all for change—especially the joy it brings.
(T+) I won't be talked out of trying the new.
(T+) I feel like a winner. I like me during bad and good times.
(T+) *When I talk in optimistic and accurate ways to myself, I feel more positive, focused and hopeful!*

PASS ON THE NEGATIVES— PICK UP THE POSITIVES

Can you feel the difference between the negative talk and the positive talk? I bet you can! I feel the difference when simply writing the words and speaking them to myself.

Factually speaking about positively supporting your communication E-type or I-type style:

1. *Empathizers do best when they feel supported by a guide as they travel through the deserts of their negative, inaccurate thinking.*

2. *Instigators do best when they feel supported by a guide as they travel through the swamps and bogs of their inaccurate emotions.*

3. *Additionally, E-types need to let go of thinking that their emotions are always accurate and useful.*

4. *Likewise, I-types need to let go of feeling that their mind is splitting apart when emotions occupy center stage.*

E-types need to let go of thinking that their emotions are always accurate and useful.

I-types need to let go of feeling that their mind is splitting apart when emotions occupy center stage.

Once you internalize these concepts, get ready for your eyelids to be lifted upward, and for your eyes to be opened outward. Using the four communicator modes, in accurate negative and positive ways, will give you new life-changing solutions and new financial solutions that have proven to work for my communications clients, and they come from all walks of life and ethnic backgrounds.

THE TWELVE DIFFERENCES IN FRAME OF REFERENCE FOR EMPATHIZER (E-TYPE) AND INSTIGATOR (I-TYPE) COMMUNICATORS

1. Interpersonal sensitivity vs. interpersonal insensitivity

- E-types negatively believe they are too sensitive and hurt too easily, while I-types negatively feel that they are too insensitive and hurt others unnecessarily.
- E-types are either introverts (ETI's) or extroverts (ETE's), just as I-types are either introverts (ITI's) or extroverts (ITE's).
- E-types suffer from *Relationship Attention Surplus Disorder*, while I-types suffer from *Relationship Attention Deficit Disorder*.
- E-types are more prone to picking up or taking on negative emotions in a speaker, while I-types might not pick up on subtle cues that account for emotions in a speaker.
- E-types use emotional intuition to cope with anxiety or stress, while I-types use intellectual precision to cope with anxious times.
- E-types feel intimidated by I-types' bluntness, while I-types feel irritated by E-types' sensitivity.

2. Listening vs. half-listening

- E-types listen *empathetically*, while I-types listen *strategically*.
- E-types seek first to listen in order to understand the speaker better, while I-types want to give advice quickly to solve a problem.
- E-types listen *inclusively* (listen with three ears) while I-types listen *selectively* (listen with one ear while multi-tasking).
- E-types like to spend time in dialogue, while I-types dislike wasting time in "idle chitchat" in order to make every second count more.

- E-types can relax and enjoy a conversation, while I-types' minds are busy thinking of several things at once.
- The approach of *"active listening"* works well with E-types, while the approach of *"directive questioning"* works well with I-types.
- E-types are negatively perceived by I-types as not getting to the point fast enough, while I-types are negatively perceived by E-types as tuning out what they don't want to hear.
- E-types are natural-born, carry-forward team builders, while I-types are natural-born, start-up idea leaders.

3. Behind the scenes vs. star of the show

- E-types tend to feel on the outside of social life looking inward for failure, while I-types feel in the middle of social life looking outward for success.
- E-types don't feel as socially popular as I-types do, while I-types strive to be socially powerful.
- E-type introverts and I-type introverts (ETI's/ITI's) may habitually feel socially shy and avoid being the center of attention, while E-type extroverts and I-type extroverts (ETE's/ITE's) may habitually feel socially outgoing and enjoy being the center of attention.
- E-types negatively believe that their I-type counterparts are self-centered, selfish and attention seeking, while I-types negatively feel that their E-type counterparts are too relationship-centered, selfless and victim thinking.
- E-types are more prone to be a victim of interpersonal bullying, while I-types are more prone to be an unintentional perpetrator of interpersonal bullying.
- E-types need to be more *independent and focused on self happiness,* while I-types need to be more *dependent and focused on the happiness of others.*

4. Interpersonal cooperation vs. interpersonal competition

- E-types feel best when cooperation is present, while I-types prefer a spirited contest, such as a debate or sporting event.

- E-types might not insist on getting their needs met, while I-types don't feel guilty about insisting that their needs be met.
- E-types don't keep score, while I-types feel more stimulated by a counting system that denotes winner/loser.
- E-types are prone to take on blame or feeling at fault, while I-types are prone to find that the fault for a communication breakdown resides in the other person or in the situation.
- E-types perceive I-types as being too hard and pushy, while I-types perceive E-types as being too soft and pushovers.

5. Talking about a problem vs. fixing a problem

- E-types firmly believe that talking about a problem is the solution, while I-types strongly feel that strategic planning is the solution.
- E-types prefer to *understand a problem before fixing on a solution,* while I-types prefer to *formulate a plan to understand and then fix a problem.*
- E-types negatively perceive I-types as being too confident, hasty and dogmatic in their opinions, while I-types negatively perceive their E-type counterparts as behaving too unconfidently, slow and wishy-washy.
- E-types value problem-solving talks that are emotionally honest, while I-types will bend the truth to avoid hurting others' feelings.
- E-types dislike many of the suggestions their I-type counterparts give them, while I-types dislike many of their best ideas returned to sender with "Yes, but . . ." excuses.

6. Relationship locus of control vs. internal self locus of control

- E-types feel the power to resolve a problem resides somewhere with both members of a relationship, while I-types believe the power to resolve a problem resides solely within the self.
- E-types feel rejected when their I-type co-communicator violates "obvious" right way vs. wrong way relationship/emotional rules, while I-types feel indignant when their E-type co-communicator violates "obvious" right way vs. wrong way communication/logic rules.

- E-types like to feel connected and feel worried when a disconnect occurs, while I-types like to feel in charge and worry when they are not in control of a situation.

7. Low self-esteem vs. high self-esteem

- E-types judge their I-type counterparts as being *aggressive positive thinkers,* while I-types judge their E-type counterparts as being *passive negative thinkers.*
- E-types' energy is more positive when they *promote positive and accurate thinking,* while I-types' energy is more positive when they *promote positive and accurate emotional talking.*
- *Empathizer-type introverts (ETI's)* act shy around people they don't know well or first meet, while *Instigator-type introverts (ITI's)* can force themselves to be outgoing and appear confident around people they first meet and don't know well.
- E-types have more confidence than they give themselves credit for, while I-types exude confidence that sometimes is tomfoolery or fakery.
- E-types are more likely to feel that their self-confidence glass is half-empty, while I-types confidently believe their glass is half-full and getting fuller.

8. Change resistive vs. change promotive

- The leading strength of an E-type communicator is *empathy,* while the leading strength of an I-type communicator is *genuineness.*
- E-types approach change too cautiously, while I-types can be too enthusiastic about change.
- E-types believe their I-type counterparts can be too unfocused with too many irons in the fire, while I-types feel E-types can get over-focused and fail to see the forest for the trees.
- E-types enjoy the exciting ideas, novelty and personal growth adventures created by I-types, while I-types enjoy the emotional warmth, steadfastness and loyalty of E-types.
- E-types pick at themselves for overreacting emotionally to a relationship imbalance and for not being more self-assertive, while I-types feel guilty for not being more relationship-centered and compromising.

9. Hopelessness vs. powerlessness

- E-types struggle with the repetitive negative emotion of sluggish sadness, while I-types struggle with the repetitive negative emotion of angry impatience.
- E-types' *emotional health suffers from negative emotions that stem from relationship distress,* while I-types' *physical health suffers from negative emotions that stem from relationship distress.*
- E-types' positive energy drains out of them when ongoing feelings of *interpersonal hopelessness* occur, while I-types' positive energy drains out of them when ongoing feelings of *interpersonal powerlessness* occur.
- E-types are vulnerable to giving in and giving up, while I-types are vulnerable to running over and getting their way at the expense of a positive interpersonal relationship.
- E-types negatively believe that I-types are "control freaks," while I-types negatively feel that E-types are "love freaks."

10. Achilles' heel loneliness vs. Achilles' heel boredom

- When under stress, E-types are more prone to experience *loneliness,* while I-types are more prone to experience *boredom.*
- When lonely, E-types talk to themselves in very negative ways. When bored, I-types stir things up by indulging in negative actions.
- E-types and I-types alike may co-create relationship crises to logically explain away and rationalize these two individually painful or "dark" emotions of loneliness and boredom.
- E-types *feel guilty when their talk doesn't match the walk of their emotions,* while I-types *feel guilty when their actions don't match their lectures.*
- E-types are more easily manipulated by guilt trips, while I-types don't fall as fast for guilt trips but carry equally heavy loads of guilt that interfere with enjoying life and feeling loved.
- E-types perceive I-types as being too close-minded, direct and stubborn, while I-types perceive E-types as being too open-minded, uncertain and never able to make up their minds.

11. Past focus vs. future focus

- *E-types focus on the past* because they like to see where they have been before moving ahead slowly, while *I-types like to focus in the future* and move on fast.
- E-types feel frustrated when I-types say, "Just forget about it and move on!" Conversely, I-types feel sad when E-types say, "I'm not just going to let you forget about it!"

12. The emotional brain vs. the logical brain

- E-types prefer to access and use the Emotional Brain more often, while I-types prefer to access and use the Logical Brain more often.
- E-types perceive their I-type counterparts as too data-driven, too analytical, cold and worshipping of statistics, while I-types perceive their E-type counterparts as too touchy-feeling driven, too moody, too fuzzy and too attached to chitchat talking.

Now that you've got that didactic outline for E-types and I-types, it's time to end this chapter on an inspirational note. Why? The goal of positive communication is to develop and nurture an inspired life, for the rest of your life.

The goal of positive communication is to develop and nurture an inspired life, for the rest of your life.

CELEBRATING YOUR LIFE TODAY

How have you celebrated being alive today?

If God were to ask you: "How have you loved being alive today?" "Who have you touched with the grace of your smile?" "Are you grudge-full or grate-full?" "Have you seen me in our child's beaming face?" "Do you work in the Church of Joy or the Church of Misery?" What would your honest answers be to these heart-hitting questions? Don't allow yourself to be chained to a false prophet called negative thinking and negative talking. Start celebrating your life instead.

There's no better time than today to tap into many, many, tiny moments of joy.

Celebrate the fact that you can't change anyone but yourself.

Celebrate the awareness that you can make a new choice at any time.

Celebrate the reality that only you have the power to control your own mind.

Celebrate the wisdom of God, who keeps you safe and loves you unconditionally.

Celebrate the importance of having joy in this one life to live.

Celebrate the capacity to open your mind to new insights.

Celebrate finding ways to enjoy yourself despite failure.

Celebrate that you're a fully feeling human being.

Celebrate being surprised.

Celebrate having faith.

Celebrate having friends.

Celebrate having another day to express who you are.

Celebrate bags of resentments dropping off like heavy rocks.

Celebrate revenge boomerangs being knocked away.

Celebrate accepting yourself after being rejected.

Celebrate the joys of partnering and parenting.

Celebrate starting, persevering, swerving, finishing.

Celebrate lives lost and lives bravely led.

Celebrate balancing a sour reality with your sweetest dreams.

Celebrate the healing power of a sincere apology.

Celebrate the mystery of creation.

Celebrate being forgiving in order to be forgiven.

Celebrate life by speaking words of caring when you don't feel like it.

Celebrate any love you've ever been blessed to receive.

Celebrate a small child's glorious intuitions.

Celebrate the wisdom of your elders.

Celebrate getting your anger out in healthy ways.

Celebrate life by trusting, risking and reaching out when there is no logical reason, whatsoever, to do so.

Be sure to celebrate your life today.

It's the only life that you've got, and you just might not be guaranteed another life more. Then, again, you may.

NEXT UP: POSITIVE TALKS

Well, we've been having a great time together so far, haven't we? But we're not over and out of here yet.

In Chapter 5, we'll find out just why your mind(s) is a terrible thing to misplace. Moreover, we'll take a wide-eyed look at a variety of challenging life issues that can be positively impacted by this new communicator theory, and why accurate negative and positive transactions are so important for you and yours.

So let's talk positively and accurately for a change!

V

POSITIVE TALKS

Negative Talks: Negative out...negative in.

Positive Talks: Positive out...positive in!

TRAINING GOAL

How talking positively encourages a positive mood and opens up new avenues for change

TALKING POSITIVELY...FOR A CHANGE

Let's start this final chapter by taking a little drive on the communications highway. It doesn't feel so scary now, does it?

Now that you've learned about the communication styles and habits of the other drivers you'll encounter, you'll no longer approach communication the way a newly licensed teenage driver approaches that first attempt at parallel parking. Now that you understand your own communications behavior, you feel more in control and less vulnerable to the other drivers. A sense of trepidation is replaced with a rush of experience. That rush of adrenaline is replaced by a rush of positive thinking and a "can-do" attitude. No longer fearful of crashes, flat tires, potholes and unpredictable lane-changers, you can now concentrate on a nice, pleasant, scenic drive with plenty of rest stops along the way.

The "are we there yet?" groan that often emanates from the back seat from anxious voices can now be replaced with "we're getting there sooner than I thought"...because now you have the knowledge AND the skill to master the communications highway far better than when you picked up this book.

Now, your goal is to start changing your own communication style and behavior...right *now* and *today,* even if it's only two minutes today and five minutes tomorrow. Eventually, it will become *your* way of communicating in life.

It's been fun feeling as if we're two birds sitting on a wire and talking to one another, hasn't it? Now it's high time to talk positively for an improvement in mood!

TWO RIGHTS DON'T MAKE A WRONG

It's been fun feeling as if we're two birds sitting on a wire and talking to one another, hasn't it? I really appreciate you and the work you're doing here! (I love to talk positively *and* truthfully!) Now it's high time to talk positively for an improvement in mood!

I love the positive proverb (T+): "Two wrongs don't make it right."

If you translate this rule as it relates to relationships, it goes something like this: "When someone is talking negatively (T-) or behaving negatively (B2-), don't just mindlessly strike back in reactive negativity, because you might become stuck in a swamp of hate."

You are learning that positive talking when you are feeling negative helps pick up your spirits. Anxiety, anger, the blues, guilt and *love* are some of the larger alligators you must wrestle with daily in the swamp. But I don't want you to feel that positive talking is an added pressure. Instead, consider it a release.

But I don't want you to feel that positive talking is an added pressure. Instead, consider it a release.

There is some correspondence between your mood, and how you talk to yourself and how you talk to (and about) others. Often talking and thinking positively don't hurt your mood and can, in fact, help your mood. And you know me by now: I don't believe you have to feel good to be okay. I believe when you feel "bad" you are still "good." Feelings don't make you good or bad; they just are winds of change. Choosing to use all of your emotions in effective and ethical ways is the ideal we are striving for here.

And you know me by now: I don't believe you have to feel good to be okay. I believe when you feel "bad" you are still "good." Feelings don't make you good or bad; they just are winds of change.

"Getting even" is another reaction that puts you behind. Punishing someone else is rarely a very good use of your time and energy, because two wrongs never come up right. Yes, I know negative people reject and hurt you, and they rip off your attention by complaining too much, especially about matters they have the power to change. Nonetheless, you probably want to talk positively because it encourages emotional honesty and relationship effectiveness by "accentuating the positive." The blame game comes around to hunt you down and haunt you every time. In addition, you have learned that chomping on a manure sandwich, or taking on the negative emotions of others, is toxic.

Some things you cannot make work, and these include mismatched or loveless relationships. In my opinion, two-thirds of relationships are loveless. No wonder so many people have problems and take it "on the chin with a grin." As children, we spend more hours training how to spell words correctly than how to pick a positive partner for the rest of our lives. My heart goes out to all of us! The biggest heartbreaks occur on the turf of love. For example, whenever you expect a relationship to make you feel good about yourself, you are in for a big awakening.

As children, we spend more hours training how to spell words correctly than how to pick a positive partner for the rest of our lives.

One thing I know for sure is that we are all struggling much of the time inside ourselves and outside in our relationships. As proof positive, look how often we act out our inner-personal emotional struggles on the relationship stage and go for revenge by punishing our partners. We just don't speak openly about our feelings or power-packed emotions, even if we have a sense of being strapped naked to a rocket ship of anger.

The main purpose of positive talking is to work through your own negative and positive emotions, refuse to pass along negatives to others and refuse to take negatives onto the self.

I believe (B1+) now you are the leader of your own life to a greater than lesser extent!

POSITIVE TALKING— POSITIVE THINKING— POSITIVE CHANGING

The main purpose of positive talking is to work through your own negative and positive emotions, refuse to pass along negatives to others and refuse to take negatives onto the self.

Negative paybacks are hell, while positive paybacks are swell. If you think you aren't a payback artist, think again.

Negative paybacks are hell, while positive paybacks are swell. Thus, I steadfastly believe (but cannot always practice) that interpersonal paybacks to "make even a perceived rejection" are ultimately ineffective in the attainment of your positive goals and are likewise quite self-defeating.

If you think you aren't a payback artist, think again. In truth, *Empathizers are prone to giving paybacks in the form of negative behaviors (B2-) that create negative feelings (E-), while Instigators are prone to giving paybacks in the form of negative talks (T-) that create negative thoughts (B1-).* Negatives beget negatives, while positives beget positives, exponentially.

What's the point really, of talking positively, especially when no one else does?

1. *Positive talks create rapid change or "the light bulb" effect*
2. *Positive talks compassionately acknowledge all of us are hurting and learning, just in different ways*
3. *Positive talks put salve on the sting of rejection*
4. *Positive talks dissipate unhealthy victimizing resentment or negative anger*
5. *Positive talks implies clear boundaries to bullies*

6. *Positive talks pass on the knee-jerk and "me-jerk" reactive retribution*
7. *Positive talks take a 2,000-pound Guilt Gorilla off your back*
8. *Positive talks empower you to have faith in doing the positive, especially when you're sinking in swampy relationship muck*
9. *Positive talks require you to be factual and accurate, even when you don't feel like it*
10. *Positive talks take you out of The Anger Game and put you smack in the middle of The Joy Game*

I believe wronging another as you think you have been wronged doesn't make anything right! Furthermore, I believe that what you just heard is an accurate and positive belief (B1+) that when transformed into words (T+) and actions (B2+) is emotionally healing (E+). You then are changed from the inside out.

In short, positive talks make you more open-hearted *and* more open-minded and more change-minded. You will find that people treat you more affectionately and respond in spontaneous new ways toward you. Today, in fact, one of the toughest men I know stood before me with tears in his eyes, reached out and gave me a great big bear hug. Talk about the spontaneous and positive! Therefore, I'm asking you to quit keeping score of who does what for whom. Vow to never again spend energy trying to figure out who requires a positive or negative payback from you.

So, talk positively to yourself, right now, and say aloud: "I believe wronging another, as I think I have been wronged, doesn't make anything right for anyone!"

So, talk positively to yourself, right now, and say aloud: "I believe wronging another, as I think I have been wronged, doesn't make anything right for anyone!"

POSITIVE TALK CHECKLIST

Let's take a minute to determine how accustomed you are to speaking and writing positively. Your negative mind (B1-) will tell you that positive talk is simply "kissing up" or "pseudo-optimism" designed to manipulate or control an outcome. Negative thinkers consider positive talk a big batch of fakery. Actually (and unfortunately), speaking genuinely and positively violates the social norm that you are supposed to keep your positive thoughts or compliments to yourself and toughen up.

How do you measure up on these positive talk attributes today?

- Are you talking positively to yourself right now? (T+)
- Are you talking positively about others right now? (T+)
- What have you said positively today to others? (T+)
- What have you said positively today to yourself? (T+)
- What notes have you written today that show caring or love? (T+)
- What voice mail did you leave today that is a pick-me-up for the receiver? (T+)
- About whom did you talk positively on purpose today, even though that person was not present to hear your good words? (T+)
- Have you gone out of your way recently to relay why you are satisfied as a customer with the services you just received? (T+)

Have you gone out of your way recently to relay why you are satisfied as a customer with the services you just received?

- Are you able to speak positively about yourself when you feel down or lacking in confidence? (T+)
- Do you have a communications coach with whom you accurately share your negative/positive beliefs and from whom you receive accurate negative and positive feedback? (T+)
- Does speaking positively raise your spirits up? (T+)
- Are you able to be accurate about painful realities and remain on-focus with your positive talking goals? (T+)

It's probably not entirely fair to expect another person to be positive toward you when you are negative toward yourself or others, or is it? If many of those statements or propositions were new or scary to you, it'll take some time to start thinking about them seriously and incorporating them into your everyday life, routine and communication/talking patterns.

When you start "dropping in" positives, you might have the peculiar experience of a "flash of emotional intimacy" that might be quite awkward, especially with strangers. It's uncomfortable to do the new, to speak the positive, with the positive intent to accentuate the positive and accept the negative without whining. But it's worth it!

When you start "dropping in" positives, you might have the peculiar experience of a "flash of emotional intimacy" that might be quite awkward, especially with strangers.

WALKING THE POSITIVE TALK

You can walk the path of positive talk to benefit everyone. *I define "positive talks" or "positive talking" as an open display of sincere verbal or written affection without any expectation*

I define "positive talks" or "positive talking" as an open display of sincere verbal or written affection without any expectation of a return.

of a return. Ergo: You give a verbal or written gift of love with no strings attached.

The negative mind (B1-, T-) will fire back: "Yeah, I get the new talk program. (B1-, T-)" "*BUT* how am I acting genuinely when I force myself to fake being positive all of the time?" (B1-, T-) "That's just not possible." (B1-, T-) "This positive talking stuff is simply telling people what they want to hear. . .which I am strictly against." (B1-, T-) "What sense is there in acting nice when you don't approve of what's going on?" (B1-, T-) "If I've learned anything at all, (B1-, T-) I've learned that people don't listen (B1-, T-) unless you're blunt and talk tough." Now hear this accurate negative feedback, my dear reader: Aren't all of those reactions a bunch of tough talk bunk? How narrow-minded and negative can people get?

I believe relationships function best when people freely exchange positives—about an equal amount of positives going out and an equal amount of positives coming back in. I'm asking you to let go of expecting anything in return when you talk positively. Why?

WHY TALK POSITIVELY

1. ***A big reason for positive talks is first to be good/kind to yourself (E+, B1+, B2+, T+)***
2. ***Another big reason for positive talks is to be good/kind to yourself when you feel bad (E-, T+)***
3. ***An even bigger reason for positive talks is to be good/kind to yourself when you think you are bad (B1-, T+)***
4. ***Another reason for positive talks is to be accurate and positive about those times in relationships when someone behaves badly (B2-, T+) and to learn and live***
5. ***And the biggest reason of all for positive talks (T+) is to be good/kind to yourself (E+, B1+, B2+, T+) when you absolutely think and feel (B1-, E-) you are a bad person who deserves bad happenings (B2-) to befall you***

Take time today to sit yourself down and give yourself a good/ positive talking to.

PRACTICE TALKING POSITIVELY

Hey, if you can practice talking positively for 20% of your day, that's all the time it takes to check it out. Think of it as the real-life version of an amusement-park ride called the "Drop Zone," and your task is to drop genuinely positive words into the relationship mind. In fact, one of the best times to send a positive e-mail, place a positive phone call (to point out a good deed done unto you), or send a humorous card is when you feel awful and disconnected instead of awe-filled and connected.

One of the best times to send a positive e-mail, place a positive phone call (to point out a good deed done unto you), or send a humorous card is when you feel awful and disconnected instead of awe-filled and connected.

Additionally, Empathizers highly value and more easily integrate *positive words* through the five senses, while Instigators highly value and more easily integrate *positive actions* through the five senses. *Thus, E-types can hear, smell, see, touch and taste words more easily while I-types can hear, smell, see, touch and taste actions more easily.* Since you have been adopting the strengths of your opposing communicator style, you now value accurate and positive words and deeds through all the E-type and I-type senses. Things are probably looking a whole lot different by now.

Still having a hard time grasping this new communication mindset? In the next section, I've selected a few e-mails and examples of positive talk verbal and written deeds that I've recently encountered to give you a grasp of positive talking. You, too, can practice these every day if you're of a mind to.

POSITIVE TALK LIVE

Do people really talk this way? Indeed, they do. Following are some positive words that I've sent to others recently and positive words that others have sent to me to illustrate the out-in and the in-out tide of talk exchanges.

They demonstrate the talk principle *"positive out. . .positive in."* The adjacent talk principle is *"negative in. . .positive out."* The psychological translation of "positive out. . .positive in" is: "As a rule, when I am feeling and thinking negatively I will consider doing a positive oral or written deed to remind myself that I can be a friend to myself during stormy, dark passages and riotous moods."

Let's talk positively *right now:*

POSITIVE TALKING: Words I said (T+) to a **beloved teenager** struggling in confusion:

"I am proud of you because you're not running away or trying to escape these painful and confusing feelings."

POSITIVE TALKING: An e-mail to me (T+) from an **appreciative client:**

"Thank you for always being so patient and so generous with your time and guidance. I appreciate your insights and wisdom. I read a card not long ago and I thought of you and all the significant people in my life—it read 'acts of kindness warm the heart, soothe the soul and make the world turn more gently.' I am forever grateful."

POSITIVE TALKING: Words spoken (T+) by me to an **early career mentor** of mine:

"I must have been a riot to teach way back when I knew-it-all. I want you to know how much I deeply appreciate your support then, and even more now twenty-plus years later."

POSITIVE TALKING: An e-mail (T+) sent to me from my **best male buddy:**

"Gary Player, the golfer, always believed this to be true, 'The harder you work, the luckier you get.' Let's see how lucky we can get in our business and personal lives!"

POSITIVE TALKING: One of many brief e-mails of thanks (T+) I wrote to my **editor:**

"Thanks for all you are, and all you do. This book is full of heart and soul thanks to you."

POSITIVE TALKING: An encouraging e-mail my editor sent to me during a discouraging time:

"It's good. . .really tied a lot of things together. I particularly liked the conversations and sample Directive Questioning exercise. I think those, more than anything, help hammer home what really happens in negative/positive communication in real life. And every time I read a new chapter, I learn a little more about me. And that's good! Hang in there. . ."

POSITIVE TALKING: Phone call I made to the **general manager** of a BP Amoco Service Station:

"I've got to register an acclaim. Your team really helped me out of a jam the other day when my car blew up. Do you mind if I turn your team in for good behavior to headquarters?"

POSITIVE TALKING: Letter received from BP **Consumer Relations:**

"We appreciate your kind call complimenting the employees at a corporate BP Amoco Service Station. It sounded like an unfortunate situation for you, however, a little easier to handle with the positive attitude of the employees."

POSITIVE TALKING: Funny card I recently received from my **brother and sister-in-law** that read:

"Wouldn't it be nice if our lives were like VCRs. . .and we could 'fast forward' through the crummy times?"

POSITIVE TALKING: A sticky note left on my office desk from my then **five-year-old youngest daughter:**

"Hiy Dad. . .haw are you doin. . .that is ol that I watid to tel you."

POSITIVE TALKING: A note from my then **11-year-old oldest daughter** left on the nightstand:

"Dear Daddy, I love you so much! You have to stay off work and stay home longer. I really miss you! Psychologist question: 'Why mislead fear, for fear will mislead you!'"

POSITIVE TALKING: Positive talk (T+) with **my dog:**

"You're a good dog, Sierra. Thank you for being the protector of this home and family. I didn't know dogs could have such a great sense of humor!"

POSITIVE TALKING: The **telepathic canine response** (T+) sent back to her human:

"Okay, Dennis. Now walk over to the pantry. Open the pantry door. Reach inside and pull out my dog treats. Reach inside the bag and pull out two treats. Now feed me the treats while I reward you by wagging my tail. You're a good human, Dennis. I didn't know humans could take dogs so seriously!"

POSITIVE TALKING: Verbal comments made to me (T+) from an **ITI grandmother and an ETE grandfather** who are rich-in-love:
"You're a miracle worker, Dr. O'Grady. All our goals have been achieved. If I had a million dollars I'd give it to you for the peace of mind I've received."

You get the idea. Whenever you feel "bad," treat yourself to some "good" talk either in live verbal or written formats. Talk out loud to yourself if you want to, because it doesn't mean you're crazy. Moreover, use every talk avenue at your disposal. For example, I love dishing out positive voice mail instead of being frustrated by hitting an answering machine. I even sing oldies songs on my mother's voice mail for kicks. Mom saves and replays them!

It's especially a huge blast to leave positive voice mail to lighten the burdens of a listener's day while simultaneously trying to lighten your own.

ADOPTING THE STRENGTHS OF YOUR OPPOSING COMMUNICATOR STYLE

You no doubt have already been adopting many of the strengths, and perhaps, a few of the weaknesses of your opposite communicator style. Sometimes the process can feel like your eyelids are ripped open and your brain is infused with new insights. I'm glad you've been breathing deeply and don't need to be in control always and all ways!

Here are five cardinal rules of the changes you are going through:

1. *When Empathizer communicators feel free to operate equally effectively in the negative or positive Beliefs (B1-/+) mode, change happens.*
2. *When Instigator communicators feel free to operate equally efficiently in the negative or positive Emotions (E-/+) mode, change happens.*
3. *Empathizers who adopt the Instigator strengths of exploring and working in the Beliefs (B1-/+) talk mode, change fast.*
4. *In contrast, Instigators who adopt the Empathizer strengths of exploring and working in the Emotions (E-/+) talk mode, change fast.*

5. Moreover, when E-types and I-types trade off favored ways of traveling by adopting the strengths of their opposing communicator style—positive change happens in a big way for everyone.

E-TYPE CHANGE AVENUES

Now and then, you have been walking in the shoes of your opposing communicator for many miles. You let yourself go and have become far more interested in your opposite communicator viewpoint. Before now, you thought there was only one way to travel on a one-way miscommunication highway. And "they" said it couldn't be done. Well, "They say" are the world's biggest liars!

By now, you have learned as an E-type, you can get "the light came on" effect when you purposefully switch talk lanes from Emotions (E) to Beliefs (B1). That's why I coached you to be the steady Tortoise vs. the hyperactive Hare. I knew you would be changing so fast you might flip in! After all, many changes aren't easy but queasy. Hurray! You dared to go into the "discomfort zone" for a change.

Positive change occurs, for E-type styles, as depicted in Figure 30.

E-TYPE Change Avenues

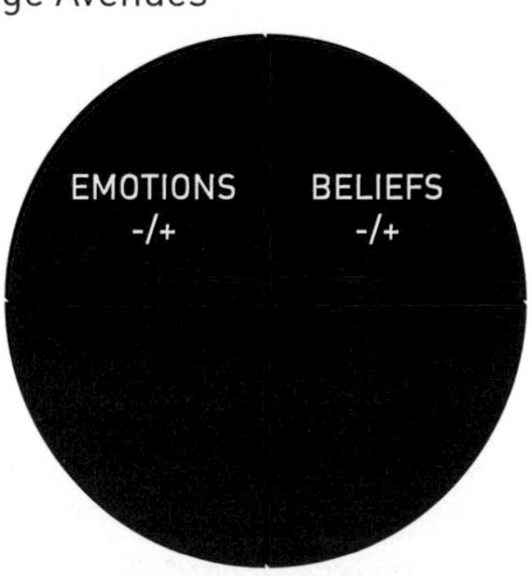

figure **#30**

E-types are prone to wearing thin with this positive belief: "I can make it work!" Empathizers can become stuck in inaccurate, negative beliefs (B1-), a negative mental thinking rut called Low Self-Esteem (LSE).

Empathizers are so very emotionally courageous and tuned-in because they can put their emotional relationship matters over the mind. Empathizers *think* they are very vulnerable when they realize how unconditionally thought of they are by others. *However, the suppressed positive thoughts of E-types are diamonds in the rough that create contentment and happiness. In coaching meetings with me, I gently prod my beloved E-types to fly in the sky of logic.*

However, the suppressed positive thoughts of E-types are diamonds in the rough that create contentment and happiness. In coaching meetings with me, I gently prod my beloved E-types to fly in the sky of logic.

And, of course, this violates the cardinal Empathizer rule of: "Why *not* keep talking about negative and positive emotions?" E-types who explore accurate negative and accurate positive beliefs reinforce positive actions (B2+) and invite you to come to The Communication Table.

I use the metaphor of The Communication Table with my trainees. What do I mean by this? Actually, the *intent of talking* is as important, and perhaps more important, than the *content of talking.* I recommend you pick a place in your home, such as the kitchen table, to be the sacred center of your serious talks. I do not recommend the bedroom, or talking willy-nilly anywhere or anytime, you feel like it. Your feelings and ideas warrant a serious sit-down melding of the emotions and mind. Actually, The Communication Table is that invisible space between you and your co-communicator where you respectfully place your issues. Maybe it's a tabletop. Maybe two favorite chairs. You pick the place that's best for you.

You and I now are sitting down at an invisible Communication Table in your and my emotional and logical minds. That's how talk works.

I-TYPE CHANGE AVENUES

I-types are prone to becoming too thick-skinned *thinking* this positive belief: "I won't mind my emotions!" Instigators can become stuck in inaccurate, negative beliefs (B1-: "I don't trust what I feel but I do trust what I think because...") that can keep them stuck in a negative emotional rut called Excessive Self-Esteem (ESE).

Instigators are so very intellectually courageous and attuned because they can put their mind over emotional-relationship matters. Instigators *feel* very vulnerable when they realize how unconditionally loved they are. *However, the suppressed positive*

However, the suppressed positive emotions of I-types are diamonds in the rough that create contentment and happiness. In coaching meetings with me, I gently prod my beloved I-types to take a dive in the ocean of emotion.

emotions of I-types are diamonds in the rough that create contentment and happiness. In coaching meetings with me, I gently prod my beloved I-types to take a dive in the ocean of emotion.

Positive change occurs, I-type style, as depicted in Figure 31.

I-TYPE Change Avenues

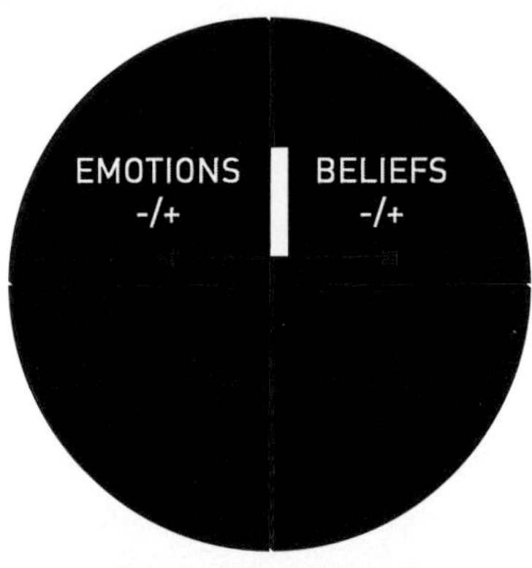

figure **#31**

And of course, this violates the cardinal Instigator rule of: "Why get into negative emotions only to lose your mind?" I-types who explore accurate negative and accurate positive emotions reinforce positive talks (T+) and invite you to come to The Communication Table.

The Communication Table is where you become who you didn't think you could ever BE, namely your opposite communicator style. Done bravely, you open new doors of awareness. *You judge less, love more. If you are an Empathizer communicator, you tend to* <u>*feel as much but think more*</u>*, for a change. If you are an Instigator communicator, you tend to* <u>*think as much but feel more*</u>*, for a change.*

Who says you and I cannot talk more positively? Just you try it and see.

E-TYPE AND I-TYPE CHANGE AVENUES

So here's the moral to the talk story that I know you can hear: Do the opposite of what you're accustomed to doing and you will get "the light switch was turned on" effect that I have been telling you about.

If you are an Empathizer communicator, *feel* (E-/+) what you do, for gosh sakes, and then explore open-mindedly what you might *think* (B-/+) to make your dreams come true. *For E-types, overall, that means working in and talking from the accurate negative/positive Beliefs (B1-/+) mode more often to affect positive change.*

Positive change occurs, E- and I-type style, as depicted in Figure 32.

E-TYPE AND I-TYPE Change Avenues

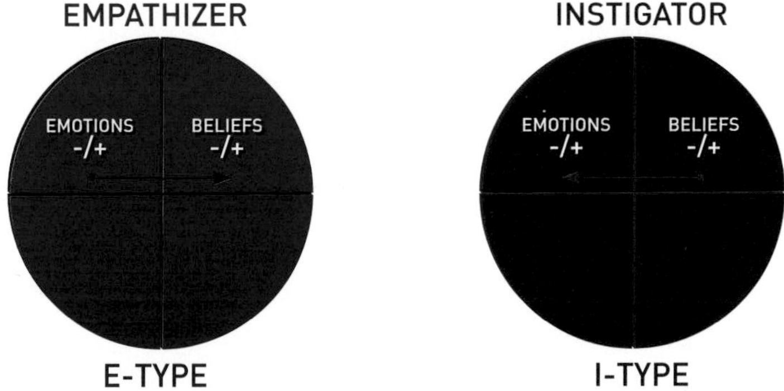

figure **#32**

If you are an Instigator communicator, *believe* (B-/+) what you do, for gosh sakes, and then explore open-emotionally what you might *feel* (E-/+) are your dreams come true. *For I-types, overall, that means working in and talking from the accurate negative/positive Emotions (E-/+) mode more often to affect positive change.*

I think it's really cool that by adopting and using the talk strengths of your other self, you are paid handsomely in terms of positive personal changes and a more positive relationship atmosphere for everyone.

A MIND IS A TERRIBLE THING TO *MISPLACE*

You've probably heard this mind-opening phrase: "A mind is a terrible thing to waste." I agree, and add this heart-opening phrase: "A mind is a terrible thing to misplace!"

So do these dual ideas really mean?

- *Negative Talks (T-): Negative out, negative in.*
- *Positive Talks (T+): Positive out, positive in.*

Positive talks work, don't take much work, and everyone benefits if they are of a mind to.

ENERGIZING THE FOUR TALK MODES

In short, the four talk modes operate as a world-wide broadcasting system, sending out your desires and receiving back your wishes much of the time. "Energy out. . .Energy in" is like breathing. You get to choose, somewhat, whether that energy is positive or negative. In my mind, focusing on positive energy is a challenge for us all.

Here's what I energetically mean by the positive/negative fueling of the four talk modes:

1. *Negative energy can be sent out from you, and negative energy can be sent to you.*
2. *Positive energy can be sent out from you, and negative energy can be sent to you.*
3. *Negative energy can be sent to you, and positive energy can be sent out from you.*
4. *Positive energy can be sent out from you, and positive energy can be sent to you.*

Often, the best choice is to talk positive when negative is in abundance. That way, you take a stand, especially during dark times that speak of the light.

And here's the reality: Your mind is more powerful than a worldwide broadcasting station. Under ideal circumstances, your mind has the ability to use hope and love to lift up humanity by adopting the mantra "Negative in. . .Positive out." Imagine the possibilities. . .in families, schools, businesses, health care, environmental awareness, personal relationships, communities, governments, international diplomacy. . .the possibilities are endless!

TWO ENERGIZING COMMUNICATION RULES

This is my message for your ears only: When you send negative energy out through your four communicator modes, you might just be unintentionally encouraging the negative to come your direction in a self-fulfilling way. The positive news: When you send positive energy out through your four communicator modes—you may receive back more positive feedback than you are accustomed to receiving.

When you send positive energy out through your four communicator modes—you may receive back more positive feedback than you are accustomed to receiving.

In other words, you grow more open-hearted and more open-minded using these two communication rules:

TALK RULE 1: Talking negatively creates and results in negative going out from you, and it encourages negative coming back in to you.

TALK RULE 2: Talking positively creates and results in positive going out from you, and it encourages positive coming back in to you.

When you send out negatives to other people, other people will many times respond in kind to your negative missives. Likewise, when you choose to send out positives to other people, other people will many more times respond in kind to your positive intentions with positive contributions. When you feel negative but talk positively—positive change happens fast.

I took my Mazda RX8 into the dealership for an oil change today. The fellow at the service desk asked me if I liked my car and I said I loved driving it. He even remembered my old car that had blown up. I said full of pep and a grin: "Man, you even remember that old car? What a mind you've got!" I seriously joked. He replied, "I remember when people are nice to me, and I forget those people who aren't!" Spoken like a true Instigator extrovert who can let the negative drop away. He then went about carefully giving me all sorts of valuable tips on how to take best care of my car, all from a causal positive conversation. And we both left the interchange feeling more positively charged than negative.

"I remember when people are nice to me, and I forget those people who aren't!"

Positive talks (T+) work, when you "go on easy."

ACCURACY MATTERS IN THE WORLD OF POSITIVE COMMUNICATION

Accuracy matters. Being exact in word and deed unleashes more of the abundant powers of your two minds. All too frequently, people unintentionally use inaccurate negatives the most.

In business or love, many of us have been burned by positive thinkers and positive talkers who use their rhetorical skills to sell us something they don't deliver.

In business or love, many of us have been burned by positive thinkers and positive talkers who use their rhetorical skills to sell us something they don't deliver. In fact, positive people who are *inaccurate* are very effective in getting their way but with consequences—they tend to be negative in their world outcomes and they tend to blow up many interpersonal relationship bridges as they march along. Keep in mind, *accuracy matters!* Being accurate about negatives and positives is where it's at.

For example, people who have panic attacks often feel like they are having a heart attack or going crazy. What kind of feeling-thought is that? Well, the panic is a very negative fear (negative Emotions mode or E-) of the negative inaccurate thought (negative Beliefs mode or B1-) that a person is dying right here and now, on the spot. How terrifying! The emotional mind and the intellectual mind are such powerhouses, both of them able to be such foolers some of the time! Our minds are ever-busy chatterboxes. Nonetheless, *we are wise to pay attention to our minds to mine positive results* by using both the emotional/logical brain(s) in accurate and positive ways within the communicator mode broadcasting system.

In the world of negative communications: Empathizer communicators are vulnerable to inaccurate/negative thinking (B1-) that pulls down their emotional mood. On the other hand, Instigator communicators are vulnerable to inaccurate/negative feelings (E-) that runs down the battery of their physical health.

In the world of negative communications: Empathizer communicators are vulnerable to inaccurate/negative thinking (B1-) that pulls down their emotional mood. On the other hand, Instigator communicators are vulnerable to inaccurate/negative feelings (E-) that runs down the battery of their physical health.

Either way, accuracy counts. To abuse a gun-and-target metaphor: "Fire. . .ready. . .aim?"

ACCURATE NEGATIVES AND POSITIVES (–/+)

Positive communicators seek foremost to be accurate about the negative and positive communicator modes (E-/+, B1-/+, B2-/+, T-/+) in order to know what to do about reality.

If you wish to be sane, not vain, here's how to tell who's talking in all of the talk transactions you say and hear:

1. ***Inaccurate or accurate negative vs. positive feelings or Emotions mode (E-/+)***
2. ***Inaccurate or accurate negative vs. positive thinking or Beliefs mode (B1-/+)***
3. ***Inaccurate or accurate negative vs. positive actions or Behaviors mode (B2-/+)***
4. ***Inaccurate or accurate negative vs. positive words or Talks mode (T-/+)***

Who's minding your mind? I hope you are because it's high time to fill your mind with positives and mine the gold that it harbors at the same time. Now you can more easily categorize in your mind whether or not a communication is inaccurate/accurate or negative/positive and from which mode the conversation is originating.

Now you can more easily categorize in your mind whether or not a communication is inaccurate/accurate or negative/positive and from which mode the conversation is originating.

BUT...

Rarely can one simple word make a big difference in any conversation, but it's possible to do a fun mental twist-and-turn with one negative word called BUT. There's magic in the spoken word and world of BUT, isn't there?

Take this new communication rule into your mind: *"In your spoken thought-sentences, the word BUT erases what you said before it, and it reinforces what you say after it."* Now promise me you won't be a fanatic and start picking on every BUT a person uses (or both of us will be butts!)

Let's take on this next subtle negative transaction for fun:

THE MAGIC OF BUT

I really want to be a far more positive communicator and get along a whole lot better BUT I'm pretty tied up at work right now. (B1+/T+, B2-/T-)

ANALYZE THIS

Imagine that the sentence above is appearing on your computer monitor. Put your cursor on the word BUT and highlight everything that has come before the BUT. Now push delete. What's been erased?

What has been deleted is this positive (B1+) thought: *I really want to be a far more positive communicator and get along a whole lot better. (B1+/T+)*

And what negative outcome or life result is reinforced because it comes after the word BUT in the transaction above? "… BUT I'm pretty tied up at work right now." (B2-/T-) Thus, you have unwittingly instructed your subconscious mind with your plucky assistance to tie together your legs and arms with tethers and then throw you in a deep pool with instructions to swim five laps. It's just not possible, no matter how strong and inspired you are.

YOUR SUBCONSCIOUS MIND IS ONLY TOO GLAD TO OBLIGE

Your four communicator modes are glad to be working for you non-stop, waking or sleeping. What you say to yourself and to others are equally powerful, especially when energized with strong emotion.

Together, let's repeat the transaction above and expand on it to imagine what your subconscious mind might interpret as the marching instructions that stem from your inaccurate/negative talk:

THE REALITY OF BUT

I really want to be a far more positive communicator and get along a whole lot better BUT I'm pretty tied up at work right now. (B1+/T+, B2-/T-)

"My dear subconscious mind: Thank you in advance for your untiring support. Here are my marching instructions for you: I need your help in the biggest way because I really don't *want to be a positive communicator and I really* don't *want to develop a loving relationship nor raise my interpersonal I.Q. I prefer instead to be frustrated and depressed. I'm serious! Thus, I might not mind a negative relationship* and *I want you to keep me very tied up at work* and *I have to feel negative for the foreseeable future by doing 'first things last' (if ever!) Got it? Likewise, when I return home from work, I want your support to complain about how nice guys and gals finish last instead of first. You're awesome, possum! Thanks for honoring my unintentional negative requests that don't accurately reflect my true desires!" (T-)*

Now I know you're going to holler loud right about now: "BUT that's not what I really meant!" Yes, with one simple word, you've just erased your true, positive intentions from being broadcasted by your four positive communicator modes.

Hey, I'm having a real fun time talking with you. I hope and trust that you are, too. Don't be too fanatical about this BUT thing, just stay focused in positive ways and many of your dreams will come true. By the way, my dear trainee, in the last sentence what positive message was *amplified (T+/B1+/B2+)* and what negative message *erased (T-/B1-/B2-)?*

PSYCHO BUT CUTE

My last client, a street-smart teen with a bag full of challenges but no troubles, was wearing a shirt with this saying on it (one that makes a startling statement in her peer world): CUTE BUT PSYCHO.

My last client, a street-smart teen with a bag full of challenges but no troubles, was wearing a shirt with this saying on it (one that makes a startling statement in her peer world): CUTE BUT PSYCHO.

You are learning the rule: The word BUT *deletes* the cute and *accentuates* the psycho. Suppose the words were transposed? Would a PSYCHO BUT CUTE message broadcast a different message to her peer world? You know the positive talk rule: A positive teen will *delete* being psycho and *accentuate* being cute. Perhaps you are becoming cute and maturely sane as we speak, too! I'm just teasing, and if I were an Instigator communicator I would add: "I was just kidding. . .don't take it so personally!"

Who among us can't love our teens for their sense of humor and grace? I know I do (T+) because I desire (E+) to.

POSITIVE TALKS EXERCISE: GIVING YOUR "BUT" A REST

Here are a few positive BUTS you can use to turn a negative into a positive. Remember, all the words that come before the word BUT in a sentence are erased, while the request that comes after the word BUT is bolded or doubled-up in your subconscious mind.

Remember, all the words that come before the word BUT in a sentence are erased, while the request that comes after the word BUT is bolded or doubled-up in your subconscious mind.

What do you request to appear in your life? What change would you like to see happen for you? Just fill in the blanks in the following and then let the power of the four communicator modes make it happen for you.

Letting It Happen: The Four Communicator Modes

I don't think I can do the new **but...**<u>*I am going to*</u>

I've been feeling bad and hopeless **but...**<u>*I will*</u>

I'm disorganized **but...**<u>*I can learn to*</u>

It's been impossible to **but...**<u>*I can*</u>

I don't want to complain **but...**<u>*I'll do anything to*</u>

You can't teach old dogs new tricks **but...**<u>*I will do*</u>

Catch it? The negative thoughts that came before the word BUT in each sentence are erased or deleted. The word BUT can be put to positive use too. Did you catch the last twist? The message "BUT can be put to positive use" has been reinforced.

I realize it might sound hokey to you, as if I'm just playing around with words. . .BUT I'm trying to make a positive point here. Your words really materialize and matter to everyone—to you and to others. So whenever possible, think and speak positively and accurately, especially during negative trials and tribulations when you and yours are tromping through the wretched and gut-wrenching emotional swamp. This is why accuracy and positive interpersonal conduct really do matter in the universal scheme of things.

THE 10 CORE OPPOSING TRAITS OF EMPATHIZERS AND INSTIGATORS

You can't be anyone other than who you were meant to be or are. Nonetheless, you are an Empathizer or an Instigator communicator and you are either an introvert or an extrovert by nature.

Let me distinguish caringly and carefully the 10 major communicator differences that truly matter to you and me so we can better understand how E-types and I-types drive down different lanes on the two-way communicator highway. Let us not judge rashly, nor flip off one another.

Quickly, 10 opposing communicator traits of Empathizer and Instigator communicators you have been feeling and thinking about lately are:

1. Interpersonal sensitivity vs. interpersonal insensitivity

Empathizers live in an ocean of emotion when tuning into their interpersonal relationships. Instigators prefer to live in the intellectual world and are insensitive to challenging emotions, preferring instead to give them no mind. E-types impose their mood on other people, while I-types impose their thoughts on other people.

2. Attentive listening vs. selective listening

Empathizers listen attentively with the goal of understanding the co-communicator's frame of reference and walking in their shoes. Instigators, on the other hand, listen selectively with the goal of coming up with a plan or advice to fix a problem.

3. The need to be liked vs. the need to be powerful

Empathizers strive to be liked and approved of, while Instigators strive solely and only to be powerful change agents. E-types try to be nice and politically correct, preferring not to stir up trouble, while I-types always want to be right and in the thick of all the action.

4. Accepting and including vs. qualifying and excluding

Empathizers seek to accept and include all co-communicators' viewpoints, while Instigators carefully qualify their opinions and exclude others' opinions that aren't logical or helpful to the issue at hand. E-types thus view I-types as hurried and intolerant, while I-types view E-types as moving too slow, and being too open-minded.

5. Discussing vs. debating

Empathizers dislike heated debates and instead prefer to discuss calmly the issues at hand and not to get too emotional about it all. Instigators, on the other hand, are great debaters and are more comfortable being aggressive and verbally standing up for a point of view they believe in.

6. Winning isn't everything vs. winning is all there is

Empathizers want everyone to win in the relationship, even if it might be at their own expense. Instigators keep a scorecard in all of their endeavors to determine if they are getting ahead. E-types are more mood-centered, while I-types are more thought-centered.

E-types are more mood-centered, while I-types are more thought-centered.

7. Let's problem solve now vs. the problem will resolve itself in time

When Empathizers feel upset, they want to talk about the problem *now* to solve it as quickly as possible. Instigators believe if you let off steam about a problem and give it time, the problem may not be as important in the *future.*

8. Anger-in vs. anger-out

Empathizers feel bad when they feel mad, whereas Instigators feel good when they feel mad. E-type introverts and I-type introverts alike are more prone to hold grudges and believe less in forgiving and forgetting. Instead, they believe that getting even and evening the score puts them ahead.

9. Change cautious vs. change friendly

Empathizers struggle with changes beyond their control and are conservative when considering major life changes such as investing, pursuing a business enterprise, re-careering or moving. Conversely, Instigators pursue change with a passion and can even change what they shouldn't touch with a 10-foot pole.

10. Tense under pressure vs. cool under pressure

Empathizers struggle to stay calm during a crisis, while Instigators are psyched up by the pressures of a crisis. E-types' psychological energy is drained by unsettling crisis events, while I-types' psychological energy is pumped up when the heat is on.

These 10 attitude skills are just a few of the interesting differences that make co-communicators such a diverse lot.

I want you to be a flexible communicator who uses the core strengths (and weaknesses) of your opposing Empathizer or Instigator communicator style in order to accomplish positive talks and to do it well. Adopt the strengths, and respect the Achilles heel, of your opposing communicator/personality type. That day will come.

And when it does, it will be a day of bewilderment and wonder.

Next, I wish to cover the topic of avoidable communication accidents that happen too often...and the regrettable relationship bridge blow-ups that happen too often as well.

NEGATIVE TALKS VS. POSITIVE TALKS

When you feel anxious or afraid, you are more likely to make communication mistakes by cutting across talk lanes.

Empathizers who feel negative are prone to *doing something negative (B2-)* that blows up the relationship bridge. In contrast, Instigators who think negative are prone to *saying something negative (T-)* that blows up the relationship bridge. The cardinal rule, therefore, is this: whenever possible, do not do or say anything to make matters worse when you feel anxious and stressed.

The main point of talking positively is to continue the use of the Directive Questioning tool. Does it matter whether the negative statements are accurate or inaccurate? Yes, it does, and that's one of the reasons for asking more questions to get at the truth. Get a sense of how you can feel (E-) negatively and believe negatively (B1-) BUT also how you can still respond flexibly and positively.

POSITIVE TALKS EXERCISE: CHANGING NEGATIVE TALKS TO POSITIVE TALKS

In this exercise, I am combining the negative Talks (T-) mode and the positive Talks (T+) mode with the Directive Questioning tool. The combination of all three makes this exercise far more complex and complete.

Negative talk creates debates that go round and round. They also put off genuine talks and can become emotional escalations or competitions. Positive talk, on the other hand, seeks to hear the truth in a spirit of brainstorming solutions to problems, while showing caring and respect.

Hurtful words and negative tit-for-tat debates occur in the negative Talks (T-) mode. Likewise, your non-verbal "skull talk" is either negative or positive, typically some of both. Confronting negative talks positively involves these five steps:

1. *Hearing the negative transaction (T-)*
2. *Framing a follow-up question to confront the negative without arguing (B1+)*

3. Asking a directive question (T+)

4. Listening to the answer (E+/B+)

5. Asking another directive question if desired (T+)

Ready for some proactive talk practice? Get the feel for *responding vs. reacting* to these negative transactions with positive exploratory questions. As idealistic as these examples sound, they seek to make the point that you can ask a question in response to a declarative that is inaccurate and negative. Here we go:

A. Negative Talks Mode (T-): What have I done to make you hate me so much?
Directive Questioning Tool (T+): Why do you assume I hate you? How do you know I hate you—by what actions? In your mind, what have you done to make me hate you? What do you see me doing presently that is hating vs. loving?

B. Negative Talks Mode (T-): You're playing mind games with me.
Directive Questioning Tool (T+): Why do you think I'm playing mind games with you? What mind games am I playing? How are you affected by the mind games? What emotions are we avoiding by playing mind games?

C. Negative Talks Mode (T-): Why don't you ever talk to me?
Directive Questioning Tool (T+): Why do you think that I don't value talking to you? What would you like to talk about? What topics do you feel I avoid discussing? What issues are on your list that we need to discuss?

D. Negative Talks Mode (T-): It's all your fault.
Directive Questioning Tool (T+): What's my fault? Why do you think I'm to blame? What have I done to make you think I'm to blame

for all this? In your opinion, how did I make this happen? How would we act or talk differently if this issue weren't the fault of either one of us?

E. Negative Talks Mode (T-): You don't find me attractive anymore.
Directive Questioning Tool (T+): What do you think makes you unattractive? What have I said or done that makes you think I don't find you attractive any more? Is there some part of your appearance that makes you feel I don't find you attractive any more? Are you feeling attractive? Are you trying to make me feel guilty to push me to change something?

F. Negative Talks Mode (T-): That was a cheap shot and a low blow.
Directive Questioning Tool (T+): What did I say that was a cheap shot in your mind? How do you think I'm fighting unfairly? What would you rather have had me say? What low blow do you feel I discounted you with? What suggestions do you have so we can fight more fairly?

G. Negative Talks Mode (T-): You aren't being fair or doing your fair share around the house.
Directive Questioning Tool (T+): Why do you think I'm being unfair and unequal? Tell me, what do you consider to be doing my fair share around here? What's on the top of your list that needs doing around here that you would appreciate help with? Is there anything I can do to make our relationship feel more fair and equal to you right now?

H. Negative Talks Mode (T-): After all I've done for you, this is how you treat me?

Directive Questioning Tool (T+): What do you think you've done for me that I don't appreciate? Are you doing too much and then resenting it? Do you think I want to take advantage of you? What are you thinking I owe you in our relationship? What bad treatment are you talking about, and what type of treatment would you prefer? If I don't agree with you, do you think I'm treating you badly, and feel mad?

I. Negative Talks Mode (T-): You don't have time for me.
Directive Questioning Tool (T+): Why do you feel I won't make time for our relationship? What have I done or said to make you feel ignored? What type of positive time would you like to spend together? What makes you think I won't make time for you to do pleasurable activities? Does this make you feel you are unimportant to me?

J. Negative Talks Mode (T-): Why do you keep trying to control me?
Directive Questioning Tool (T+): Why do you think I want to control your life? How do you think I want you to behave differently to please me? Why would I want to anger you by controlling you? Control you how, in your view, to change what? What would you like to see me change? Why do you think I want to make you become someone you aren't?

K. Negative Talks Mode (T-): There you go again making excuses about why we can't be romantic tonight.
Directive Questioning Tool (T+): What type of romance are you expecting tonight? Why do you think I make excuses not to be close? What excuse are you referring to that I typically use? Are you disappointed or

angry with me? Are you suggesting we have a date night? In your opinion, what keeps us from enjoying intimacy more often?

L. Negative Talks Mode (T-): Your mood is about as much fun as a den full of rattlesnakes.
Directive Questioning Tool (T+): What mood do you sense I'm in? What am I doing or saying that indicates to you I'm in a bad mood? How does my mood bring down your mood? Are you saying I bring home my work woes through the door? Do you have any suggestions about what we can do to pick up the mood around here?

M. Negative Talks Mode (T-): You won't ever be happy!
Directive Questioning Tool (T+): Why wouldn't I want to be happy? What do you hear me being so unhappy about? Do you think I'm unhappy with you? How do you hear me being unhappy in our relationship? Do you see me being resistive to happiness? Do you feel happy in our relationship?

N. Negative Talks Mode (T-): You'll never be satisfied!
Directive Questioning Tool (T+): Why wouldn't I want to feel satisfied and contented? What do you hear me being so dissatisfied about? Do you think I'm dissatisfied with you? How do you see me as discontented in our relationship? Do you see me being resistive to contentment? Do you feel satisfied in our relationship?

O. Negative Talks Mode (T-): You just don't understand!
Directive Questioning Tool (T+):
What don't I understand? How am I misunderstanding you? How could I

understand you better? What could I do to make you feel more understood? How do you feel confused about me? What can we do to make our relationship more positive? What positive goals do we need to set and move forward on?

Positive questions are better than negative answers most of the time when both parties talk around The Communication Table. Directive questions seek to tie down a misunderstanding during tense times so both communicators can be accurate and negative or positive depending on the situation.

Positive questions are better than negative answers most of the time when both parties talk around The Communication Table. Directive questions seek to tie down a misunderstanding during tense times so both communicators can be accurate and negative or positive depending on the situation. Accuracy counts for so much!

You will know you have grown enormously in your ability to communicate when one day, as you drive along the communication highway, you see a signpost. That signpost will appear the moment you feel like saying the negative *BUT* say the positive, instead! It is about time for some positive change, isn't it?

COMMUNICATOR TYPECASTING

I've typecast personality by asking this single question to a person: "Are you more ingoing or introverted or more outgoing or extroverted?" I've found this simple question to be a reliable indicator of personality type.

I typecast my co-communications into one of four categories whenever possible: Empathizer introverts, Empathizer extroverts, Instigator introverts, Instigator extroverts. I liken them to the four fingers on my left hand. I've typecast personality by asking this single question to a person: *"Are you more ingoing or introverted or more outgoing or extroverted?"* I've found this simple question to be a reliable indicator of personality type. Often, a person may seem one way but be the other way.

By now, you are processing both intuitively and intellectually a communicator/personality profile for Empathizer and Instigator communicators (including introvert and extrovert types) of people you work and play with. Way to *GO!* And by now, you realize the type of communicator that you are is the best communication fit that you can ever be for the one and only you. Nonetheless, you are also adopting the strengths (and sometimes the weaknesses) of your opposing communicator type.

Let me more deeply explain how you are in relation to four different communicator/personality combinations that do really matter in matters of work and romance.

TYPECASTING: THE FOUR COMMUNICATOR SUBTYPES

As you've learned, there are four communicator subtypes when you combine Empathizer-type communicator together with introvert or extrovert type and when you combine Instigator-type communicator together with introvert or extrovert. Naturally, the four communicator subtypes have all four communicator modes to talk through in either positive or negative ways.

No subtype is better or worse, they're just different ways of experiencing the world. Our purpose here is to create new places in your mind where you can hold these four subtypes of communicators. You can do it! I have faith in you, and ask you to have no doubt about it! I have been discovering that certain subtype pairings seem to be more effective in business and romance.

These, then, are the four communicator/personality types that you are in daily interaction with:

1. ETI or Empathizer-type communicators who are introverts

ETI's are emotionally strong E-types who are deep as an emotional ocean. They are interpersonally tuned in, have a high interpersonal I.Q., enjoy solitude and retreat, and like being alone in their own company. ETI's need to recharge after social events, can be leaders if they believe in the cause, and can come across interpersonally as shy or pushovers unless they know you well. Mindset: "There are no right or wrong emotions where I come from." In romance, ETI's may need a fellow introvert, usually but not always, also an E-type. In business, ETI's are frequently behind-the-scenes workhorses who have a tremendous ability to focus and get a job done well.

2. ETE or Empathizer-type communicators who are extroverts

ETE's are emotionally strong E-types who can see and understand complex interpersonal and social issues. ETE's comprehend and put to positive use relationship rules of good conduct because they are inter-relationally so tuned in. ETE's have a high interpersonal I.Q., enjoy togetherness and interaction, like the company of others, recharge in social events, can be leaders if they believe in the cause and can come across interpersonally as a little intense or moody.

Mindset: "Where I come from, even shallow is deep." In romance, ETE's may need an extrovert, usually but not always, an I-type. In business, ETE's are frequently team leaders who have a tremendous ability to motivate colleagues/coworkers through their example of hard work, humor and smarts.

3. ITI or Instigator-type communicators who are introverts

ITI's are mentally strong I-types who are in-going, creative entrepreneurial geniuses, natural-born leaders, and who tend to be abrupt and prone to going to extremes. Interpersonally they can come across very blunt or forceful. Mindset: "Don't waste my time, either lead or get out of my way." In romance, ITI's are more likely to be with a coupled co-communicator who is an E-type whether ETI or ETE. In business, ITI's synergistically (1+1=3) team up particularly well with ITE's.

4. ITE or Instigator-type communicators who are extroverts

ITE's are mentally strong I-types who are socially very out-going, go-forward entrepreneurial geniuses, natural-born leaders who come across very positively interpersonally. Mindset: "There are no strangers because I make friends wherever I go." In romance, ITE's may need a fellow extrovert, usually, but not always, an E-type. In business, ITE's synergistically (1+1=3) team up particularly well with ITI's.

Wow! Aren't these some fascinating differences when looked at this way? And don't these four communicator subtypes hold some fascinating implications for marriage/divorce, parenting, business partnering, teacher-learner matching, finding the person of your dreams, entrepreneurship, adolescence, and many other life challenges? You bet.

TYPECASTING OPPOSES STEREOTYPING

Typecasting is the opposite of stereotyping. Typecasting requires an open mind whereas stereotyping requires a closed mind.

I hope you are now typecasting those you know and love as you go about your daily school routine or workday. It's a blast when you're able to put people in the communications limelight in positive ways without stereotyping! It's also an *effective* and *ethical* way to build a bridge between your mind muscle and heart muscle.

As you might have suspected, I typecast all of my clients and likewise typecast the close people in their lives with whom they may struggle. *Currently, I have discovered that about 40% of communicators are Empathizers and 60% of communicators are Instigators.* It makes the work so much easier and positive and results happen in our first meeting together! Moreover, I did a little out-of-office typecasting myself today for the fun of it. I mentioned to you earlier in this work about my healer chiropractic physician friend who has helped thousands move out of pain. He is in independent practice, the star of the show, an Instigator-type extrovert, or ITE, who has really amounted to something *big.*

I have discovered that about 40% of communicators are Empathizers and 60% of communicators are Instigators.

Guess what I found when I typecast his three positive female office staff? All three of his female officemates are Empathizer-type extroverts, or ETE's. From the four subtypes above, do you think the team is probably hitting on all 12 cylinders although imperfect? Yes, you probably could tell. Certain types seem to work together best in certain situations. These E-type females are focused, customer friendly and unafraid of hard work and thus make the doctor's healing show a public happening from behind-the-scenes.

YOUR DIRECTOR'S CHAIR

Of course, you have a large say in how you direct the movie script of your life. Eric Berne and Claude Steiner, in developing the theory of "life script," made sure we knew we have a large say in what we say and do.

Let's bring it on home for now. Let's get personal. Are you talking and behaving like an Empathizer communicator or an Instigator communicator today? As well, on the personality spectrum, are you more ingoing or introverted or more outgoing or extroverted today? Let's typecast you and yours in the storyline.

Pick a director's chair to sit in from these four chairs:

1. *Are you TALKING (T) AND ACTING (B2) like an <u>Empathizer introvert</u> communicator today?*
2. *Are you TALKING (T) AND ACTING (B2) like an <u>Empathizer extrovert</u> communicator today?*
3. *Are you TALKING (T) AND ACTING (B2) like an <u>Instigator introvert</u> communicator today?*

4. Are you TALKING (T) AND ACTING (B2) like an Instigator extrovert communicator today?

When you know your communicator style, you can pick up the strengths of your opposing style while more fully appreciating your own strengths without embarrassment. How can it get any better than this?

Get this: Positive communicators don't drive down the two-way communicator highway with their wheels off.

Get this: Positive communicators don't drive down the two-way communicator highway with their wheels off.

TAKING A TURN AT NON-BLAMING TYPECASTING

Would you like to take a turn and try your hand at typecasting without condemning or boxing someone into a bloody corner?

How about this positive mental exercise: Chances are that you have children or grandchildren who are in school or college. If you don't have kids or grandkids, develop a mental image of a nephew or niece or a close friend's child. Now which one of the four subtypes above would you say best typecasts the child or grandchild? Doing so can be a little tricky because you can't ask them directly if they are more introverted (ingoing) or more extroverted (outgoing). And I've found that the person himself or herself is a better estimator of being an introvert or an extrovert than family members.

Nonetheless, start with the Empathizer vs. Instigator communicator designations in first and second order in the structure of the following sentences:

- Is she/he more *sensitive or insensitive?*
- Is he/she more *emotional or logical?*
- Is she/he more *thin-skinned or thick-skinned?*
- Does he/she dislike *arguing or enjoy debating?*
- Is she/he more *easy-going or a strong personality type?*
- Does he/she *compromises easily or competes fiercely?*

If your loved one is sensitive, emotional, thin-skinned, dislikes arguing, is easy-going and compromises easily, then your co-communicator is likely an Empathizer communicator.

Of course, the first part of each question is the E-type preference while the second part of each question is the I-type preference. *If your loved one is sensitive, emotional, thin-skinned, dislikes arguing, is easy-going and compromises easily, then your co-communicator is likely an Empathizer communicator.*

On the other hand, *if your loved one is insensitive, logical, thick-skinned, enjoys debating, is a strong personality type and competes fiercely, then your co-communicator is likely an* *Instigator communicator.* Now all we have to do is add the personality type. Is she/he or he/she more ingoing (introverted) or outgoing (extroverted) in his or her inner-personal world in your opinion?

If your loved one is insensitive, thick-skinned, enjoys debating, is a strong personality type and competes fiercely, then your co-communicator is likely an Instigator communicator.

Now do you know your loved one's communicator type? Are you able to work with it? Stretch with me here: I know it can be a little tricky because you can't ask loved ones directly this instant if they are more introverted (ingoing) or more extroverted (outgoing). Moreover, some of them may be too young to understand the terms. Nonetheless, does your child, grandchild, niece or nephew tend to be more ingoing or more outgoing?

This mental exercise cues your mind to distinguish between communicator type and personality type, affording a new category in your brain. Personally, I have taken scores of outstanding classes and read dozens of fine books on personality and I have not had a single class in communicator types and modes of communication.

I believe there is "know" better moment than the present one.

I believe there is "know" better moment than the present one.

TYPECASTING TODAY IN THE FOUR COMMUNICATOR/PERSONALITY SUBTYPES

Let's make our best guess and typecast the person in your mind one at a time into one of the four communicator/personality categories. Don't fret if you make a mistake because it shall soon be corrected.

Here are the four communicator/personality subtype categories, again with a brief description of each one:

Communicator Type 1: An Empathizer-type (E-type) communicator who is an introvert or **ETI.** The *Empathizer introvert* is a communicator who is emotionally sensitive, prefers emotional solutions to logical solutions, and is interpersonally intuitive.

Communicator Type 2: An Empathizer-type (E-type) communicator who is an extrovert or **ETE.** The *Empathizer extrovert* is a communicator who is emotionally sensitive, prefers emotional solutions to logical solutions, and is interpersonally effective.

Communicator Type 3: An Instigator-type communicator (I-type) who is an introvert or **ITI.** The *Instigator introvert* is a communicator who is emotionally insensitive, prefers the mind rule over emotions, and is interpersonally intuitive.

Communicator Type 4: An Instigator-type (I-type) communicator who is an extrovert or **ITE.** The *Instigator extrovert* is a communicator who is emotionally insensitive, prefers the mind rule over emotions, and is interpersonally effective.

So let's put this together a little tighter now. Let's begin with your communicator and personality subtype to reinforce your thinking and to encourage you to visit and explore these four communicator categories daily.

POSITIVE TALKS EXERCISE: SUBTYPE THIS!

When I was first learning the theory, I subtyped myself and then I subtyped my wife and kids, family and friends, clients and work associates.

In fact, as I wandered around in my mind and life I thought: "What subtype was Forrest Gump?" "I wonder what subtype Marilyn Monroe was?" "I wonder what subtype Elton John is, someone who sang so poignantly about Marilyn Monroe and the demise of Princess Diana?" (I met Elton John early on in his career in the early 70s and he was *so* genuine!) Get this: I think Rocky (both the boxer and the squirrel) was an Instigator introvert. I think Rocky's beloved, Adrianne, was an Empathizer introvert (and was she hot, Rock!) But who can tell for sure? I also think Beatle legend John Lennon was an Instigator introvert while Beatle teammate Paul McCartney was an Instigator extrovert. What a perfect match-up in the entrepreneurial world! I raved about Paul's confession that all the Beatles music that needed to have been sung was done. Let's move on, mate!

In these next four brief questions, I will simply ask you to typecast only your communicator/personality subtype, your oldest child's, your grandchild's, your niece's/nephew's subtype to keep it simple.

Here we go:

Communicator/Personality Subtype				
My subtype is:	ETI	ETE	ITI	ITE
My oldest child's subtype is:	ETI	ETE	ITI	ITE
My oldest grandchild's subtype is:	ETI	ETE	ITI	ITE
My oldest niece/nephew's subtype is:	ETI	ETE	ITI	ITE

Given your collective subtypes, how close together in fit are you? Do your subtypes clash or mesh really well? Now read the categories above again with your special people in mind. Are your loved ones accurately portrayed in the subtype overview descriptions?

Here we go a-typecasting!

FAMILY OF ORIGIN TYPECASTING

Family of origin is something we all hail from, for better or worse. You can choose your friends but you can't choose your family.

In my case, I grew up in a traditional blue-collar family with high pride. Don't get my Irish up! Let's typecast for a change of view and venue.

What type is/are your mom(s)?

My mom is an Instigator-type extrovert or ITE because she fiercely led the household as a stay-at-home mom and she liked to socialize with extended family and neighbors.

What type is/are your dad(s)?

Dad was an Instigator-type introvert or ITI because he mindfully financially provided for the family by working at General Motors and was a man of few words who loved to tromp in nature. Thus, mom and dad matched on communicator type, and were opposite on personality type.

What type is/are your brother(s) or sister(s)?

Brother Al is an Instigator-type extrovert or ITE, matching exactly our mother's type. When Al was a teenager, I remember him announcing that he would retire in his early 50s and move to Florida. I-type Al led that charge and is now retired in Florida enjoying friends and flying.

What type are you?

And my type? Have you guessed it yet? You should have a pretty darn good idea by now and I'm still not saying!

My oldest daughter, Erin, typecast me perfectly on April Fool's Day. I made her vow to keep it a secret. Now don't fret if you're puzzling about the exact typecast of those you know and love. . .or those you wish you didn't know but frustrate you. You will make it right sooner than later.

More proactive practice is on the way! Sooner than sooner, you will come up with the correct typology. Take it slowly because we are in no hurry. Remember, nice guys and gals always finish first even though they may lag behind for a while in the race between the tortoise and the hare.

Remember, nice guys and gals always finish first even though they may lag behind for a while in the race.

Anyway, typecast away today and listen for differences in talks that you never heard or noticed before.

TALKING ABOUT TALK

Now let's have a little fun, shall we? Each talk mode has positive or negative consequences, and each mode is inaccurate/accurate and negative/positive. That's how it all works out all right, right?

Check it out in Figure 33.

Negative And Positive TALKING

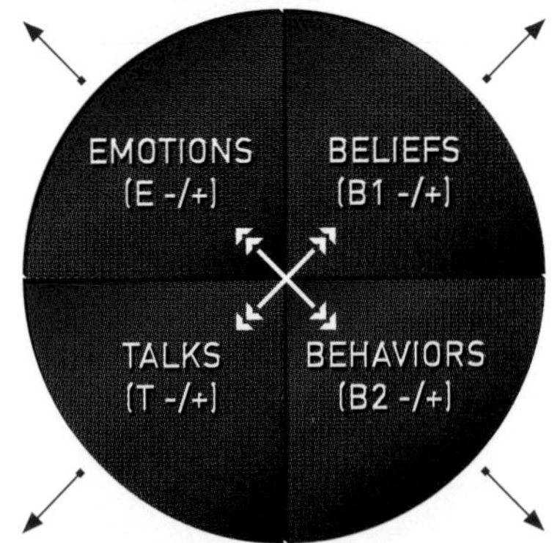

figure **#33**

So what might each communicator mode say during a car ride when they participate individually in a group chat?

EMOTIONS (E) TALK MODE

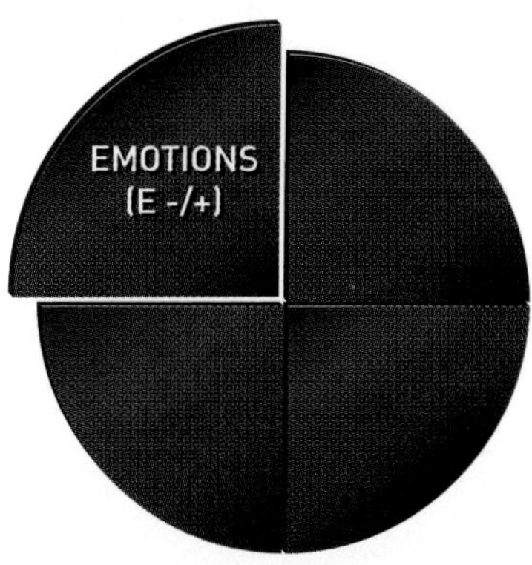

figure **#34**

Hi, my name is Emotions (E)

I am driving. My name means that I speak in terms of *feelings,* whether negative/positive or inaccurate/accurate. I have all kinds of big and small feelings such as sad, mad, scared and glad. I can overpower Beliefs (B-/+), but not always. I am very sensitive and tuned in. When I change talk lanes too fast, I zip into negative Behaviors (B2-) by doing something unexpectedly negative, which guarantees my fellow co-communicators will *feel* mad at me.

I fight with negative Beliefs (B1-) about who has the power and who should be in charge. When I team up with positive Beliefs (B1+) and we work together as a team—positive change happens fast. Can you believe it?

BELIEFS (B1) TALK MODE

figure **#35**

Hi, my name is Beliefs (B1)

I am driving. My name means that I speak in terms of *thoughts,* whether negative/positive or inaccurate/accurate. Since I don't have feelings, I have all kinds of big and small ideas about how to fix things and make things better. I can overpower Emotions (E-/+), but not always. I am very logical and analytical. When I change talk lanes too fast, I zip into negative Talks (T-), and say mean things that will cause my fellow co-communicators to be mad at me and *think* poorly of me. I fight with negative Emotions (E-) about who has the power and who should be in charge. When I team up with Emotions (E-/+) and we work together as a team—positive change happens fast. Can you believe it?

BEHAVIORS (B2) TALK MODE

figure **#36**

Hi, my name is Behaviors (B2)

I am riding. My name means that I speak in terms of *actions,* whether negative/positive or inaccurate/accurate. Since I don't feel or think, I am free to do what I want for better or for worse. I can overpower Talks (-/+), but not always. I am very action-driven and data-defined. Why would I mind taking a back seat to Emotions (E-/+) or Beliefs (B1-/+) when nothing of importance can happen without me? Talks (T-) fights with me in the backseat because both of us know *actions (B2-/+) speak louder than words (T-/+).* What's all the commotion about? I am the "motion" in *emotion* and the "be" in *beliefs* and nothing takes action or flight without ME. When I team up with Talks (T+) and we work together as a team—positive change happens fast. Can you believe it?

TALKS (T) TALK MODE

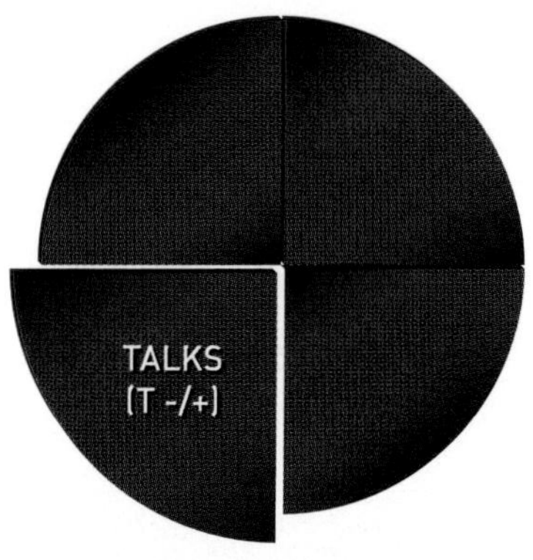

figure **#37**

Hi, my name is Talks (T)

I am always taking a back seat to everything and everyone. My name means that I speak in terms of *words,* whether negative/positive or inaccurate/accurate. Sitting in the back seat, I sometimes feel excluded, unwanted and lonely. I enjoy talking about anything to anyone about everything, but who goes out of their way to talk or listen to me? I love the exact usage of words. I feel excluded by Behaviors (B-/+), and I feel more than a little abused by Beliefs (B-/+), both of whom use me to make negative points on their behalf. I enjoy it when everyone is talking intelligently and passionately at the same time, because words do matter. I don't claim to be particularly emotional or brainy, so don't take offense when I'm just joking! I know I can promise you the moon but sometimes deliver dirt. I never mean to be mean, so why won't you believe me when I tell you it's not my fault? When I team up with Behaviors (B2+) and we work together as a team—positive change happens fast. Can you believe it?

Whoa. I would have never guessed that interpersonal talks (T) would play the poor-me victim violin and feel so rejected. In fact, negative/inaccurate Talks (T-) sounds awfully like the talk mode of the abused stepchild, ever abandoned and left out in the cold without clothes. Who would have figured that the spoken word, whether negative or positive, would carry such a wallop? Now we know.

Let's pull together now for plenty of positive talk (T+). We need it now more than ever because there is precious little time to lose or abuse.

WHEN YOU SLING MUD, YOU LOSE GROUND

H. L. Connelly, my high school speech teacher and early-on psychology mentor, was fond of thoughtful quotes that could make you feel differently, think differently and act differently. One of my all-time favorites: "When you sling mud, you lose ground."

One of my all-time favorites: "When you sling mud, you lose ground."

Translated, "When you sling mud, you lose ground" means that whenever you or I focus…focus…focus on the negative, we lose out! And we really lose out big time when we over-focus on the inaccurate negative or all those internal half-truths fueled by fear and blame.

Whenever you blame someone else or you blame yourself, you lose ground. A colleague, Dr. Jimmy Johnson, who co-led forensic psychiatry groups with me, was fond of saying: "When you sling back manure that has been thrown at you, who is responsible for making your hands dirty?"

Although you know in your heart that revenge is sweet and terribly fattening, you punish others you judge as not doing what you want or expect. You and I want it our way, and if we can't have it our way, we want the inferior one (whoever that is) to hit the highway! We rationalize (B1-) that it's the only way to teach the offender a proper lesson (B2-) and to let the offending co-communicator really know how bad they've made you feel. But isn't your feeling bad (E-), bad enough?

What a storyline: "If you hurt me I have the right and the duty to hurt you back and then some!" in order to educate you in proper relationship protocol. Once again, it's a manure sandwich disguised as a bologna sandwich that is pure baloney.

E-types are prone to stuffing or saving their anger (E-/+) while I-types are prone to releasing or distributing their anger (E-/+). E-types who stuff their anger and hide their heads in the sand like ostriches aren't any better off than I-types who puff out their chests in anger and thump them like baboons. There is a time, place and season to hold or fold your anger, hand-hold positive anger and work through negative anger as best you can.

E-types are prone to stuffing or saving their anger while I-types are prone to releasing or distributing their anger. E-types who stuff their anger and hide their heads in the sand like ostriches aren't any better off than I-types who puff out their chests in anger and thump them like baboons.

Usually, slinging negative anger around hurts you (the bearer) and everyone (the receiver) equally poorly most of the time. Look at it this way: If I give you my negative anger, it is a gift that keeps on giving. Or look at it differently: If you hold onto my negative anger, I don't have to, which isn't fair to me at all (and not fair to you either?)

THE BOOMERANG EFFECT: "WHAT GOES AROUND COMES AROUND!" (INCLUDING POSITIVE PAYBACKS)

Negative talks (T-) tend to make you and your co-communicators feel mad and disconnected, while positive talks (T+) tend to make you feel glad and connected, no matter whether you are an Empathizer or Instigator.

Negative Talks (T-) tend to make you and your co-communicators feel mad and disconnected, while positive Talks (T+) tend to make you feel glad and connected, no matter whether you are an Empathizer or Instigator.

"What goes around comes around, including positive paybacks" is a rule I've found to be true in my life experience. I see it as a razor-sharp boomerang I throw out, either positive or negative, that later comes circling back around to help or hinder me. This positive belief encourages me to think before I strike back in blind anger. Thus, I'm requiring myself to use my anger in healthy ways that buttress relationship bridges instead of blowing them up. Honestly, I misspeak too often for my own good, but I keep trying to manage my mouth better.

Your life is a mixture of negatives and positives, coming into you, going out from you. Your mind is in constant communication with the world, a huge broadcasting system to make your positive goals come to life. You want to minimize "noise" or distractions and maximize positive output. In general, I think we all agree that dealing in the negative expands the negative, while dealing in the positive expands the positive.

In general, I think we all agree that dealing in the negative expands the negative, while dealing in the positive expands the positive.

"Negative in. . .positive out" could mean you deal constructively, responsibly and responsively with negatives tossed your way and dish out positives as you go along your life highway. This isn't a guilt trip or some type of religious propaganda meant to make you behave, either. I simply trust that I've made the case to you that when you send positives out into the world, there is a greater likelihood that you will receive a "boomerang" effect of receiving more positives flying right back into your life.

I simply trust that I've made the case to you that when you send positives out into the world, there is a greater likelihood that you will receive a "boomerang" effect of receiving more positives flying right back into your life.

The rejection syndrome is a circular series of communicated negative emotions (E-) and negative beliefs (B1-) that send your mood and self-esteem spiraling downward quickly into a vast vortex. But by accepting yourself, you unleash positive changes. *Empathizers change faster when they switch from Emotions (E-) mode to Beliefs (B1+) mode, while Instigators change faster when they switch from Beliefs (B1-) mode to Emotions (E+) mode. The power of change works in reverse for the two types.*

Likewise, begin to wonder if sending out negatives or sounding like a broken record of complaints might just co-create more negatives coming back into your life. The talk exercises I have given throughout this book are enormous lifelong challenges to help you talk about love instead of hate. Do not be dismayed when recipients of your positive talk may daze off in amazement or puzzlement.

Do not be dismayed when recipients of your positive talk may daze off in amazement or puzzlement.

That's okay because you're talking positively first for yourself, and secondly for the wellbeing of others. You come first. Only when you begin to take care of and pay attention to yourself first can you begin to take care of and pay attention to others.

LET'S TALK ABOUT HEALTHY ANGER

The intent of healthy or useful anger is never to destroy. Negative anger is the major culprit that undermines positive interrelations.

"Good" or positive anger motivates you to make "good" or positive happenings for you and yours. In particular, healthy anger strives to: Force a change in the status quo, to get someone to do something differently, to let go of the old, to make something new happen in your business or personal life, to receive a response instead of being ignored, to be treated as an equal instead of a subordinate, to make your family function better as a team, to live a life of meaning instead of a life of quiet desperation, to make your voice count, to leave the world a better place, to redress grievances through healthy discourse.

In short, positive anger (E+) claims that when things go wrong (B2-), they can be fixed (B2+). Bill Cornell, a Training and Supervising Member of Transactional Analysis, outlines how women and men can choose to think negatively (B1-) or positively (B1+) and inaccurately or accurately about their healthy anger:

Positive anger claims that when things go wrong, they can be fixed.

1. Good feelings make you good. (B1-)

2. Bad feelings make you bad. (B1-)

3. People who make you feel good are good. (B1-)

4. People who make you feel bad are bad. (B1-)

5. Anger is a bad feeling. (B1-)

6. When I feel angry I am bad. (B1-)

7. People who are angry with me are bad. (B1-)

8. When I'm angry, there's something wrong with me. (B1-)

9. When you are angry at me, something is wrong with me or you. (B1-)

10. I must hold my anger back because no one will tolerate it. (B1-)

The Empathizer belief, "I must hold my anger back because no one wants to hear it," causes interpersonal rejection and the stowing of resentment. In contrast, the Instigator belief, "I've got to speak my mind right now," causes interpersonal rejection and the stewing of resentment.

What does it take for human beings to feel priceless instead of worthless when we experience the very real feelings that humans are supposed to feel?

Tune in your heart-mind with these positive thoughts: "I choose to use my anger to solve problems, not cause them." "Women and men are equally powerful when it comes to using their anger wisely."

So many times each day, my clients say: "Something's wrong with me. I shouldn't be feeling so much. My back's pressed up against a wall because if I express what I feel, it just creates conflict and I don't want conflict."

What does it take for human beings to feel priceless instead of worthless when we experience the very real feelings that humans are supposed to feel?

POSITIVE TALK ABOUT HEALTHY ANGER

Tune in the broadcasting power of your mind with these positive thoughts: "I am good enough." "I choose to use my anger to solve problems, not cause them." "Being angry doesn't make me a bad person." "Women and men are equally powerful when it comes to using their anger wisely."

Based on the 10 steps previously mentioned by Bill Cornell, here might be a more effective way to think about your feelings when you are mad or otherwise thinking of yourself as a "bad" person:

1. Good feelings don't make me good. (B1+)

2. **Bad feelings don't make me bad. (B1+)**
3. **People who make me feel good have positive and negative traits. (B1+)**
4. **People who make me feel bad have positive and negative traits. (B1+)**
5. **Anger can be a positive feeling. (B1+)**
6. **When I feel angry, I am good. (B1+)**
7. **People who are angry with me are good. (B1+)**
8. **When I'm angry, there's something right with me. (B1+)**
9. **When you are angry at me, something is right with you and me. (B1+)**
10. **I must express my anger assertively because everyone will welcome it. (B1+)**

Bad feelings, be they guilt, anxiety, confusion, depression, frustration, shame or whatever, don't make you a "bad" person, do they? After all, you can't enjoy your relationships for very long when you are emotionally shut down, constricted or tied up in knots.

LAST UP BUT NOT LEAST

Last up is, *Will you be good to me?,* a poem that empathizes and emphasizes what the experience of interpersonal rejection vs. acceptance often feels like. The first stanza illustrates positive talks (T+) while the second stanza is the negative mirror image that illustrates negative talks (T-) and interpersonal rejection. How does each type of talk make you feel as you read it?

WILL YOU BE GOOD TO ME?

Will you let me know in little ways how important I am to you each day?
Will you see me through fresh new eyes each morning?
Will you hear my words with non-judgmental ears?
Will you give me a hug when I feel overwhelmed without my asking?

Or will you be too busy to call me from work...
Look at me through cold, cynical eyes in the morning...

> *Judge me as too needy if I need to talk to you...*
> *Scold me for wanting a hug without asking!*

Will you still love me when I disagree respectfully with you?
Will you still remember that I'm a good man or good woman when you're mad at me?
Will you accept my disappointments without becoming defensive?
Will you accept my vulnerability and not attack or lambaste me?

> *Or will you put me down when I disagree with you...*
> *Call me bad names when you're mad at me...*
> *Give me grief instead of hearing my grief...*
> *Disappear when I'm distraught!*

Will you confront me when I shred your self-esteem?
Will you remind me how I'm good enough when I doubt myself?
Will you make regular deposits in our bank account of love?
Will you forgive me for being far less than I can be?

> *Or will you ignore my complaints...*
> *Lay a guilt trip on me that I'm being too selfish...*
> *Treat the dog better than you treat me...*
> *Blame me for not living up to your expectations!*

Will you kiss me when you don't have time to?
Will you be happy and excited to buy me presents?
Will you set limits with me when I talk stupidly?
Will you hold my hand in the grocery store?

> *Or will you love me when you're not so busy...*
> *Get more thrilled about the bills than me...*
> *Stuff your anger and steam when I speak stupidly...*
> *Walk in front of me when we're out together!*

Will you be good to me?
And love me even when I don't show up to love myself?

Now when the interpersonal going gets tough, you no longer play the blame game reflexively. Instead of having an anger attack between you and any of the four co-communicator subtypes, you instead keep an open mind by reminding yourself: "That's so narrow of me!"

TALK WORKS

CONCLUSION

Negative Talking: "It's my way or no way!"

Positive Talking: "It's my way...your way... OUR way! Okay?"

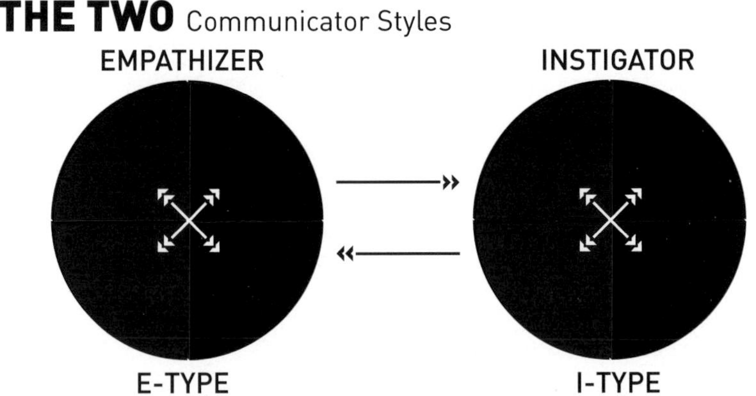

figure **#38**

WHEN THE GOING GETS TOUGH... LET'S GO ON EASY

My high school football coach thundered during half-time pep talks: "When the going gets tough, the tough get going!" That's a bit of inaccurate positive thinking (B1+), in the humble opinion of this 50-something personal coach to communications trainees of all ages.

I think it is far more honest and accurate to use these words of wisdom: *"When the communication going gets tough, let's go on easy!"* If you have read just one-third of this book by now you know exactly what I mean. You are going on easy down the two-way communicator highway. *Your* light has turned on bright, your eyelids are ripped open, and you have traveled on a rocket ship of positive change to new destinations. Who would have believed it possible?

If you have read just one-third of this book by now you know exactly what I mean. You are going on easy down the two-way communicator highway. Your light has turned on bright, your eyelids are ripped open, and you have traveled on a rocket ship of positive change to new destinations. Who would have believed it possible?

Now don't take me for some perfectionism pundit, either. Your relationship *life* still is far from perfect. Nevertheless you are feeling deeply satisfied and connected. Now you can imagine a journey on which the sun is shining, you feel self-assured, your communicator car window is rolled down on this balmy day and the scenery is breath-giving. Although the road of your life still has many twists and turns (and a few potholes), only rarely do you now listen to the spirit-sickening music of the "victim violin" or eat a "manure sandwich" for lunch.

"Way to go!" says Coach O'Grady. "I knew you could do it." I knew you would, if only you gave a few of these new communication tools, like directive questioning, a chance.

Moreover, the negative people in your life don't drive you half as crazy as they used to, now do they? You've also learned to raise your glass to life and make a toast whether it's "half empty or half full." Speaking of your life energy: Don't you feel more tuned in, understanding and compassionate? Do you feel like "a love-it-all" vs. "a know-it-all," especially warmly supported during dark, stormy nights of the soul? And how! And you thought these striking results were out of reach.

Do you feel like "a love-it-all" vs. "a know-it-all," especially warmly supported during dark, stormy nights of the soul? And how! And you thought these striking results were out of reach.

So look who's talking now! Now you know how to *Talk to Me,* because you factor into the talks whether you are talking to an Empathizer-type communicator or an Instigator-type communicator. Your communicator table has become a rich dialogue and personal interchange of positive news.

So look who's talking now!

UNCOMMON RESULTS

Thank your God—whoever he/she is—that you have been open to the miracle of change.

I'm so proud of you because you have changed a lot without whining or backing off! Wasn't it especially sweet when your changes brought about positive changes for others without trying to control anyone? I love how you write and talk positively now. Your positive talking habits are irrepressible and irresistible. And, oh, isn't the light bright and your eyes opened wide when you talk positively? What a new life view!

Let's hear from some of my communications trainees whose achievements make me so happy for them:

- *I am far less judging and far more loving*
- *I am more genuine, more present…less grumpy*
- *I accept myself more and reject myself and others less*
- *I saved my marriage*
- *I don't feel like I'm a dummy at communication anymore*
- *I go for my goals without fear*
- *I use new talk solutions to "fix" old problems*
- *I like my communicator style and understand my opposing communicator style so I don't get stuck as often in communication ruts*
- *I feel more contented and "at home in my skin"*
- *I use the four talk modes to lace a difficult day with humor*
- *I've been receiving positive feedback about my e-mails… I'm told they add hope and subtract hate*
- *Although I still don't like my talk nemesis, I don't allow him to bring me down for days on end*
- *I don't eat "manure sandwiches" fed to me by bullies*
- *"It's all your fault!" is no longer in my thinking or actions*
- *I use the 50% co-responsibility rule to change what I can*
- *I've adopted the strengths of my opposing communicator style*
- *I wrestle the largest alligators in the emotional swamp first*
- *I don't feel blue, anxious, angry or guilty as much as I used to*
- *New positive people have come into my life*
- *I'm enjoying my life and enjoying change for a change*

You have learned to spare your precious energy and time trying to drain the emotional swamp of negative emotions *or* negative thinking. You have discovered that you are far better off wrestling the biggest alligators in the swamp, setting off in a new direction and then getting the heaven out of there. Once out of that stinky emotional swamp, you have plunked down your behind in a five-star hotel Jacuzzi with an oceanfront view. And you can afford room service, now!

Haven't you learned the new communication moves MUCH faster than you thought you would? You have become less judging, and more loving, by bridging your emotional brain and intellectual brain.

THE ONLY CONSTANT IN LIFE IS CHANGE

Thomas Jefferson said that the only constant in life is change. I couldn't agree more with the word parody and paradox. Change happens with or without you. I prefer you be the director of positive changes in your communication life.

You've learned how to prevent many "maddening" talk accidents. You accept now that Empathizer communicators become anxious when their preferred lanes of Emotions and Talks are blocked. On the other hand, you also understand now that Instigator communicators become angry when their preferred lanes of Beliefs and Behaviors are cordoned off. So you try to accommodate these talk preferences whenever you can. You "get" that neither communicator type is better or superior—just different. Big changes! You no longer allow anyone to treat you like dirt.

You've learned how to prevent many "maddening" talk accidents. You accept now that Empathizer communicators become anxious when their preferred lanes of Emotions and Talks are blocked. On the other hand, you also understand now that Instigator communicators become angry when their preferred lanes of Beliefs and Behaviors are cordoned off.

In my first book *Taking the Fear out of Changing,* I discussed the *five fears of change* that a person must travel through to get from here to there.

THE FIVE FEARS OF CHANGE

- Fear of the Unknown
- Fear of Failure
- Fear of Commitment
- Fear of Disapproval
- Fear of Success

I also candidly discussed the *five emotional stages of change* we must all pass through on our change voyages.

THE FIVE STAGES OF CHANGE

- The Crisis Stage (Stage I)
- The Hard Work Stage (Stage II)
- The Tough Decision Stage (Stage III)
- The Unexpected Pain Stage (Stage IV)
- The Joy and Integration Stage (Stage V)

By interacting with this new communicator theory, you will continue to accrue many positive changes. Indeed, now "the past is the past!" as you create the new in your near future and future. Yes, there is some anxiety attached when you move into and explore unknown regions, which is true for every human being. While writing this book, for example, I let go of much and allowed much to come into my life. It was not a comfortable process, but a necessary one.

The biggest prize: You also have learned how your opposing talk style fairly and unfairly criticizes the core strengths and Achilles Heel of your talk style. Empathizers can be too sensitive! Instigators can be too insensitive! By now, you don't critique your opposite talk style, and instead, appreciate and enjoy your lovable Empathizer or Instigator communicator far more. After all, our families typically have both types. And like me, you've had the unexpected pain (over and over again) of missing the communication target in spite of your best positive intentions. "Learn and live!" I say. In spite of every change resistance, you have made major positive changes in your mood and attitude, too. "Bravely done!" says Coach O'Grady! You are courageous.

The biggest prize: You also have learned how your opposing talk style fairly and unfairly criticizes the core strengths and Achilles Heel of your talk style. Empathizers can be too sensitive! Instigators can be too insensitive! By now, you don't critique your opposite talk style, and instead, appreciate and enjoy your lovable Empathizer or Instigator communicator far more.

Choose to talk again positively today for a change of pace.

DRIVING ON THE TWO-WAY COMMUNICATOR HIGHWAY

It is a two-way communicator highway! And how! Two colors of cars, two styles of driving, no need to fight or argue about our differences or preferences.

Now when you speak to Empathizer communicators, you respect their need to use emotional language and words to draw a picture that the E-type can accept. When you speak to Instigator communicators, you respect their need to use logical language and actions to draw a picture that the I-type can accept. It matters too whether your co-communicator is an introvert or extrovert, and you respect that preference as well.

This is for the good of all, not for the purposes of manipulation, but for the purposes of positive communication. To summarize what you now already know so much more about:

1. **You know there are two communicator types called Empathizer (E-type) and Instigator (I-type) communicators.**
2. **You understand far better the unique frame of reference of Empathizer (E-types) and Instigator (I-types) communicators and contain in your brain a thumbnail sketch that distinguishes the two types that you confer with every day.**
3. **You speak and write far more positively, especially when you are feeling or thinking negatively.**
4. **You can easily recite in order the four communicator modes verbatim, and you can hear them loud and clear when your co-communicator speaks to you or you are speaking to yourself.**
5. **You are using your under-used communicator modes far more often. If you are an Empathizer, you are speaking and writing far more often in the modes of Beliefs (B1+) and Behaviors (B2+). If you are an Instigator, you are speaking and writing far more often in the modes of Emotions (E+) and Talks (T+).**
6. **You also know that Empathizers (E-types) and Instigators (I-types) can either be introverts of extroverts, neither one being better than the other. Typically, the person him/herself knows if he/she is an introvert or extrovert.**
7. **You now do typecasting in these four categories: Empathizer-type introvert (ITI), Empathizer-type extrovert (ETE), Instigator-type introvert (ITI) and Instigator-type extrovert (ETE). Speaking of leaders: ITI's are start-up entrepreneurs, while ITE's are go-forward entrepreneurs,**

but not always. Thus, you and yours are an ETI, ETE, ITI, or an ITE. By typecasting, your co-communicators feel intimately understood and their difficulties accepted.

8. **You now listen with three ears. You have realized exponential results (2x2x2x2x2=32). You know that one size talk shoe doesn't fit all. You realize the coaching method I use, or the new therapy method based on my theory is called Cognitive Emotive Therapy or CET. I have been using CET with all of my communications clients since the summer of 2004 with astonishing results.**
9. **You can name in order the four negative or positive communicator modes of Emotions (E-/+), Beliefs (B1-/+), Behaviors (B2-/+) and Talks (T-/+), and you now distinguish and use them in accurate vs. inaccurate ways.**
10. **You've witnessed how Empathizers are prone to cutting across the talk lanes of negative Emotions (E-) to negative Behaviors (B2-), causing a hurtful talk accident when they are under a great deal of relationship distress. You are avoiding this type of talk collision more often because you are responsive instead of reactive.**
11. **You likewise have witnessed how Instigators are prone to cutting across the talk lanes of negative Beliefs (B1-) to negative Talks (T-), causing a hurtful talk accident when they are under a great deal of relationship distress. You are avoiding these talk accidents more often because you are responsive instead of reactive.**

12. Overall, if you are an Empathizer communicator you are now able to think more accurately and positively, and if you are an Instigator communicator you are now able to feel more accurately and positively.

My concluding point is this one: I want you to be a flexible communicator who can use the core strengths of either the E-type or I-type communicator style to get the talk job done more effectively and ethically as any good leader would.

My concluding point is this one: I want you to be a flexible communicator who can use the core strengths of either the E-type or I-type communicator style to get the talk job done more effectively and ethically as any good leader would.

All is right, we HAVE traveled a long and enjoyable way together. And more new sights and insights await us around the next curve on the two-way communicator highway. Using the map of your opposite communicator type has turned the light switch on in your mind to make change happen fast.

TRAVELING ALONG ON THE NEW EMPATHIZER AND INSTIGATOR CHANGE HIGHWAY

You now know you are either an E-type or I-type expert communicator. You also accept as *factual feelings:*

1. *You are aware of who's talking to you by type*
2. *You have adopted the strengths of your opposing communicator style*
3. *You have experimented with the weaknesses of your opposing communicator type*
4. *You flexibly use the mode(s) of talk that work best for the task at hand*
5. *You speak accurately and positively, and you write accurately and positively*
6. *If you're an E-type, you explore change through the Beliefs (B1-/+) mode of accurate communication*
7. *If you're an I-type, you explore change through the Emotions (E-/+) mode of accurate communication*
8. *You are being and doing something new each day and feeling quite excited*

You speak accurately and positively, and you write accurately and positively.

Now, you freely choose talk quadrants that consistently and persistently respect the negative while honoring the positive.

Now, you freely choose talk quadrants that consistently and persistently respect the negative while honoring the positive.

BEGINNINGS, ENDINGS AND BEGINNINGS AGAIN

I first made acquaintance with this new communicator theory in Cabo San Lucas while on a heart-mending vacation with my wife and three daughters in the summer of 2004. Not too much later, I was embroiled in many heart-breaking events. I don't mean to suggest to your subconscious mind that sadness follows gladness. Both exist in life as we courageously and steadfastly travel along our two-way communicator highway.

While enjoying the Mexican folk art in the store *Desert Moon,* my eyes fixed upon an art piece that was a circle cut into four quadrants. I didn't want to buy it, although it wasn't expensive. I asked the storekeeper what it meant, and I learned that the four quadrants in Mexican lore represented the power elements of Earth, Wind, Fire and Water. After dinner, I returned to the store and purchased the piece. As I stood nearby full of curiosity, the art piece was meticulously wrapped in bubble plastic to insure a safe journey home to Ohio. It is now hanging on my family room wall.

Back in the Midwest, and while on my knees in church, the communicator mode names came to me. There is nothing fishy about it. The four quadrants took life in this way both in my emotional mind and in my logical mind:

1. Earth (Emotions communicator mode) [E-/+]
2. Wind (Beliefs communicator mode) [B1-/+]
3. Fire (Behaviors communicator mode) [B2-/+]
4. Water (Talks communicator mode) [T-/+]

Nothing fancy here. When I returned home from church, I drew the circle and cross in-between, and wrote the four names of Emotions, Beliefs, Behaviors and Talks. I wasn't sure if I should think of them in clockwise or counter-clockwise fashion, but I eventually decided on the Western approach during long walks of pregnant thought. Frankly, I wasn't sure at all what was going on but I felt tremendously engaged in the process.

Now, I *am* quite sure what I'm doing! After only a few months of practice I was on my way to communicating more positively and effectively. I now know from my experience that this communicator theory works. . .wonders. In truth, every single communicator, regardless of communicator/personality type, has complete access to drive in all of the four talk modes if they care to.

Don't be psyched out by yellow lines that cue your subconscious mind to steer around productive lanes of travel! Every talk lane is useful at times to get you where you/we need to go.

Let's travel together down the two-way communicator highway to enjoy this bountiful life, replete with breathtaking vistas and bountiful challenges. I will travel together with you, all ways and always. Because of our journey, we will be enriched and our lives will be infused with new insights and new energy.

Dr. Dennis O'Grady
Communications Psychologist
www.drograndy.com • (937) 428-0724

SPECIAL ACKNOWLEDGEMENTS

Trained in transactional analysis, body-centered psychotherapy, and psychoanalysis, William F. Cornell, M. A. is author of 30 journal articles and book chapters, many which explore the interfaces among interpersonal, body-centered, and psychoanalytic modalities. He is coeditor of the *Transactional Analysis Journal* and of *From Transactions to Relations: The Emergence of Relational Paradigms in Transactional Analysis.* For more information go to *http://www.analyticpress.com* and *http://www.itaa-net.org.*

Sue MacDonald, currently the marketing manager for a Cincinnati technology firm, is a former newspaper journalist who specializes in health and self-help issues. With her husband Richard Rossiter, she is the co-author of a manual to help people overcome the aches and pains of everyday living through powerful two-person stretches known as The Rossiter System. *Surgery Sucks: Fix Your Body Without Needles, Knives, Scalpels, 'Scopes, Lasers or Other Sharp Stuff!* is available at *http://surgerysucks.com.* Sue is the proud mother of two children, Sara and Tim.

James P. Rafferty, Ph.D., is a licensed clinical psychologist and Associate Professor in the Department of Family Medicine at Wright State University School of Medicine. Dr. Rafferty serves as Director of Family Practice Development in the Office of Family Practice Education and Development at Miami Valley Hospital, Dayton, Ohio. He focuses on strategic planning and professional development issues for physicians. Dr. Rafferty also maintains a part-time consulting practice. For more information go to *http://www.wright.edu* and *http://www.mvh-familypractice.org.*

ACKNOWLEDGEMENTS

Alfred Adler, Bob Alberti, Melody Beattie, Ellen Beck, Russell Bent, Eric Berne, Robert Bly, John Bradshaw, Dan Brazleton, Robert Brooks, Nina Brown, Joseph Campbell, Pema Chodrin, Jean Illsley Clark, H.L. Connelly, Sean Covey, Stephen Covey, F. Ann Crossman, Carl DeCaire, Kevin Lamb, Paul DeLuca, Elaine Donnelson, Richard Doty, Kenneth Drude, Richard Duncan, Wayne Dyer, Albert Ellis, Duke Ellis, Milton Erickson, Erik Erickson, Jim Finke, Suzanne Finke, Susan Forward, Ron Fox, Victor Frankl, Sigmund Freud, Erich Fromm, David Garner, Maureen Garner, Kerry Glaus, Bob Goulding, Mary Goulding, John Gottman, John Gray, Denny Gump, Louise Hay, Napolean Hill, Bill Hilt, Joyce Hogan, R.T. Hogan, Jacque Horney, Karen Horney, Christina Howard, Muriel James, Jimmy Johnson, Carl Jung, Taibi Kahler, Gershen Kaufman, Sam Keen, Robert Kiyosaki, Bruce Kline, George Kohlrieser, Dick Kooser, Larry Kurdek, Marti Laney, Pamela Levin, Bruce Linebaugh, Drue Lollis, William "Bud" Marsteller, Bob Martin, Justine McDevitt, Phil McGraw, John Mould, Augustus Napier, Al O'Grady, Ginny O'Grady, Emmett Orr, Shirley Panken, M. Scott Peck, Fritz Perls, Karen Peterson, Preston Pulliams, John Rabius, Max Raines, Marge Reddington, Theodore Reich, Jerry Rex, Sheri Rex, Tony Robbins, Bill Roberts, David Roer, Carl Rogers, John Rudisill, John Ruffolo, Neil Sanders, Virginia Satir, Bob Seufert, Cathy Simonton, Rachel Simmons, Claude Steiner, Deborah Tannen, Pat Torvik, Brian Tracy, Leon VandeCreek, Neale Donald Walsch, Kevin Ward, Carl Whittaker, Dennis Wholey, Oprah Winfrey, Zig Ziglar.

The Dayton Daily News, Dayton Development Coalition, *The Detroit Free Press,* Miami University, Miami University Middletown Campus, Muskegon Community College, Sinclair Community College, Sinclair Community College Corporate Center, *The Cincinnati Enquirer, The Columbus Dispatch, The Xenia Daily Gazette,* Wright State University, Wright State University School of Professional Psychology, University of Dayton, *USA Today.*

And especially to all of my esteemed communications clients over these 30+ years who have taught me so much about change management, stress (anger) management and communications management! My warmest thanks and eternal gratitude to each and every one of you.

SELECTED READINGS

Alberti, R. E. and Emmons, M. L. (1970). *Assert yourself—it's your perfect right: A guide to assertive behavior.* San Luis Obispo: Impact Publishers.

Aron, E. N. (1996). *The highly sensitive person: How to thrive when the world overwhelms you.* New York: Broadway Books.

Aron, E. N. (2002). *The highly sensitive child: Helping our children thrive when the world overwhelms them.* New York: Broadway Books.

Barnes, G. (Ed.). (1977). *Transactional Analysis after Eric Berne: Teachings and practices of three TA schools.* New York: Harper and Row.

Basch, M. F. (1980). *Doing psychotherapy.* New York: Basic Books.

Bayne, R. (1995). *The Myers-Briggs type indicator: A critical review and practical guide.* London: Chapman and Hall.

Beattie, M. (1989). *Beyond co-dependency: And getting better all the time.* San Francisco: Harper/Hazelden.

Becker, E. (1973). *The denial of death.* New York: The Free Press.

Berne, E. (1964). *Games people play.* New York: Grove Press.

Berne, E. (1970). *Sex in human loving.* New York: Simon and Schuster.

Berne, E. (1972). *What do you say after you say hello?* New York: Grove Press.

Benfari, R. (1991). *Understanding your management style: Beyond the Meyers-Briggs type indicator.* Lexington, Mass.: Health and Company.

Bettelheim, B. and Rosenfeld, A. (1993). *The art of the obvious: Developing insight for psychotherapy and everyday life.* New York: Alfred A. Knopf.

Blumstein, P. and P. Schwartz. (1983). *American couples: Money, work, sex.* New York: William Morrow.

Bly, R. W. (1988). *A little book on the human shadow.* New York: HarperCollins.

Bradshaw, J. (1990). *Homecoming: Reclaiming and championing your inner child.* New York: Bantam Books.

Branden, N. (1983). *Honoring the self: The psychology of confidence and respect.* New York: Bantam Books.

Brill, A. A. (Ed.). (1938). *The basic writings of Sigmund Freud.* New York: Modern Library.

Brooks, R. and Goldstein, S. (2001). *Raising resilient children: Fostering strength, hope, and optimism in your child.* Chicago, IL: Contemporary Books.

Buckingham, M. and Coffman, C. (1999). *First, break all the rules: What the world's greatest managers do differently.* New York: Simon and Schuster.

Buckingham, M. and Clifton, D. O. (2001). *Now, discover your strengths: The revolutionary program that shows you how to develop your unique talents and strengths—and those of the people you manage.* New York: The Free Press.

Bugental, J. F. T. (1976). *The search for Existential identity.* San Francisco: Jossey-Bass.

Buscaglia, L. F. (1972). *Love.* Thorofare, N.J.: Charles B. Slack.

Carnegie, D. (1936). *How to win friends and influence people.* New York: Pocket Books.

Campbell, S. M. (1980). *The couple's journey: Intimacy as a path to wholeness.* San Luis Obispo, CA: Impact Publishers.

Campbell, S. M. (2001). *Getting real: 10 truth skills you need to live an authentic life.* Novato, CA: H.J. Kramer Books.

Campbell, S. M. (2005). *Saying what's real: 7 keys to relationship communication and success.* Novato, CA: H.J. Kramer Books-New World Library.

Chapman, G. and Chapman, G. D. (1992). *Five love languages: How to express heartfelt commitment to your mate.* New York: Moody Press.

Chodron, P. (1995). *Awakening compassion: Meditation practice for difficult times. (Audio program).* Boulder, CO: Sounds True Audio.

Chodron, P. (1998). *When things fall apart: Heart advice for difficult times.* Boston, Mass.: Shambhala Publications.

Chodron, P. (2001). *The places that scare you: A guide to fearlessness in difficult times.* Boston, Mass.: Shambhala Publications.

Clarke, J. (1978). *Self-esteem: A family affair.* MN: Winston Press.

Conway, J. (1978). *Men in midlife crisis.* Colorado Springs, CO: Cook Communications.

Cornell, W. and Hargaden, H. (Eds.). (2005). *From transactions to relations: The emergence of Relational paradigms in Transactional Analysis.* Great Britain: Haddon Press.

Covey, S. R. (1989). *The seven habits of highly effective people: Powerful lessons in personal change.* New York: Simon and Schuster.

Covey, S. M. (1997). *The seven habits of highly effective families.* New York: Golden Books.

Covey, S. (1998). *The seven habits of highly effective teens.* New York: Fireside.

Covey, S. R. (2004). *The eighth habit: From effectiveness to greatness.* New York: Free Press.

Dobson, J. C. (1983). *Love must be tough: New hope for families in crisis.* Dallas, TX: Word Publishing.

Dominian, J. (1993). *Dynamics of marriage: Love, sex, and growth from a Christian perspective.* Mystic, CT: Twenty-Third Publications.

Dowling, C. (1981). *The Cinderalla complex: Women's hidden fear of independence.* New York: Summit Books.

Dreikurs, R. (1946). *The challenge of marriage.* New York: Hawthorn Books.

Dyer, W. (1976). *Your erroneous zones.* New York: Funk and Wagnalls.

Ellis, A. and Harper, R. (1961). *A guide to successful marriage.* No. Hollywood, CA: Wilshire Book Company.

Fenichel, O. (1945). *The psychoanalytic theory of neurosis.* New York: W. W. Norton.

Farrell, W. (1988). *Why men are the way they are.* New York: Penguin Group.

Fisher, B. (1981). *Rebuilding when your relationship ends.* San Luis Obispo, CA.: Impact Publishers.

Fleet, G.L. and Hewitt, P. L. (Eds.). (2002). *Perfectionism, theory, research, and treatment.* Washington, D.C: American Psychological Association.

Forward, S. with Frazier, D. (1997). *Emotional blackmail: When the people in your life use fear, obligation, and guilt to manipulate you.* New York: Harper Collins.

Forward, S. (2002). *Toxic In-Laws: Loving strategies for protecting your marriage.* New York: HarperCollins Publishers.

Freud, S. and Brill, A. A. (Ed.). (1938). *The basic writings of Sigmund Freud.* New York: Modern Library.

Friedman, R. J. and Katz, M. M. (Eds.) (1974). *The psychology of depression: Contemporary theory and research.* New York: John Wiley and Sons.

Fromm, E. (1941). *Escape from freedom.* New York: Holt, Rinehart and Winston.

Fromm, E. (1947). *Man for himself: An inquiry into the psychology of ethics.* New York: Owl Books.

Goldberg, H. (1976). *The hazards of being male: Surviving the myth of the masculine privilege.* New York: Signet Classics.

Goleman, D. (1995). *Emotional intelligence: Why it can matter more than intellectual I.Q.* New York: Bantam Books.

Gottman, J. M. and Markman, H. and Gonso, J. and Notarius, C. (1990). *A couple's guide to communication.* Research Press Company.

Gottman, J. M. (1999). *The seven principles for making marriage work: A practical guide from the country's foremost relationship expert.* New York: Three Rivers Press.

Goulding, M. M. and Goulding, R. R. (1979). *Changing lives through Redecision Therapy.* New York: Brunner/Mazel.

Goulding, M. (1996). *A time to say good-bye: Moving beyond loss.* Watsonsville, CA: Papier-Mache Press.

Gray, J. (1992). *Men are from Mars, women are from Venus: A practical guide for improving communication and getting what you want in your relationships.* New York: HarperCollins.

Gray, J. (1995). *Mars and Venus in the bedroom: A guide to lasting romance and passion.* New York: HarperCollins.

Gray, J. (2000). *How to get what you want and want what you have: A practical and spiritual guide to personal success.* New York: HarperCollins.

Harris, T. A. (1967). *I'm OK—You're OK.* New York: Harper and Row.

Hay, L. L. (1984). *You can heal your life.* Santa Monica, CA: Hay House.

Hill, N. (1965). *The master-key to riches.* New York: Fawcett Crest.

Hendrix, H. (1988). *Getting the love you want: A guide for couples.* New York: Harper and Row.

Hogan, R., Curphy, G.J. and Hogan, J. (1994). *What we know about leadership: Effectiveness and personality.* American Psychologist, 49 (6), 493–504.

Horney, K. (1937). *The neurotic personality of our time.* New York: W.W. Norton and Company, Inc.

Hubble, M.A. and Duncan, B.L. and Miller, S.D. (1999). *The heart and soul of change: What works in therapy.* Washington, D.C.

Ignersoll, B. D., and Goldstein, S. (2001). *Lonely, sad, and angry: How to help your unhappy child.* Plantation, FL: Specialty Press.

James, M. Jongeward, D. (1971). *Born to win: Transactional Analysis with Gestalt experiments.* Menlo Park CA.: Addison Wesley.

Jamison, K.R. (1995). *An unquiet mind: A memoir of moods and madness.* New York: Random House.

Jampolsky, G. (1979). *Love is letting go of fear.* Millbrae, CA.: Celestial Arts.

Jampolsky, G. and Cirincione, D. (1990). *Love is the answer: Creating positive relationships.* New York: Bantam Books.

Jewell, J. E. and Abate, F. (2001). *The New Oxford American Dictionary.* New York: Oxford University Press.

Johnson, S. (1999). *Who moved my cheese? An amazing way to deal with change in your work and in your life.* New York: G. P. Putnam Son's.

Jourard, S. M. (1964). *The transparent self.* New York: Van Nonstrand.

Jung, C. G. (1923). *Psychological types.* Routledge, London.

Jung, C. G. and Campbell, J. (Ed.). (1971). *The portable Jung.* New York: Viking Press.

Kaufman, G. (1980). *Shame: The power of caring.* Cambridge: Schenkman Publishing Company.

Kroeger, O., and Thuesen, J. M. (1989). *Type talk: The 16 personality types that determine how we live, love, and work.* New York: Dell.

Kroeger, O., Thuesen, J. M., and Rutledge, H. (2002). *Type talk at work: How the 16 personality types determine your success on the job.* New York: Dell.

Kurdek, L. A. (1983). *Children and divorce.* San Francisco: Jossey-Bass.

Kurdek. L. A. (1984). *Nature and correlates of relationship quality in gay, lesbian, and heterosexual cohabiting couples.* In B. Greene and G. Herek (Eds.), *Contemporary perspectives on gay and lesbian psychology: Theory, research, and applications* (pp. 133–155). Beverly Hills, CA: Sage.

Kurdek, L. A. (1995). *Divorce effects on children.* In D. Levinson (Ed.), *Encyclopedia of marriage and the family.* New York: Macmillan.

Kushner, H. (1986). *When all you've ever wanted isn't enough: The search for a life that matters.* New York: Pocket Books.

Laing, R.D. (1960). *The divided self: An existential study in sanity and madness.* Middlesex, England: Penguin Books.

Laney, M. O. (2002). *The Introvert advantage: How to thrive in an Extrovert world.* New York: Workman Publishing.

Lederer, W. J. and Jackson, D. D. (1968) *The mirages of marriage: A profoundly original look at the marital relationship with no–nonsense procedures to help solve its problems.* New York: W. W. Norton.

Lerner, H. G. (1985). *The dance of anger: A woman's guide to changing the patterns of intimate relationships.* New York: Harper and Row.

Maslow, A. H. (1968). *Toward a psychology of being.* New York: D. Van Nostrand Company.

May, R. (1969). *Love and will.* New York: W. W. Norton and Company, Inc.

McGraw, P. C. (2000). *Relationship rescue.* New York: Hyperion.

McGraw, P. C. (2001). *Self matters: Creating your life from the inside out.* New York: Hyperion.

McLaughlin, J. T. and Cornell, W. (Ed.). 2005. *The healer's bent: Solitude and dialogue in the clinical encounter.* Relational perspectives Book Series, Vol. 30. New York: The Analytic Press.

McKay, M., and Davis, M., and Fanning, P. (2004). *Messages: The communication skills book.* New York: New Harbinger Publications.

Napier, C and Whitaker, C. (1988). *The family crucible.* New York: Harper and Row.

O'Grady, D. E. (1992). *Taking the fear out of changing: Guidelines for getting through tough life transitions.* Dayton, OH: New Insights Communication.

O'Grady, D. E. (1997). *No hard feelings: Managing anger and conflict in your work, family, and love life. (Audio program).* Dayton, OH: New Insights Communication.

O'Grady, D. E. (2005). *Talk to Me: Communication moves to get along with anyone.* Dayton, OH: New Insights Communication.

Panken, S. (1973). *The joy of suffering: Psychoanalytic theory and therapy of masochism.* New York: Jason Aranson, Inc.

Paolino, T. J. and McCrady, B. (Eds.). (1978). *Marriage and marital therapy: Psychoanalytic, Behavioral and Systems theory perspectives.* New York: Bunner/Mazel.

Peck, M. S. (1978). *The road less traveled: A new psychology of love, traditional values and spiritual growth.* New York: Simon and Schuster.

Peck, M. S. (1978). *People of the lie: The hope for healing human evil.* New York: Simon and Schuster.

Peck, M.S. (1987). *The different drum: Community making and peace: A spiritual journey toward self-acceptance, true belonging, and new hope for the world.* New York: Simon and Schuster.

Peplau, L. A. and Perlman, D. (1982). *Loneliness: A sourcebook of current theory, research and therapy.* New York: John Wiley and Sons.

Perls, F.S. (1969). *In and out the garbage pail: Joy, sorrow, chaos, wisdom the free-floating autobiography of the man who developed Gestalt Therapy.* New York: Bantam Books.

Reich, W. (1942). *The function of the orgasm: The discovery of the orgone.* New York: The Noonday Press.

Rogers, C. (1972). *On becoming a person.* New York: Houghton Mifflin Co.

Satir, V. (1972). *Peoplemaking: Because you want to be a better parent.* New York: Science and Behavior Books.

Satir, V. (1978). *Your many faces.* Millbrae, CA: Celestial Arts.

Schloff, L. and Yudkin, M. (1993). *He and she talk: How to communicate with the opposite sex.* New York: Plume.

Simmons, R. (2002). *Odd girl out: The hidden culture of aggression in girls.* New York: Harcourt, Inc.

Smalley, G., Trent, J. T. and Silvestro, D. (Ed.). (1992). *Love is a decision: Thirteen proven principles to energize your marriage and family.* New York: Simon and Schuster.

Smith, M. (1985). *When I say no I feel guilty.* New York: Bantam Books.

Spring, J. A. and Spring, M. (1997). *After the affair: healing the pain and rebuilding trust when a partner has been unfaithful.* New York: HarperCollins Publishing.

Stuart, R. B. (1980). *Helping couples change: A social learning approach to marital therapy.* New York: Guilford Press.

Tannen, D. (1990). *You just don't understand: Women and men in conversation.* New York: Ballantine Books.

Textor, M. R. (Ed.). (1989). *Handbook of divorce and divorce therapy.* New York: Jason Aronson.

Trimpey, J. (1996). *Rational recovery: The new cure for substance addiction.* New York: Pocket Books.

Walsch, N. D. (1995). *Conversations with God: An uncommon dialogue book 1.* New York: G. P. Putnam's Sons.

Walsch, N. D. (1997). *Conversations with God: An uncommon dialogue book 2.* Charlottesville, VA: Hampton Roads Publishing Company.

Walsch, N. D. (1998). *Conversations with God: An uncommon dialogue book 3.* Charlottesville, VA: Hampton Roads Publishing Company.

Wilber, K. (1993). *Grace and grit: Spirituality and healing in the life and death of Treya Killam Wilber.* Boston, Mass.: Shambhala.

Wholey, D. (1997). *Miracle of change: The path to self-discovery and spiritual growth.* New York: Pocket Books.

Winfrey, O. (2005, February). *What I know for sure: A healthy relationship brings joy—not just some of the time but most of the time.* Oprah Magazine, p. 234.

Zimbardo, P. G. (1977). *Shyness: What it is what to do about it.* Reading, Massachusetts: Addison-Wesley.